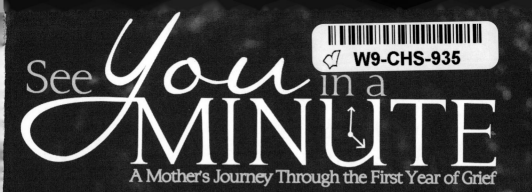

See You in a MINUTE

A Mother's Journey Through the First Year of Grief

BY MISTY NOVAK

FOREWORD BY SANDI PATTY

See You in a MINUTE

A Mother's Journey Through the First Year of Grief

BY MISTY NOVAK

FOREWORD BY SANDI PATTY

See You in a Minute:
A Mother's Journey Through the First Year of Grief
Copyright © 2012 by Misty Novak
All Rights Reserved.

Cover design by Abby Beard
www.abbybeard.com

FOR ZACHARY
Your music forever resonates in my heart and soul
You left the world a better place
It is my prayer that I'll
See You in a Minute

FOR MY HUSBAND, DAN
You are the better half of my life
God's love and patience reflects through you

FOR MY CHILDREN, JOEL AND BRYTNI
You continue to make me proud as you let
God's light shine through your lives

**FOR MY GRANDCHILDREN, CAMDEN ZACHARY,
LILY ANN, KENDALL JO, CONNOR LAIRD**
You are the blessings of my days,
May you always know that you are the light of the world

Table of Contents

Foreword by Sandi Patty

I have had the privilege of knowing Misty Novak for almost 25 years. My first introduction to her was as the kindergarten teacher to our oldest daughter, Anna. I was so struck by her joy, her smile, her vivaciousness... but mostly I fell in love with her heart. This was a woman who loved children... not just hers but those children that walked through her sacred door every morning saying, "Good morning Mrs. Novak."

As the years have passed 6 out of our 8 children have had Mrs. Novak for their teacher. To say that she has impacted our lives and the lives of our children would be an understatement. We have been so deeply and profoundly blessed.

As Mrs. Novak became "Misty" to me, (when the kids weren't around), we would often share "kid" stories – who was doing what. Like many moms do when they are genuinely proud and blessed by their children. Misty's son Zack became a regular topic between us because Zack seemed to have an amazing and unusual musical gift. Each year that our kids were in her class, the school would host a Christmas luncheon where families could come and eat lunch with the kids. Zack Novak was regularly the "piano music" as he played live the many songs he had learned through piano lessons and those songs that he was currently "writing". With 6 children under the tutelage of Mrs. Novak, I got to see Zack each year grow as a young man and grow as a musician and pianist.

When Zack made his decision for college, I was so pleased he had decided to attend Anderson University in Anderson, Indiana (my alma mater). AU was blessed to have him as a student. I would frequently run in to Zack on campus or I would hear him play piano and sing when there were performances that I attended.

I say that in this foreword because I guess I want you, the reader, to understand that these people weren't just friends.... they became family! We watched out for each other. Celebrated the many joys and yes grieved the losses.

I will never forget that dark day when Misty and her husband Dan just showed up at our home having learned of Zack's death. I remember it so clearly as there were no words at all that either of us could say. Don, my husband and I along with Misty and Dan just held each other – for the longest time. There was no need for words.

As we all began to gain our composure, Misty shared briefly with me some things that I already knew – Zack had so looked up to me, I was kind of an extra mom to him. Would I be willing to sing at his funeral? Zack always loved when I sang The Lord's Prayer.

And sing I did, through tears, through memories, FOR Misty and Dan and FOR ZACK! It's what he would have wanted.

I am so proud of my friend Misty for putting this journey through grief in a book. I know it has been part of her healing but I also know this – there will be many people who will be blessed and encouraged and challenged by reading these pages. They will know they are not alone. And that someone else experienced the worse loss possible, and has come through it. There will always be a hole... that will never go away. But Misty has found that in the "new normal" she can grieve and love at the same time. She can cry and rejoice at the same time. That God has been, and will continue to be in all that she is – until that day she can hold again her precious Zack!

I love you Misty Novak – you remain a hero in our family!

Sandi Patty

Preface

Being a mother, the thing that I feared the most in my life happened. I lost my child. No matter how old the child may be, if you outlive the child, the world seems to be tilted incorrectly or perhaps you seem constantly disoriented. Your world has been thrown off balance. You feel that each day is an awful nightmare from which you can't seem to wake up. And life as you have known it, will never be the same.

My son, Zachary Joseph Daniel Novak, 25, died April 20th, 2006 when a small six-seated Cessna plane crashed while attempting to land just south of Monroe County Airport in Bloomington, IN. Zachary was on the plane with four other talented musicians: Chris (Christy) Carducci, Garth Eppley, Georgina Joshi, and Robert Samels. All five of the victims were students of the Jacobs School of Music at Indiana University and were returning from a Lafayette Bach Chorale rehearsal late on a Thursday evening.

The need to express my grief and to tell the journey of my grief seemed more like a requirement to me. I had a need to revisit places in my heart and soul that seemed to keep me restless. Perhaps God has a plan in this for me, I have thought over these past few years.

Zachary passed more than five years ago. Even as I write the words, I still feel as though it was a lifetime ago and yet at the same time it feels like yesterday. Could telling this story be of help to someone else who has or is walking this path? Would my story help clarify the pain a mother suffers due to the loss of her child? These past two years, I felt as if God were nudging me to get this story out. Perhaps, if only to record the sequence of events that occurred so that Zachary's nieces and nephews might know and understand about their

"Uncle Zack." Just maybe I might find some peace within my soul through writing.

How can I go back through the pain? Am I really able to write about the nightmare of my life? Will the writing be cathartic? These questions whirl like a cyclone through my head keeping me up at night. As the writing began, I found myself continually reverting to the music he had recorded. Music, for me, is reflective as well as healing. Music was inseparable from Zachary's personality as he often walked into a room singing or responded to a question with a phrase from a song. Each chapter echoed a song from Zachary's past and his music became an outline to follow as I wrote about the path of grief. Listening to music has helped me *see* Zachary and remember the happy times we shared.

Life flies by as quick as a breath. It seems like yesterday when I watched my own three children playing within the confines of our fenced yard. Now I am the grandparent of four smart, sweet, beautiful youngsters, all under the age of five. Time happens fast. It is by faith that I live hoping that I will once again see and hold my first born, Zachary. When people leave each other, some say these words: "See you in a minute!" Will I see Zachary in a minute? "To God, a minute is an eternity, and an eternity is but a minute" (a quote from Zack's journal, I'm unsure of its origin). The speed of life as we age seems to mark this as a reality.

May those who read this book better understand the weight of loss and this mother's first year's passage through the grief of losing a child. And so the journey begins…

Misty Novak

On the Street Where You Live

April 21, 2006 – my life changed forever on that date.

"Is he hurt? Well, he's not dead, is he?"

It was a typical Friday. I woke up, showered, and got ready to go to school. I was a sixth grade teacher in a middle school not more than five minutes from our home in Anderson, Indiana. Most Fridays during the school year, I met a good friend, Sylvia, at school for an early breakfast. My husband, Dan, had a meeting that morning at 8:00 a.m. which allowed him a little extra time to sleep.

I turned on the television to watch and listen to the news as I did each morning. While I was putting on my make-up, I heard the news of a plane crash in Bloomington, Indiana. My oldest son, Zachary, attended Indiana University (IU). I turned, as if in slow motion, toward the TV. A cold chill shot through me. This chill went from the top of my head to the tips of my toes… a chill that rocked me to the core of my being, and I felt a twinge of panic.

My mind raced as I thought about Zack taking that trek from Bloomington to Lafayette, Indiana to perform with the Lafayette Bach Chorale. Yes, Zack did follow that path, but he would not be on the plane. After all, he always drove. Zachary had spoken with me about a girl who had her own plane and had flown to practices, but at this point in time, I was unaware of how good of friends Zachary actually was with Georgina, the pilot. I shut the thought of Zachary being on the plane out of my head. It's funny how often you disregard certain hard-to-comprehend inconceivable thoughts even when you have a premonition. I'll never forget that chill or that dizzy, slow motion feeling of that morning as long as I live.

I began to think that Zack must know the crash victims because of the flight pattern mentioned on the news. My spirit told me that the crash was connected to him in some way but my head talked me out of it being any more than that. I went on to school without mentioning the crash to my husband. I left him sleeping soundly in bed.

***

We had seen Zachary on Easter just four days before today. He had to leave our house early to go to the Bach rehearsal in Lafayette. Zachary was at the car getting ready to leave with his girlfriend, Jillian. I was crying that day when he left. I didn't know why because I'd never cried when any of our kids had left before that day. Zachary got out of the car, came back and hugged me.

Zachary asked me why I was crying and I said, "I don't know why. I simply don't want you to go." I knew I needed to control myself. After all, Zachary was 25... not a child anymore. It's funny what your spirit knows and your mind won't accept.

"Don't cry, mommy. I'll be home in two weeks. We'll do lunch, go to the pool...it will be fun," Zachary said. I stood on the porch, hugging him while Dan was over at the side of the porch giving me the cut-it-out sign with his hand going back and forth under his chin.

"Get a grip," I said to myself. "Dan's right. Cut it out." I have thought back on this moment so many times...millions of times. Oh, how I wish that I hadn't let go of him!

As I watched him climb back into his black Malibu, Zachary spoke the last words I'd hear him say to me, "Bye! I love you! I'll see you soon!" He shut the car door and backed out of the driveway. To this day, I never watch anyone leave the drive. That Easter, I watched as Zachary and Jillian drove away together, *down the street where we live*, and out of the neighborhood. Dan hugged me and asked what had gotten into me. I simply said, "I don't know. I just miss him."

Zachary had driven between the cities many times, but on that Easter evening, it was storming so Dan called him a few times to make sure that he had made it safely back to his apartment. He often called each of our children when they were on the road. (Dan continues to do this today even though they are married and out on their own.) Zack had told us that he would be making the drive again on Thursday. Of course, that stormy, Easter night, he made it back to Bloomington… safely. I wish he had driven April 20th instead of flying.

***

While eating our breakfast of bagels and hot chocolate at a small table in my classroom, I asked Sylvia if she had heard about the plane crash on the news that morning. I told her of my cold chill like no other and how it rocked me to my core. I told her that I felt sure Zack must know the victims and I would call him right after school to talk with him about it. I let it go at that. Odd how your mind works…how it simply won't let you believe anything that could be this traumatic could possibly be connected to your life. Besides, wouldn't I already have been notified if Zachary was involved?

The day went on. You see, I love teaching and kids in general. Each year of my 31 years of teaching has been a treasure. That particular school year, 2005-2006, I was teaching six sessions of Language Arts to approximately 160 students. I had worked hard on a class game over the last few days. The game was similar to the television shows *Jeopardy* and *Who Wants to be a Millionaire*. It summarized skills we had worked on all six weeks and was a fun, learning way to end the grading period. I had entered the six-weeks-grades into the computer and the game seemed like a great release to the students and me. After all, it was Friday, and this game did incorporate the Language Arts standards. The students and I were really involved and enjoying the game. I feel the need to tell this because it shows how disconnected I was to the next sequence of events. How far away I had put my thoughts of the morning news and that soulful chill behind me.

At approximately 2:15 p.m., the assistant principal came to the classroom and told me that the principal needed to see me in the office. I looked at the time and asked if it could possibly wait until after school since the day would end in fifteen minutes. He said that it was necessary for me to go now. I was concerned that I had done something wrong. I mean, this must be big to take me out of the class this close to the end of the day. Being my first year in middle school, I was nervous. What had I done? Was there an upset parent? Had I broken some rule or policy? All of these questions darted through my mind as I walked to the office. I had no clue about what was in store for me.

I entered the office. A colleague and good friend, Dan Alexander, was sitting with his back toward me as I entered the office. As he turned to look at me, I saw such sadness in his eyes. I felt even more frightened and concerned. Lucinda McCord, the principal, was behind her desk. I wondered, "What in the world did *he* do?" Dan was a pastor, a wonderful person, and an excellent teacher. I thought that this must be big trouble if he and I were both involved. Lucinda came around her desk and sat in front of me. I said, "What did I do?" I was still clueless as to what was about to transpire.

Lucinda took my hand and said that I had done nothing wrong. Her eyes spoke to me in an extremely compassionate way. As she began to speak, her eyes filled with tears, "There has been an accident... a plane crash."

Before she could go on, I interrupted and said, "It's Zachary, isn't it?"

Lucinda began to cry. I said the words that would resonate in my head for weeks to come. These words echoed in my head day and night.

"Is he hurt?" I pushed back from the desk. My tone changed, my words were almost angry. "Well, he's not dead, is he?" I searched her eyes for hope. I searched her eyes for the response that I wanted to hear.

***

Flashbacks were something I had taught in language arts, seen on television, and read in books. Now I understood them. Flashbacks became part of my existence, part of my new reality. These scenes from the past appeared out of chronological order, triggered by some sensation – a smell, a sound, a touch. At times, the flashbacks are so real that I can almost reach out and touch them. This moment in the principal's office would become one of many flashbacks.

***

Lucinda then said that she had spoken to Gwyn Richards, the Dean of the Jacobs School of Music at Indiana University. A plane had crashed and there were five people dead. At this point, I am told that I screamed. Some say it was a cry of such pain that they could not describe it, but would never forget it...I don't recall that noise...or thought...was I dreaming? Wake me up, somebody!

Everything from that point was somewhat blurry. I know that my friend, Dan, went to get my phone so that I could call my husband Dan, my sister Debby, my mom and dad, and Father Dhondt at St. Ambrose, our family church. I cried, shook, chilled, felt sick, scared, sick again… sensations and emotions I'd never felt before took over my body.

Lucinda said that they had not confirmed that it was Zachary on the plane. She asked me if Zack could be staying with someone else in Lafayette. Would he have gone somewhere else? My mind began to race. Hope set in at this point. Maybe, I thought, he would stay with his little sister, Brytni. After all, she went to Purdue University in Lafayette. No… wait…Brytni graduated and was substituting for the first time at East Side Middle School today. Zack couldn't be with her. Maybe he's with Jason, Brytni's fiancé. No…that couldn't be the case because Jason is at a job interview in Austin, Texas. Isn't it strange how the mind continues to reject the incomprehensible because of the terror? Isn't it strange how your mind searches for some rational, reasonable conclusion to try to solve the problem and yet arrive at the answer you want? Where could Zachary be? Certainly that couldn't be *him* on the plane. After all, he told us that he was driving.

I began to think about what I'd seen on television that morning. If Zachary was on the airplane, a policeman or another official of that sort would need to be here at school to tell me news of this magnitude. The way this was happening didn't make sense to me. This entire scenario gave me hope that someone had made a dreadful mistake. My Zachary, my son, must still be somewhere else. If he were truly dead, someone of official, outside authority would have to tell me, not my school principal. Something about this whole scene just didn't make sense.

At this point, all my mind could even muster up was the need to talk to my husband, Dan. Certainly, he knew all about this and would explain to me what was going on. He has always been my tower of strength. What about Brytni and Joel, our other children? Did they know? How would or *could* I tell them? We were all so close that this simply couldn't be real.

There was a definite twist of fate on this day or was it God's placement? Brytni was substitute teaching in sixth grade at my school for the first and only time, language arts, no less. I had even eaten lunch with her earlier. My mind continued to race. Thank God I can hold her when we talk! She had always looked up to her big brother who was only two years older than her. What will I say? How will I say it? This can't be true!

What about Joel? He was married, a little more than a year ago to his longtime girlfriend, Hillary. His older brother, Zack was his best man. They are only 11 months apart in age...so very close. Where is he? Oh, that's right. He's at school. I can't tell him! All of these thoughts kept coming at such a rapid pace that I felt myself begin to drift away. Where is Dan? Why wasn't he here at school when they told me? He could tell Joel better than I. After all, he coached Joel in baseball for years. I can't tell Joel. Too much pain was flooding my mind. Was I in the present or past? I felt like I was going to get sick. The room began to spin.

Just then, my colleague and friend Dan returned with my cell phone. I pushed the speed dial button on my phone. My mind went whirling out of control. Why wasn't my husband Dan here? It's so odd how irrational my thoughts were during this episode. Thank God Dan answered. I blurted out that they think that Zack is dead. I continued to tell him about a plane crash and they think that he was on that plane that went down in Bloomington. I was sobbing and yelling and simply sounding crazy. Dan said that he couldn't understand me.

"What plane crash? What are you talking about?" Dan responded. "Is there someone else I can talk to? You aren't making any sense."

I passed my cell phone to my principal. She filled him in on the details that she had been told by the Dean of Music at IU. She had written some notes on a post-it pad. For some reason, I kept her notes which read as follows:

Coroner-hangar
Zack-rehearsal at Purdue
5 left for Purdue-5 on return-no ID yet
Zack's car at airport
Private plane-student was pilot
Crashed 11:40 p.m. in wooded area beyond runway
5 boarded plane
All 5 deceased
Coroner of Monroe County has bodies at the airport
Gwyn Richard's phone number given by secretary-Jennifer

I didn't read the notes until later…even now as I type these notes, I feel the cold chill of the memories of that date and time…a nightmare in the making.

Feeling lightheaded, I sort of fell back into a chair. My mind continued to race. This couldn't be happening. *Zack's driving to the rehearsal. He can't be dead!* Those words continue to echo through the corridors of my mind.

My principal asked who else she could call to help me. What else could she do to help resolve the confusion? I proceeded to tell her to get in touch with my sister, Debby, a teacher at Highland High School, and have her come to East Side as soon as possible.

Debby was like a second mother to Zachary. I needed her here to help me sift through all this information. I just knew she'd figure out this mess. That's what Debby has always done for me throughout my life. (Later, I found out that when her principal had told her, she fell to the floor with such a loud scream that it was known as, "The Incident Upstairs.") She was told that she needed to get herself together because her sister needed her… and, much to her credit, she did.

I called my parents whose strong faith in God has always been like an anchor that I could depend on whenever I needed to be grounded. Surely they could clarify all of this. I certainly couldn't! One of my mom's favorite Bible passages flew through my head. Romans 8:28 (NRSV): "We know that all things work together for good for those who love God, who are called according to his purpose." I had always believed that and now, how could this be happening to me if I was, in fact, rooted in faith? My mom and dad must know the answer. It's odd how even as adults, we think our parents can fix anything. At first, I was sure that they didn't comprehend what I was saying. If I couldn't, how could they? My dad and mom were in disbelief and said that they would begin praying right away.

I asked my friend, Dan, if he could call Father Dhondt, our priest at St. Ambrose. Father Dhondt truly loved Zachary. I felt sure that he would be saddened greatly with this news and would know what to do.

***

I wasn't a cradle Catholic. As strange as it may sound, Dan took me to Midnight Mass at St. Ambrose for our first date. I had become Catholic when our children were small. Dan and I faithfully attended church as a family throughout our lives, even when we were in high school.

I later found out that the church office staff already knew! Our family was shocked to discover most of Anderson knew about Zachary before we did.

***

While in the midst of this tragedy, I continued to grasp at anything or anyone who might change the circumstance or at least explain it to me. I knew I had faith in the Lord and this faith must sustain me. My mind continued to search for answers.

I took my phone and began calling Zachary's number. His cell phone rang, but would roll right to his voicemail. Again and again, I pushed those buttons. I left several frantic messages about calling me ASAP. It wasn't uncommon for Zack to not respond right away to calls – sometimes he forgot to charge his phone. Again, my mind told me that Zachary had to be all right. If he had been on that plane, would his cell phone still work? My thought was that there was no way – that if he hadn't survived, his phone would surely be gone, too. Where could he be?

When Brytni walked into the office after school, she knew immediately that something was very wrong. Our eyes met. When I told her there had been an accident...a plane crash, her first response was to tell me that her fiancé, Jason was okay. She had spoken to him earlier and he was fine. Brytni told me that I should relax. Then I told her that it was Zachary. Brytni was stunned. No, this all couldn't be real! We held each other and cried. Brytni expressed her concern of how could this possibly be ...he didn't know anyone with a plane. I told her that he had talked to me about a girl that flew back and forth to rehearsals, but I didn't think that he knew her well enough to fly with her. (Parents of twenty-five year olds can't possibly know what their adult children are doing or who they know, even though we parents don't want to believe that fact. After all, we always keep in close contact with our children and their activities, right?)

Lucinda again asked if Zachary could have gone somewhere else in Lafayette. The identification of the five bodies had not yet been positively established. Brytni and I, almost in unison, stopped crying and said that this can't possibly involve Zachary. He must be somewhere in Lafayette with some other member of the Bach Chorale. The coroner must have him mixed up with someone else. We left the office feeling as if this were nothing more than a tragic mix-up.

As we walked out of the office, I can still recall the faces of the office staff…tears running down their faces and saying how sorry that they all were about Zachary. I remember telling them not to worry. The coroner must have him confused with someone else. Everything will be just fine. That's what my mind kept telling me.

I really don't remember my sister, Debby, arriving at East Side. It seems as if she just appeared. Time skipped, leaving voids of recollection. All of a sudden, we were in my classroom. I was trying to make lesson plans for the next school day, which would be Monday. I began taking down the game board which was covering my agenda board for the next week. How relieved I was that I had plans already in place for the next week. All I needed to do was make copies of the lesson. It's so strange what you feel or don't feel when you are in denial. Debby kept saying not to worry about plans. I was simply numb. My actions seemed robotic. It felt like I wasn't me anymore, that someone else was moving my body from place to place. Brytni and Debby insisted on our leaving school to go home. I couldn't understand why I couldn't finish my lesson plans. Brytni or Debby – I'm not sure who – finally snapped her fingers in my face and said we needed to go, so I relented and we left.

As Debby, Brytni, and I left the building, I heard passers-by in cars yelling from their windows how sorry they were about Zachary. How could they know? I was puzzled by their actions when I had just found out.

Again, as if by magic it seemed, my husband Dan came walking up the sidewalk. His appearance brought a sudden sense of relief to me – I began telling him it was all a misunderstanding and that there had been a mistake about

Zachary. It couldn't have been him. Dan gave me a look that I will never forget. His face was filled with sorrow. His eyes spoke the truth as he said that our worst fear had been realized. Dan had spoken with the coroner while driving here. Our Zachary was on the plane. He was "one of those bodies in the hangar at the Cook Airport in Bloomington" that Lucinda had written in her notes. I collapsed into his arms. Brytni fell to the ground sobbing. The world stopped for me. This moment was like a bomb exploding in my head – and another in my heart. How could this be real? I wouldn't and couldn't accept that Zachary was gone.

Dan asked Debby if she could drive our van to the house. He didn't want me driving. Brytni and Debby went in our van. On the way to the house, Brytni called Joel to talk to him about Zachary. She was sure that he must have heard by then.

At the time of her call, Joel was just returning to his home from school. He walked straight from the front door to the refrigerator bypassing the blinking answering machine. The phone rang and it was his wife, Hillary, who was crying so hard that Joel couldn't understand a word she was saying. She was about to tell him of this unbelievable news when Brytni's call beeped in. Joel began to sense that something was terribly wrong. Things were not normal... a blinking answering machine, a hysterical wife, a call from his sister. After hearing the news, Joel's heart sank, frozen in the moment, confused and overwhelmed. Thank God he didn't listen to the answering machine when he first arrived home. The machine contained messages from friends expressing their sorrow at Zack's passing. The machine would have told him the fateful news instead of Brytni.

Later we discovered how Hillary heard the news, and also how relieved she was not to have been the one to tell her husband. My thought was I could hardly wait to hold Joel and to see his face.

I must have gotten into Dan's car. Things just seemed to happen. I remember thinking this all must be a dream, a terrible nightmare. I would wake up soon and all of this will go away. This would be a reoccurring thought for months… no, *years* to come.

Upon our arrival home, the phone was ringing. George, the pastor of the First United Methodist Church (FUMC) in Bloomington was calling to see if he could help in any way. When I told him that we had just found out about twenty minutes ago, he seemed speechless. My sister asked me to pass her the telephone. She wrote down his number and thanked him for his concern. Zachary was one of the music directors at the church. He directed the children's choir and the Wesley Choir at FUMC.

Later that evening, that wonderful church opened its doors to the students at Indiana University. They held their arms out to a community in shock and grief. At this point, I was unaware of anything other than what was happening right around me. Everything seemed to become *all about me* for several days – even years. I could barely hold my head up let alone my arms out to anyone else in need of comfort. Everything around me was a complete blur.

The phone rang again. I don't remember if I answered or someone else handed it to me. It was my good friend, Alberta. We never needed lots of words to know what each of us thought. She asked if "it" were true. I simply replied, "Yes." She came right over and remained for the entire week. Alberta kept people at bay. She was kind and expressed my gratitude for their caring, but also conveyed that I needed some space. If flowers or food arrived, she or Debby made a note of it. I would have been lost without her help. Good friends are irreplaceable.

As quickly as possible, I went upstairs, took off my clothes and put on something else. I vaguely recollect taking the clothes I had worn to school, including my shoes and underwear, walking them to our garbage container outside and placing them inside. It was as if I could dispose of this tragedy if I could get rid of any evidence of the day. How could I ever look at those clothes again? Those clothes would have been a reminder of the mind-boggling news of the day. I wished that I could have gotten rid of events of the day as easily as those clothes.

I returned to the upstairs bathroom and got sick. Not the kind of sick that I had ever experienced before this day. In a robotic fashion, I would get sick to my stomach and then go about acting *normal*. This would happen over and over again during the course of the evening.

A huge hole had begun to develop. This *hole* is real! It became a part of me; over time when I mentioned this to other mothers who had lost children, they knew about this hole. It is feeling that never quite goes away, but the severity does lessen. The edges around the hole, after a few years, seem to not be as piercing. The feeling is a cross between being sick and being hungry…a true stomach ache that just can't be healed. This *hole* can't be cured or alleviated. There simply isn't a treatment.

All I knew is that I wanted Zachary home. I wanted my world to be the way that it had always been… before now. I wanted things to be *normal* again.

Joel and Hillary arrived soon after. I clung to Joel and sobbed and sobbed. My mind went blank at this point. Natalie and Adam Farmer, who are Hillary's sister and brother-in-law, arrived. Natalie graduated with Zachary and had sung with him in Highland Singers as well as at Joel and Hillary's wedding just a summer ago. We were together in our living room. Zack's piano and family photographs became a focal point for me. The thought that "this can't be happening" was a dominant message floating through my brain. I don't remember conversations…just tears.

I thought of all the people who loved Zack…then I thought of David Sturgeon, my sister's oldest son. Even though there was a ten year difference between David and Zachary, time wasn't a barrier. They vacationed together and often just hung out. Where was David? Dutifully, he was helping chaperone a class in Washington, D.C. David reacted quickly when he found out, got a ticket on the next flight home, and came straight to our house. David and I stood by the front curb of our street, held each other, and dissolved into tears.

Then the train of people and mounds of food began arriving at the house. Their thoughtfulness was astonishing… extraordinary. Our family was blessed to have been encompassed by such a flood of giving. But eating or even drinking was the very last thing on my mind.

Close family members arrived and positioned themselves where they felt that they could be most helpful. Ray-Ray, Dan's youngest brother and his wife, Natalie came to be with us as did Dan's sister, Jodi, her husband, Pat and daughter, Amy. Zack had been Amy's piano teacher as well as her oldest cousin. My sister's husband Ervin, and their youngest Steve, made trips in and out of the house checking on the needs of each family member. My parents came to pray. The family sat in the backyard as guardian angels, watching over us. We are blessed to be such an extraordinarily close knit family.

Grief causes you to do some strange things. It seemed that I lost about two hours of time that I can't recall anything that happened. (I do believe that my memory has not been as clear as it once was prior to this tragedy.) I went outside and swept the back patio. My sister told me later that I swept it so many times that she had lost count. I also pulled weeds in the backyard. I just wanted to be left alone. I remember thinking, maybe if I do something normal, everything will *be* normal. Every now and then, I would go upstairs, get sick and then resume whatever chore I had left outside. Joel and Alberta kept the throng of people away from me, forming a protective barrier. Could someone make these people understand that my world had been forever changed? I just didn't want to talk to anyone. Besides, my feelings were that Zachary would be okay. Everyone else must be confused. My life had always been so right. I must be dreaming all of this. Wake me up, somebody, please!

***

There is a true touch of irony. We live only about a mile from the Anderson Municipal Airport. When the weather permits, small planes are constantly flying over our home. I've always enjoyed watching them take off…and land. About a year later, Dan told me that he said a prayer for those flying. From that day through today, I, too, always pause to say a silent prayer for the safe landing of each of those planes.

***

That beautiful, sunny spring day, small planes seemed to fly over our house constantly. Looking up at the bright sky, I paused to glance skyward. My thoughts were blank except to think perhaps Zack was nearby, flying near to comfort me. Then I would want to pull the aircraft out of the sky. My mind shifted back and forth. (Covering my ears at the sound of a plane became a habit for several years.)

As I was pulling those crazy weeds, I was keenly aware that someone was always nearby. Sometimes, it was my sister. Other times, it was my niece, Kati, or her fiancé, Justin. I felt as if those who were near thought that I shouldn't be left alone. Joel seemed to be standing guard over me, too. How odd that my son, whom I had protected throughout his childhood, had now turned the tables. Vague thoughts of him talking on his cell phone and looking pale drifted in and out of my mind. Such thoughts felt as if they were floating on a piece of time somewhere outside of my reality. Time and space merged into one single element for me. Everything seemed surreal. Memories are such a fragile part of your mind.

Dan left to tell his mom and dad. Brytni went with him. He knew that this kind of news was best heard in person. He knew all too well that news of this magnitude heard over the phone is dangerous. After all, I had told him over the phone. Dan drove from Noblesville to Anderson in twenty minutes just to get to me at East Side. This trip usually takes around forty minutes. He had no idea how his mom, Zachary's grandmother would take the news of losing her first and oldest grandchild. Yes, this must be something Dan would do face to face. I don't recall Dan or Brytni leaving the house. My mind couldn't hold a thought.

Sometime when I was mindlessly sweeping the back patio, Father Dhondt, and Connie Jo, our pastoral assistant, came into view. The conversation between us was brief. They said that they would pray for me. Both of them looked at me not knowing what else to say. I think they thought I was too far gone to discuss the details necessary after someone dies. At this particular point, I am sure they were right. Making their apologies, Father and Connie Jo excused themselves and went inside the house. Later, I found out that they went into our living room to wait on Dan's return.

After Dan returned from telling his parents, I was told that he had a conversation with Father Dhondt and Connie Jo about Zachary's funeral arrangements. Dan and I had not discussed this. How could we when I still couldn't accept the news of the crash? My poor husband had to face the truth right away. Father Dhondt told Dan that he couldn't have the service at the church. Dan was puzzled and challenged the statement. Father said that we must look into getting a place off site because neither Catholic Church in Anderson would be large enough to accommodate the crowd of people anticipated to come to the funeral. Dan's initial response was pure disbelief. Zachary was only 25. How many people could he have known in his short life? Father Dhondt was insistent. We later found out how right he was about this issue.

Dan stated that he would ask Hillary's dad, Joe, to talk to Anderson University (AU) about Reardon Auditorium which holds a little more than 2,000 people. AU is a Church of God University. We would want Zachary to have a Catholic Mass. How could this happen? Zachary was an AU graduate and was going to fill in as adjunct music professor for Dr. Richard Sowers while he was to be on sabbatical in the fall of 2006. Yes, he was to be part of the staff, but this was a lot to ask.

Joe Royer was employed at the university as director of facilities. Dan discussed the matter with him and said he would broach the subject with the president of the university. Much to our amazement and overwhelming gratitude, the president of Anderson University, Dr. James Edwards, did not even hesitate to offer the auditorium. Dr. Edwards was willing to accommodate our wishes and would do anything to help. The so-called stage was set. At this time, I was unaware of these arrangements. I was still in my own little crumbling world.

Jason, Brytni's fiancé, arrived at the house in the early evening. Debby had told him about Zachary over the phone. Jason had gone to Austin, Texas to interview for a job. He had done intern work for a company over the past two summers and they were offering him a job. Dan greeted him in the driveway, hugged him, and told him to take care of Brytni. She'd need him.

When I saw Jason, I cried and hugged him, too. Then I pleaded with him not to take my baby to Austin. Sobbing, I pulled away from Jason expressing that asking him to change his job site was so selfish of me. He should go where the job market called him, but I hoped that his job would land him closer to home. Much to his credit, Jason began looking for a job in Indiana. I will be forever grateful for his willingness to think more of our family than himself. To me, Jason truly became part of the family that day. His selflessness was astounding.

Plans were now put into motion for the most gruesome, dreadful event a mother could imagine…preparing to bury her child. How could we do this? Zachary's life was so wonderful, with a bright future ahead. This service must be a celebration of his life. Somehow, Dan and I would have to make this beautiful… as beautiful as Zachary.

In the Wee Small Hours
of the Morning

Sleep. What a simple pleasure I had taken for granted for years. I loved to nap and had always enjoyed eight hours of sleep. Now sleep became a rare commodity that could only be attained in short increments. Sleep still eludes me even after five years. Some nights, I still find myself taking an over-the-counter sleep aid. My doctor offered to prescribe something to help me sleep, but I decided against it. Odd how something which was so easily accomplished in my "past life" seems like a luxury now.

As the song says, "The whole wide world is fast asleep. You lie awake and think"…think about him…about Zachary. How could this be happening? How far away is he? Is Heaven really some arbitrary place way up in the sky? I found myself talking to Zachary as if he were right beside me. Questions like, "Where are you? How far away are you?" and praying that he would answer me. Sometimes my mind would yell the same questions, thinking maybe he can't hear me so I'd better speak up.

The whole world seemed at rest; yet, I couldn't fathom the thought of resting without the knowledge of my family being safe and sound. My family was no longer whole.

Dan was such a patient and compassionate help. I would jolt up into a sitting position, gasping for air in the middle of the night. Dan would very calmingly, as if the hand of God

Himself was reaching out to me, rub my back. Sometimes I would get up out of bed and state that I just had to go for a walk. Again, being such a kind husband, Dan would say that he'd go along, too, even though he had to go to work the next day. As I look back on my behavior, I feel so selfish. At the time, it seemed to be a survival technique. I needed to just get out! Escape. Run away, or should I say, walk away from the living nightmare.

***

The evening news came on. Everyone gathered around the television as we were told that the news would announce the names of the crash victims. I didn't want to see or hear the news, but Dan thought that we should watch it together. Staring blankly, I saw those five young, talented students' pictures flash on the screen. Odd, Zachary didn't have his professional head shot like the others. I thought how embarrassed he would be that his looked like a random photo. I'd have to take care of that…my mind still was unable to grasp that Zachary was part of those who were gone. What an odd perception…if I could fix the picture, maybe the situation would be repaired.

Later that evening, after everyone had gone home, Joel, Hillary, Brytni, Jason, Dan and I gathered in the den. I didn't want any of us to ever leave this room. Our family was safe right now. That's how I wanted it to stay. Brytni had planned to stay the night in her old room, but now that Joel was married, I didn't know his plans. I was thrilled when he asked if he could stay home for the night. He and Hillary would sleep in the boys' old room. Of course, I was relieved and thrilled to have us together. We all needed to get some rest.

Dan and I tried to go to bed. I do mean *tried*. We both were crying and holding on to one another. We couldn't sleep. How would we ever sleep again? We prayed for guidance to help us try to figure out our next step.

***

The word, step, seemed to be the most appropriate word. I have been a walker for most of my married life. My next-door-neighbor, Nancy, and I walked about two miles every morning before work – 5:15 a.m. was our usual time. Walking had been an enjoyable pastime for me. It's also been a good way to get in some much needed exercise and fellowship prior to starting the day. Exercising in the crisp morning air usually allowed me to see problems in a clearer fashion and Nancy had been my friend since our college days at Anderson University. Sometimes, it would seem that we would solve our problems and the problems of the world as we walked around our neighborhood.

***

The time was around 1:00 a.m. Sleep would not come. I told Dan I needed to walk. Perhaps we could get a focus on what we should do. The morning was so beautiful. The sky was full of stars. One star seemed particularly brighter than the others.

***

For the next few early mornings as well as the next few years, I would go outside and look up and say, "Good Morning, Zack." In my mind, I could hear him respond, "Morning, Mom." Oh, how many times I'd wish that it was him next to me, but then again, maybe he really was.

***

Before we began our walk, we noticed a potted tree had been placed by our mailbox. The card was from other parents who had lost their child, too. It had a simple message, "Welcome to the club that no one wants to join. Call us if you need us. You are in our thoughts and prayers." Dan and I looked at each other without words. There simply aren't words so many times.

As Dan and I walked that first early morning, he spoke to me about the dreadful events that awaited us: funeral arrangements, burial plots, and other such things that no mother ever wants to discuss. Each lap around the block was a new topic, full of tears and despair. How could we be talking about these things? I surely must be dreaming.

During one of our sleepless walks around the neighborhood, Dan and I decided which funeral home would take care of Zack. This was not an easy decision at first because we have connections with each of the funeral homes in Anderson. Henry Diedring of Brown-Butz-Diedring was a longtime family friend and it felt like the right choice.

I remember feeling like another person must be living my normal, wonderful life and had left me here in their place. This couldn't be my world!

Dan remained in the moment, always strong and steady. I, on the other hand, was not. Dan spoke of establishing a scholarship in Zachary's name at Anderson University. The university had played such a big part of who Zack had become. We agreed that would be a priority on the to-do list over the next few days. The scholarship would be given for future aspiring musicians with exemplary work ethic and outstanding academic performance. How Dan could be thinking of such an amazing legacy for our son was remarkable to me. Through my haze, I agreed that the scholarship was a fitting idea.

***

Zack had lived on campus before leasing a home from his voice teacher, Fritz Robertson. Can you imagine having professors take such an interest in you personally that they would allow you to rent a home from them? Zachary loved the university and it, in turn, loved him back.

***

Even though I remained in my distant shattered world, during one of those expeditions around the block, I insisted that we go to Bloomington. I had to retrace the steps that Zachary had taken last. I had to be where he was last. Dan agreed. When we had discussed going the night before, Dan felt that we needed to stay home and gather our thoughts as well as make arrangements. I relented then, but felt that it was more than necessary for me to be in Bloomington...for *us* to go to Bloomington.

After several more laps, we returned home and prepared to go to the crash site in Bloomington. My sister, Debby, nephew, David, and Zachary's girlfriend, Jillian also made the trip with us. Joel and Brytni felt they needed to remain on the home front to try to sort out their thoughts as well as take care of the house. Alberta remained there, too.

My mind remains foggy about the details of the day. Showering, dressing, preparing for the day seemed to be nothing but a blur. Somehow, in my mind I felt that if I got to the crash site, I might *feel* him there. That may sound irrational, but those were my thoughts.

Before we began the trip to Bloomington, Dan and I had a flat tire. Dan had an uneasy feeling about going in the first place and the flat tire seemed to be a bad omen. After some debate and a new tire, we proceeded to Bloomington with Debby, David, and Jillian accompanying us.

Very little conversation took place, but we did receive two phone calls. The first was from the funeral home director, Henry. The cause of Zachary's death was blunt force trauma. He stated that he'd pick up Zachary's body and bring him to the funeral home. Henry and Dan had spoken earlier, but I had not spoken to Henry so I got on the phone. I told Henry that Zack wanted to be an organ donor. Even in death, I knew how Zachary felt about helping others.

***

I remembered standing in line with him at the Department of Motor Vehicles when we had both gone to have our license renewed. He had noticed that my driver's license didn't say that I wanted to donate my organs in the event that something might happen to me. I told him that I'd never really given it any thought. Zack explained that if you can no longer use your organs, why not let someone else have the benefit of them. I signed up to be organ donor eligible that day.

***

Henry told me something that day that I simply could not comprehend. He paused, and then stated that there was nothing left that could be used. My mind paused, too. How can that be? What does he mean by, "Nothing left"? How bad could this crash possibly have been? In what kind of shape *was* Zachary's body? What was blunt force trauma? I shuddered. I want to see my baby was all I could think. My head just couldn't take hold of all of this information. This can't be happening. I have got to get out of this nightmare.

My head whirled I handed the phone back to Dan. Henry told us that he would take care of everything. The coroner had sent some of Zachary's things that he had with him on the plane to the hospital. Henry said that he'd pick them up, but

Dan insisted that since we were already in Bloomington that we would get them. Dan and Henry spoke a little while longer, about what, I don't know; he thanked Henry and hung up.

The second call was from my friend Gloria. She and her husband, Kevin, live in Ellettsville, which is located about a stone's throw from Bloomington. Dan and I had known them both since our junior high school days. We have kept in contact over the years and I felt comforted just hearing her voice. She was graciously extending an invitation to stay at her home whenever we were in the area. Our plans on that day were merely to make a few stops at some particular places connected to Zachary and return home to Anderson. Plans to stay at her home would be made at a later date. How very blessed I felt to have such a great friends even when my world was shaken to the core.

Upon arriving in Bloomington, Dan and I went to the Monroe County Airport. We needed to get directions to the crash site and tell them that we were taking Zachary's car home. When we pulled through the gate, we saw Zack's Malibu. I felt dumbstruck. I felt as if I was having an out-of-body experience. (This would occur many other times over the next few years.) As we piled out of the van, I felt my legs move toward his car. I felt my hands move but my mind was screaming, "Where are you? Why aren't you here?" I cupped my hands so that I could look inside. There, I could see a Wendy's bag. That was his last meal before flying? Of course it was. He was always on the run, trying to squeeze one more minute into his day. He was supposed to be driving, not flying.

***

Flashing back through time, I thought of when Zack had picked out this car. How excited he was when he drove it home. Dan and I bought him a new car because he had earned so many scholarships that we didn't have to pay a dime toward his first year of college. The look on his face when he drove it home with the sunroof open. That smile… those hugs… my mind felt as if it were a bomb ready to detonate. How can I go on without him?

***

The people working in the terminal seemed surprised to see us, but they gave us directions. We still had some difficulty finding the entrance road to the crash site so we stopped at a nearby fire station for further help. One of the firemen escorted us to the gate for the path that led to the site.

The gate to the road was open, but we were unsure how far we could drive back on the road. We opted to park the van and walk. It was only about a half a mile up the road. No problem, I thought. As we hopped out, I began almost running ahead of Dan, Debby, David, and Jillian. If I get there, I thought, Zachary's spirit might be there, too. After all, this is where he was alive last. It all made perfect sense to me at the time. I went the wrong way at first. After a few wrong turns, we trudged our way through the field and to the edge of the woods. Dan discovered the trail. There had been trucks or all-terrain vehicles that had crushed the weeds which seemed to have made a path to follow. My heart pounded with anticipation of finding him… his spirit… as Dan and I pushed through the weeds.

When we discovered the site, it took my breath away. There were pieces of the airplane scattered all around and a very large impression the nose of the plane had left upon impact. I walked around aimlessly picking up slices of broken glass and chunks of aluminum from the skeleton of the plane to take home with me. It was as if I needed to locate some part of Zachary even if through inanimate objects. Shutting my eyes, my mind called his name and asked, "Where are you Zachary? I've come to take you home." As if she had read my mind, Debby said that she didn't think that he was here. This place would be too painful of a situation for him to stay.

I prayed that the Lord would let Zack come to me. Mothers need their children. I began pleading with the Lord. Then I began calling to Him aloud to help me. The desperation to find Zachary was all encompassing.

Then I looked at my husband. He had found two sticks and some vines. Dan began making a cross and planted it at the point in front of the plane-made hole. His presence of mind throughout this entire ordeal remains remarkable to me. David, Debby, Jillian, Dan, and I held hands and said a prayer for all five of those souls as well as for God to give us strength to continue this walk of grief. Then, we left the woods. There was nothing more to do there.

Piling back into the van, my sister, who was very worried about my health, kept handing me a bottle of water. After we visited each place that day, Debby would hand Dan and me a bottle of water and say that if we were not going to eat, at least we needed to keep hydrated. Dan and I forced ourselves to choke down a few swallows. Maintaining our health was far from the focal point of my mind. After all, wasn't this just a living nightmare?

We visited his apartment next. Rachel, who was subletting a room from Zachary, let us in. She looked as if she'd seen a ghost. She knew all the students involved in the accident. How kind she was to us even though her world had been shaken. Standing in the doorway, my mind flooded with memories… moving him in, bringing him homemade chicken soup when he was sick, and other such warm recollections. When your child grows up and no longer lives with you, as a parent, you think that he will be home. Perhaps, he has just stepped out for a date or to perform somewhere.

Upon entering his bedroom, the world seemed to spin faster. My heart was coming through my chest. There was his tux shirt and jacket, draped on the corner of his full length mirror. Odd thoughts popped into my head. I was proud of him for having made his bed. He'd done his laundry, but not put it away. It was still in the basket. Slowly, I opened his closet door and went inside to try to find him, to breathe in his scent, to hold onto part of him. I clung to those clothes and cried and cried. At this particular moment, my friend, Beth called my cell phone. She, too, was crying and asked me where I was at this time. When I told her, she said that's what she'd be doing, too. There was nothing more to say.

***

Throughout this journey, Beth would become my sounding board. The person I could call day or night and she'd listen. Listening is the best gift you can give to someone who is drowning in grief. I will always hold my good friends from junior high in high regard for their willingness to give that open ear to me during my darkest hours.

***

My mind reflected back to the news broadcast and Zachary's ordinary photograph. As his mother, I knew Zack would have been upset that his professional headshot wasn't on the news. Where would he have put those head shots? I knew that the university had the other four musicians because their master's degrees were to be vocal performance. Zachary's master's would have been in choral conducting. Even though Zachary was paid to sing in many venues, his passion was what took place behind the scenes. Indiana University would not have a professional photograph of Zack because he had not been in musicals or operas there. He must have his photos for his portfolio in his apartment. Jillian went to his four-drawer filing cabinet and retrieved the folder containing those professional photos. Somehow, I felt this would have been a huge relief for Zachary. We took that folder with us.

Telling Rachel that we'd be back next week to pick up Zachary's things, we turned to leave. We did notice a typed grocery list on his big, big desk. (The desk took up more than half the room.) David, Debby, and I had to laugh out loud. Only Zachary would be so particular as to type a grocery list. Jillian said that he had gotten the list online, sort of a generic list for groceries. Still, it was so like Zachary to make us smile even at one of our lowest points. I took that list with me, too.

Arriving at First United Methodist Church (FUMC), we were greeted by his friend and associate, Mary Beth. She took us upstairs toward his office-with-the-door. The fact that it had a door was a big deal. He had pleaded his case for the door with the senior pastor, typed list of reasons in hand, and won (beating out the associate pastor for rights to that office). Zack was in a cubical for all of his first year of working at the church. He always kept things in such pristine, extremely organized fashion. Even though Zachary's intentions were to stay at FUMC for only two years, he had taken a definite interest in the church and its people.

***

The first time Zack saw the scattered piles of music, he knew that he'd reorganize all of it. Zack had taken me to the storage area where the music was kept and proclaimed that he'd fix that up before he had completed his work at the church.

By the time of our last visit with him at FUMC in March of 2006, Zachary had organized all of the music into labeled binders for the Wesley Choir. He had cross referenced the music by composer, type of music, and song title. These details were color coordinated with the category of the music to make it more user-friendly. Zachary truly had an attention to detail.

During that last visit, Zachary, Dan, Jillian, and I were going through the church so that he could show us his office-with-the-door, when we passed the pastor in the hall. He told Zachary that the workers had just hung the cross in the sanctuary, but there was a wedding rehearsal going on and he'd have to wait to see it. After the pastor was out of our sight, Zack grabbed my arm and said, "Let's go, Mom. I can't wait!"

I can still see him with his arms spread out and looking at this huge wooden cross in awe. It was 22 feet tall and 10 1/2 feet wide with a removable smaller cross in the middle. When the middle cross is removed, a golden cross imprint remains. The cross has the Star of David as a background of the three dimensional cross. A FUMC member and craftsman named David Calkins had been commissioned by the church to create this masterpiece.

"Isn't it magnificent? It's just as I imagined it would be." There was a wedding rehearsal going on at the time. The participants stopped and stared at Zachary. I told him that we needed to go, but he said that they have these all the time and just kept looking at the cross. I told him that *these people* don't do this all the time. He turned to the rehearsal party and apologized and stated once more, "But isn't it spectacular!" Everyone laughed and agreed. I'm ever so grateful that Dan and I stopped to see Zachary that day. It's one of my most treasured memories.

We later found out that this cross had been Zachary's idea, a fact that he'd neglected to tell us. The wall of the church was too bare. Several members of the congregation had tried to fill the gap but nothing seemed to work. Zack offered an idea to the committee stating, "I have a thought." He made a sketch on a napkin. (The church framed it for us later and it now hangs on our living room wall along with a photo of the real cross at FUMC.) The cross remains on the wall at FUMC in their sanctuary with a plaque under it reading simply, "The Gift."

***

We made our way through the church and into that office-with-a-door. My knees felt weak as I looked around the room. So much of Zachary's personality was evident in the office decor. He had purchased two matching lamps with his own money. Music was visible everywhere. I knew that I needed to take part of him with me right away.

Music was so much of him. I grabbed two of his black music binders. One was labeled for Brytni's wedding the following October. Zack had already begun to gather songs for his little sister's wedding. I knew that Brytni had to have that binder. How would we have her wedding without Zachary? The other binder was a collection of Sandi Patty songs that he had used since he was very young. Once again my mind flashed back to this small, towheaded boy, his two front teeth missing, belting out one of Sandi's songs, "Love in Any Language." I could hardly stand with my melting knees. Dan thanked Mary Beth and told her that we'd be back sometime the following week to pick up the rest of Zack's things. I echoed his thank you as we left the church.

After returning to the airport to pick up Zack's car, we received a call from Gwyn Richards, the Dean of Music at Indiana University. He was hoping we could stop by before heading back to Anderson. Dan and I were in Zachary's Malibu. David was driving our van with Debby and Jillian as passengers. We were on our way to find the hospital, but instead chose to go to the university.

Dean Richards was there to greet us as we pulled our small caravan onto the road beside one of the music buildings. My mind was in such a total state of shock that I seemed like another person talking when I spoke. I was clutching the file folder containing Zachary's professional head shots close to my chest. When Gwyn introduced me to the photographer, I asked if he could please replace the photograph we'd seen on television with the one I had with me. He replied that he'd take care of it right away. One problem solved. Why couldn't everything be fixed that quickly? Somebody must shake me, please! I needed to wake up.

Walking into Gwyn's office, I immediately saw Fritz. What a wonderful feeling to hug someone else I knew who truly loved my son. Maybe he can help put the pieces of this puzzle back together. What happened that night? Why was Zack on the plane? Had Fritz seen Zack or spoken to him? My life had been broken into millions of fragmented pieces like a shattered glass.

Fritz took Dan and me aside to tell us about his last conversation with those students. Fritz had been with all five of the students just the night before. He and Zack were to be the dueling tenors at the Bach performance in Lafayette. Fritz spoke of helping to load the five students into a small SUV after the Bach practice. A fellow Bach singer named Lesli volunteered to drive them to the airport. Garth claimed the front seat while the two larger young men, Robert and Chris, slid into the back seat prior to Zachary. Georgina threw herself across all three boys in the back and Fritz shut the door.

Fritz said that they were all laughing and waving goodbye and reassured us that all five of those talented singers were enjoying themselves as they drove off to the airport. He wanted Dan and me to know that Zack's final trip was full of fun and camaraderie. I clung to every word... and to Fritz. I felt the power of his words record into my memory banks. Many things about that day remain a blur, but the story revealed to us at that moment would be forever burned into my mind.

David, Debby, Jillian, Dan, and I met several people that day at the Jacobs School of Music. The president of the university, several professors, vocal instructors, secretaries, and other administrators were all present in the dean of music's office. I can't recall all their faces or their names, but I did commit to memory their genuine compassion and the depth of their kindness. (These wonderful traits still remain a constant for us whenever we are at IU.) We thanked them for their kindness and asked for directions to the hospital so that we could pick up items Zachary had with him on the plane. We then left for the hospital not fully understanding what would be waiting for us.

Henry, our funeral director, had told us that his personal effects were at the emergency room. The walk through the hallway gave me a chill. Was Zachary's body still here? No, I remembered that Henry was having someone from the funeral home pick him up earlier in the day. My mind was echoing thoughts like, "Did I really just say those words...funeral... body?" I felt dizzy and queasy.

Locating the emergency area, we asked a guard if he knew where we could pick up Zachary's things. He had us sign for the bag he had for us. After Dan signed the form, he handed us a large, black garbage bag held closed by a twist tie. We stood like statues waiting for the other person to make the first move.

Dan set the bag down on the floor emergency room lobby. He untied the bag and removed Zack's small canvas black satchel which he carried with him. It was torn, bent and covered completely with wet, pasty mud. Dan and I looked at each other and Dan's knees buckled as he fell to the ground. We held each other on the floor of the lobby and cried. The security guard looked at us in dismay. I felt sure that he was totally unaware of what was in that bag.

We took the trash bag outside and continued to look through it. We pulled out his shoes. They, too, were covered in mud, but they were also mangled and partially ripped. "My poor baby! How hard did they hit? Were his shoes ripped off his feet? I need to hold him!" I felt the world spin and I remained as an outsider looking at everything move, but me. I felt as if I were watching someone else in my place. I recall thinking that I must be dead, too.

Besides the shoes and the black satchel, were his cell phone, pieces of sheet music, a Sudoku book, and his keys. The sheet music was torn and dirty, but still legible as was the Sudoku book. Those car keys…well, they were bent and covered in dirt. Dan slowly wiped away the dirt and tried to straighten out the car keys. That was another one of those dreamlike moments. We turned on his cell phone. It still worked! The phone had many unheard messages on it. We were amazed after looking at everything else, his phone remained intact.

David, Debby, and Jillian climbed into the van. Dan and I slowly got into Zachary's Malibu. We put the most of the items back into the bag and began the long drive home. Neither Dan nor I spoke too much. I spent my time crying while I stared blankly out the window. I looked through his glove compartment, CDs, and his empty Wendy's bag in the back seat. He had debited his food that night. I thought about his lack of cash and wished I had given him money more often.

After leaving Bloomington, Dan called Henry to tell him that we were stopping by the funeral home. He had to see Zachary for himself. I had been saying that off and on all day. Henry pleaded with Dan not to come. Dan would not take "no" for an answer. Henry relented, but asked Dan to give him some more time so that he could at least stitch Zack up. I remember wondering, what condition was Zack in? The shoes, the satchel, the car keys… all that mud… how *bad* was bad? I wanted to see for myself. After all, Zachary was my baby.

"Good," I thought. "We'll both see him." I wanted so badly to touch his face, hold his hand, and all of the other comforting things that a mom does when her children are hurt.

Dan told Debby, David, and Jillian to wait in the van or just go on home. He turned to me and told me to wait in the car. I told him emphatically that I would not wait in the car. I was going to go with him. There would be no stopping me. Henry met us at the door of the funeral home. He was desperately trying to talk Dan out of seeing Zack. Dan said that if Mary could see Jesus, he could see Zack. Pausing to catch my heart and my breath, I echoed the sentiment by merely responding, "Yes".

Henry said that there was absolutely no way he would let me see Zachary. "You just can't, Misty. You need to remember your son with a smile on his face. Not like this." Henry looked at me with compassion in his eyes and said once more insistently, "You just can't."

Dan and Henry went inside one of the viewing rooms. I waited outside fuming at being told what I could and could not do regarding my son. After all, I was his mother. Mary was Jesus' mother as Dan had said. Not seeing Zack after longing to see him since we had found out seemed absurd. I hadn't wanted or asked for protection from how he had looked. I was beyond very frustrated.

When Dan came out of the viewing room, he looked gaunt and pale. He grabbed my arm to escort me out of the funeral home. We walked slowly out of the funeral home and Dan handed David the car keys. Dan climbed into the back seat of Zack's car. He told us that he couldn't drive. Debby drove the van with Jillian and I angrily got into the front seat of Zack's Malibu. I felt cheated and betrayed. I know that Henry and

Dan thought that they were protecting me, but I felt the despairing need to see Zack. My voice was not being heard.

At home, Joel, Hillary, and Brytni were impatiently waiting for us. Brytni told me that her dad more or less fell out of the car while I got out and slammed the car door. We went into the living room. The kids asked Dan to describe Zachary's appearance. I remember some of the details. My heart wouldn't hear most of the horrific information. Dan went into the bathroom and got sick. Brytni went with him to try to console him. Later she said that she watched her dad age before her eyes. His hair even began to turn grey as she tried to comfort him. I continued to be in my own zone. Nothing made sense.

Later that evening, I took Dan outside to the front east corner of the house. I fervently declared my feelings about being excluded. I gave birth to him and I needed to see him now, if only to touch his hand. He called Henry to explain my plea to see my son. To Henry's credit, arrangements were made for me to at least view his hand. One side of Zack was not as damaged as the other. Henry asked for more time to prepare for me to come to the chapel to see even his hand. Relieved and vindicated, I re-entered the house to tell the rest of the family that we could see Zachary's hand within the next few days.

Before going to bed or thinking about sleep, I had to take care of Zachary's things from the hospital. Somehow, I just had to clean up this mess. Absurd thoughts of how could I try to help Zack kept me standing. Torn between what was existing and what I wanted to control seemed a conundrum.

Yes, the whole wide world seemed fast asleep as I thought about Zachary. My mind reflected on all areas of his life. It's funny how you can recall almost every minute of even your pregnancy of your first child. The moments only a mother can know. My heart and soul relived those moments over and over again...the first sign of movement in the womb, the hiccups while inside me. And all the things a mother feels when she's pregnant. All the while I thought, "Oh, Lord God, please let me wake up! This simply must be a nightmare!"

There would be no sleep as long as Zachary's things needed cleaning. If I could sleep, I just knew when I awoke: everything would be back to the way it was. I could resume my previous life, life with my whole family back in place.

See You in a Minute

Not While I'm Around

"**N**othing's gonna harm you, not while I'm around." Those are the first words of the song. I wasn't there when the plane went down. Did he call for me like when he was a little boy? I doubt that he called my name, but I wish that I could have been with him, to hold his hand, to shelter him from harm. What went through his mind? What were his last thoughts?

Dan or I had always been around to protect our children. All three of our children were grown up. The choices and decisions they make had become their own. Oh, how I wished he'd chosen to drive like he had in the past...like what was written in his planner, but it was Finals Week at IU. I knew that Zack was merely trying to shave off some minutes. He always had so much packed into a day. I wished I could have been the one on the plane and not Zack. He was so full of life with so much talent to offer. All of those students had talent beyond their years...beyond the years of most people. What could God's plan be with this tragedy? *Is* there a plan of some kind? How could this accident possibly have happened?

***

When Zack was a little boy of eight years old, he and his brother, Joel had bunk beds. Being the oldest, Zack took the top bunk. On the weekend of his Uncle Bobby's wedding,

~ 53 ~

Zack fell off his bunk while trying to make his bed. Dan and I were scurrying around finalizing our packing for the big event. Dan was a groomsman, Joel was the ring bearer, and Zachary was to sing, "Love in Any Language." Even at that age, people requested him for weddings and he occasionally served as a cantor at church. We were all so excited for Bobby and LeDonna's big day!

Zachary walked calmly into our bedroom, holding his right hand with his left. "I think I broke my arm," he told us. His right arm was in the shape of a "U." It was obvious that his arm was broken. Dan told me to go get some ice and put it in a plastic bag. Complete panic took over and I found myself spilling more ice on the floor than in the bag. Zack never shed a tear even though I was shaking and not at all calm.

We gathered Joel and Brytni along with Zack and rushed to the hospital. I held Zack on my lap the entire ride. Even though I couldn't protect him, I could help him. I could comfort him. I could hold him.

Upon arrival at the ER, it was determined that Zachary needed to have surgery to re-break his arm and put it into a cast. While he was on a gurney being wheeled into surgery, Zachary looked at me with tears in his eyes and fear written all over his face. I reassured him that everything was going to be okay – I'd be waiting for him right after the doctors fixed his arm.

After the surgery, Zachary insisted on going to the wedding to sing. I tried to talk him into staying home to rest. After all, he had just had surgery! Zack didn't want the wedding not to have its planned music. We once again packed the van and headed for the wedding.

Although I was sorry to see him suffering, at least in this scenario I was able to offer him a mother's touch. I was there to hold him, to apply ice to ease his pain, and simply to be there with him.

***

We had been to so many places in Bloomington; each one left its own impressionable scar in my heart as well as my soul. The emergency room items were tangible reminders of the pain I felt. His personal possessions handed to us, his dad and mom, in a trash bag. The mere thought that the final possessions Zack had carried with him that day had been placed into a container used to throw away trash, things we no longer value. The act seemed like pure irony. All of the mud covering his satchel, music, keys, and…his *shoes…those special shoes.*

***

I can picture Zachary and his friend, Leah, standing in our entry way with wide grins on their faces. They had been on a shopping trip with a mission in mind: a quest to find Zack a new pair of shoes; shoes that he could wear both with dress slacks or jeans. He and Leah had returned with *the* pair; black Dockers that slipped on, no laces.

"What do you think, Mom? They are the perfect blend of casual and dress, don't you think?" Zack asked me. He struck a pose and strutted around the hallway, just a bit. He and Leah were so proud of the successfully completed task. They giggled and gave each other high fives for the job well done. I did have to agree that those shoes fit the bill to a tee.

***

I took the trash bag over to the kitchen sink and carefully removed the shoes. As I scrubbed I cried. The elastic on his cross-between-dress-and-casual shoes was ripped. The insole of his right shoe was permanently bent inward. I thought again about his shoes being ripped right off his feet. I felt my breath catch in my throat. My mind could not – nor would I let it – go there.

The depth of my sorrow was truly beyond anything I could ever write on paper or speak aloud. The pain was excruciating with an ache transcending anything physical.

I continued to sob and scrub those shoes until I removed every trace of mud I could. Yet, it seemed no matter how hard I tried, I couldn't remove all of that mud. It seemed to become part of the shoe, kind of like a stain. I tried a scrub brush, stain remover, and any kind of detergent I thought might help. It was no use. The mud remained embedded as if had become a part of the leather. I handed the shoes carefully to Joel and Brytni who stood by waiting for further instructions. Everyone knew I was at a breaking point. Inside, I wondered if I was slipping away from the world around me. I was obsessed with trying to rid those prized shoes of the muddy blemishes.

Then there was his satchel. I first emptied the contents: several pieces of torn and muddy sheet music, broken pieces of his once-sharpened pencils, his working cell phone, and a partially completed Sudoku book. Had he been working a puzzle on the plane that day? I began to scrub his torn and bent, black, canvas satchel. There was just so much irremovable mud! The sink had to be emptied and refilled countless times throughout this cleansing process.

I just kept thinking how hard they must have hit the ground in those woods. Were Zachary and the others covered with the mud, too? My thoughts were that they must have been because of the vast amount of muck. Again and again, I felt my heart catch in my throat. Some things my mind would not let me envision. I told myself not to go there. I must concentrate on the task at hand: just keep scrubbing.

The purification process continued. I washed all of the items I found at the crash site. There were so many odd things. I couldn't imagine why the police or someone conducting the investigation of the plane crash hadn't collected these items to aid in the research. We had discovered bent metal pieces of the plane projected through the mire along with fragments and chunks of broken glass, and part of a navigational map. Why had these things been left behind? Were they not important to anyone? I wanted to discover the function of these neglected parts. Surely they had served a useful purpose at one time. What had happened on that plane? Why did they fail to land?

I prayed that none of them felt anything. "Please, God, let their pain have been brief or for them to have experienced no pain at all," I prayed. I hoped that they didn't know what happened and that no one was afraid when they crashed. I thought about the other mothers and fathers. Had they washed the mud off of their child's things as I had done? The unrelenting questions within my mind were unbearable. I wanted to wash away Zachary's hurts and make him whole again, just like when he was little. I think every parent would choose to be the one in pain rather than their child suffering.

After each item was carefully washed, I asked Brytni and Joel to take care of them. They dutifully took turns placing the items on the lid of the hot tub in the exercise room. Our room had French doors that separated it from the rest of the house. Perhaps my deep-seated thoughts were that by placing these artifacts out in a separate area, I could shut the doors and separate myself and the world from the accident. (Later I found out that Joel had asked Brytni what she thought I was going to do with this stuff and what were her thoughts about my cleaning frenzy. Brytni's response was that she hadn't a clue, but she had felt that they should continue to do as I requested.) The Lord has blessed us with such kind and respectful children.

Dan's brother, Mike and his wife, Diane had arrived from out of town. Mike and Diane were Zachary's godparents. I don't recall our conversations, but I am told that they watched the attempted decontamination process. Diane cried along with me while Mike talked through the events of the day with Dan. Their sons, Craig and Matt, were present, too. All of us were in such shock. They soon decided that we needed some alone time and left to go to Jodi's house for the evening.

After every item had been washed and placed in the exercise room, we decided to try to get some rest. It was an attempt to escape from the crushing sadness. Joel and Hillary decided to go to their house while Brytni went back to the apartment she shared with Kati, her cousin. Kati's sister Lauren and her boyfriend Adam were also there to offer their support.

Dan and I made the attempt to go to bed. We laid there, prayed the prayers we used to say with the kids before bedtime, asked God to grant us some peace, and cried... hard. We cried the kind of tears that just wouldn't end. Sleep came in only small increments; five minutes here, half an hour there, and so it went that night. The night panics came in waves. Finally, I woke Dan up and told him that I needed to walk and talk again. And so we did.

As we walked, we spoke about where to bury our son. I had just not ever given any thought to finding a place to bury someone I loved so deeply. Most of my family had been buried in a large cemetery across town. The very idea that Zachary would be so far away from me was wrong. We arrived at the decision that Maplewood Cemetery, close to our home and right by Anderson University, would be the place.

What an unthinkable topic of conversation! Surely this was not my actual life. My body was moving, although my head was feeling anesthetized. Why can't my heart go numb, too?

We decided to go to Maplewood when it was light. Because it was Sunday, no one would be working at the cemetery. Going when no one was there would give us the opportunity to look for a plot in private. I couldn't believe Dan and I were speaking of tombstones and plots. Where was I? Wake me up. Please!

The next day, Dan, Joel, his bride of just over a year, Hillary, Brytni, and I went to the cemetery. Jillian went, too. We wandered aimlessly around the Catholic section which was located close to the front of the cemetery. I didn't realize that the cemetery had different sections. Dan mentioned having a large stone with our last name on it. I was simply not coherent, more like a zombie, which, looking back seemed appropriate considering our location. We decided to focus on his plot that day and think about the stone at a later date.

All at once, there was a cool breeze. We were standing under a large maple tree. It was as if we were all frozen in time. There seemed to be a calming spirit encompassing us. I knew that this was the place. The family agreed that this location seemed just right. It was next door to the dorm where he had been a resident for three years as well as almost directly across the street from the music buildings at Anderson University.

Odd thoughts came into my mind through all of this. I was glad that he'd be under a large tree. He needs to be in the shade. Zack gets sunburned easily. I knew that this thought didn't make sense but I do think that a mother worries about her child even when that child is out of reach. Being rational wasn't part of my irrational world. Nothing seemed to make sense. Why should my abstract prospective thought seem any stranger than anything else?

Dan and I decided to buy our plots, too. I wanted to be beside Dan and Zack so I was to be in the middle. Joel was married. Brytni was engaged to be married in October. It seemed inappropriate to discuss where they wanted to be buried at this time. I do think that I made a reference to it but we simply didn't go into it. The very idea that we were purchasing a burial plot for Zachary was enough for all of us.

Dan would go to Maplewood on Monday to purchase the plots.

***

That evening, I received a call from my beautician, Nicole. After expressing her regrets about Zack's passing, she extended the invitation for me to have my hair done. She had checked the appointment book and saw my name listed for the following week. Nicole wanted me to know that the shop would be closed on Monday, but she would be happy to go in and get it done so no one would be there except us. She assured me that I could just sit or talk if I wanted. Nicole just wanted to be there if I needed her.

Come in on her day off? I recall thinking how very thoughtful. My appearance was the last thing on my mind. With the shop closed, no one would be around to ask questions or to eavesdrop, which did sound peaceful. Hillary, Debby, and Brytni encouraged me to pursue the offer. After talking it over with them, I decided to go while Dan was at the cemetery office to finalize purchasing the plots.

I wondered how many other beauticians thought of their clients in such a selfless manner. Nicole is a special friend with an exceptional heart. I'll never forget her willingness to extend her time and talent to me during the worst days of my life.

***

Guests and food continued to pour in. My friend, Alberta, and my sister, Debby remained as guard and secretary. They kept people at bay and recorded who brought what dish for our family.

One visitor, however, insisted on being seen. After having been turned away on Friday, Jerri was adamant about speaking with me. She told Alberta and Debby that there was something she had to give me that I needed. She had a purpose for being so unrelenting.

***

God works in mysterious ways. We first met Jerri and her husband, also named Dan, when Joel was five years old. Their son, Chris, played on the same coaches pitch team as Joel. The two dads named Dan coached our sons' teams together for seven years. We shared many a pizza and lots of Dairy Queen celebratory treats over those years. We had a parting of the ways, so to speak, and hadn't really communicated for several years.

An amazing thing happened the afternoon before the plane crash. Jerri and I mended fences in the parking lot of the school administration building. Prior to leaving, we hugged and promised to get together soon. Our chance meeting had only happened because I had been running late, and she happened to be leaving work early. I believe God had His hand on our reunion.

***

When I saw Jerri on Sunday, she seemed relieved to see me. "Misty, I have chills. I have something to tell you. I have a side job. I do videos for people…weddings, funerals, and other events. Please, let me help you. Let me do a video of Zack's life."

I was speechless. What were the odds that our paths would cross on the very day of the accident? Although the crash happened that night, we had repaired our friendship earlier that same day. Some people might say that such things are nothing more than a coincidence, but I *know* this mended friendship was a work from God. Not only did Jerri make a beautiful tribute to Zack, but she also helped design thank-you notes I used after the funeral. I still use those notes for special mailings today. But the best thing that happened was repairing a broken, but not forgotten friendship.

Another important visitor arrived to express his grief and offer his help. Dr. Richard Sowers came into our house looking almost as grief stricken as we appeared. We escorted him upstairs where we could talk without interruption. Dr. Sowers poured out stories of how much he had valued Zachary and loved him almost like a son. He had been a mentor for Zack and helped him throughout his musical journey at AU and IU. Rick tearfully told us of his intentions to leave Zachary all of his music collection when he had died, but this was not to be. He told us that the university wanted to contribute musically to the funeral. If he or the university could help in any way, they would be willing and available. Dr. Sowers also shared with us two e-mails he had received from Finland expressing the grief felt for this loss even overseas.

Dan and I cried with him. We were in awe of the impression Zack had left. What a difference his life had made in just twenty-five short years! Of course, Zack would have been honored at this extended tribute. Dan and I were more than willing to have the choir perform.

We must find a way to celebrate his life. Music was his passion and his talent. We told Rick about the location of the funeral. He was already aware, as well as having suggestions for music they could perform at the event. Dan and I discussed the music with the knowledge that a wondrous honor was being bestowed on our boy.

After we hugged Dr. Sowers, he instructed us not to worry about a thing. The music would be under control. We felt a sigh of relief as now part of the weight had been lifted from us. What a huge blessing!

Knowing more intense days loomed, Dan and I knew we needed to go to church and pray for God's guidance, wisdom, strength, and protection. I told Dan that I could not face the people or memories at either of the Catholic churches in town. We decided to go to St. Mary's in Muncie. Dan and I had both attended Ball State. St. Mary's is close to the college campus. Maybe we would find some peace for a short while.

We were delayed at home trying to decide where to go which made us a few minutes late to church. Upon our arrival, we experienced a true miracle…one of many more to come. When we got out of the van, a magnificent tenor voice seemed to greet us. This voice beckoned us to try to find joy and to enter the church. Dan and I stopped, almost in unison, gazed at the sun filtering through the trees and listened. We looked at each other and I said, "That voice! It sounds just like Zachary's!" Dan agreed. We both thought we were hearing things. We stood outside a few minutes longer almost as if we were holding our breath, listening and yearning for our son. The closer we got to the church doors, the louder it got and more certain we became that the voice we were hearing belonged to Zachary. Was Zachary waiting for us inside?

When we entered the church sanctuary, the voice we were hearing seemed to change. It was not the same as the voice we were hearing outside the church. Dan and I looked at one another. What happened to the voice? Was that voice we had heard before entering the church meant for our ears only? What did this mean? These are some of many questions I want to ask God someday. My mind was exploding with unanswered questions.

After returning from church that Sunday evening, we told the family about what had happened at church. I could tell that the family was unsure about our story so we dropped the subject, but held that moment in time close to our hearts.

A new task awaited us. Debby, Brytni, Joel, and I began rummaging through old photo albums and mounds of past pictures for the video. Jerri was hoping to have the photos and music by Monday evening. We had not yet set a date for the funeral although we had an inkling that it was going to be later in the week.

Pouring over pieces of the past was so painful…memories of a little boy gradually becoming a man. Zack at the piano, Zack performing, Zack receiving this award or that award, always smiling, hugging his brother or sister or someone else that he loved…all these wonderful events and precious times shared as a family spilled over the pool table. We organized the photos into piles beginning with birth and progressing to the latest photos taken on Easter, the last day I saw him.

I began to think about Zachary, our gift from God. My mom had once told me that children aren't really ours, but are just on loan to us. They really belong to God. It's amazing how much smarter your parents become as we age.

Strange as it may sound, I began to feel blessed. I had had the *privilege* of being the mother of one of the nicest people I have ever known. I was just lucky enough to be his mom. I cried tears of pride and sadness, blended together. Tears for what I had known and what I would miss.

Henry and Dan had talked. We were to meet at the funeral home tomorrow morning. We left the upstairs room and decided to call it a day. I knew that my eyes were sore from the perpetual crying. Everyone seemed spent. We left the photos in their respective piles with plans of returning tomorrow to complete the task. Everyone went home to rest for another big day on Monday…funeral plans and the viewing of Zachary's hand.

Our new sleep pattern slowly began to emerge after the past two life changing nights. Dan and I would pray, hold each other and drift off for a few hours or minutes. I continued to have my nightly panic attacks until I would have to get up to walk. Shutting my eyes was just too painful. The early morning walks were always so undisturbed. It seemed to be just Dan, me, and God. It was often on those walks that we could feel that people were praying for us. I believe that those prayers held us up and kept our feet moving forward.

It was during one of those walks around 4:00 or 5:00 a.m. that we saw our neighbor, Kevin, taking his dog, Nestley, for his morning business. When Kevin first saw us, he was startled. Realizing that it was Dan and me, he broke down. He told us that he, his wife Debbie, and their church, were all remembering us in their prayers. Good friends, powerful prayers…what more can be said.

We returned home. Dan and I did finally start trying to eat. He told me that we needed our strength. We feasted on hot tea and a slice of cinnamon raisin toast. This breakfast would also become the only thing I could choke down in the morning for many weeks. We called it our comfort breakfast.

It was finally time to go the funeral home. I was more than ready to see Zachary's hand. If everyone insisted on protecting me from seeing all of my first born then at least I would have the chance to see a part of him. I felt I needed to see some part of him in order to believe that Zachary was gone from me. In a way, I felt a little like Doubting Thomas in the Bible. I needed to see and touch the proof of his identity. Maybe, I should have been more like the other disciples, but at this point, I felt like a mother bear wanting to find and protect her lost cub.

Several of us met in the parlor of the funeral home. Once again, I began to feel sick to my stomach. Henry greeted us and ushered us into a large meeting room. The seats were fashioned in a circle so that we could easily share our plans for the impending "event." The stage was set for a viewing on Wednesday and the funeral itself would be on Thursday. I sat quietly and merely listened. When asked a question, I only remember nodding my head. Words seemed empty to me. Henry said that the viewing would be from 2 to 8 p.m. Only then did I react.

"No! I just can't greet people for that long," I declared. Dan and Henry agreed that it needed to be that long to accommodate others. I unwillingly conceded. I was sure that I would not be able to accomplish this daunting task. The dates and times were now set. I would have to figure out a way to drag myself through the looming event.

Before leaving the consultation room, Henry handed me a box. It contained an oval shaped pendant on a long black cord with a silver clasp. He said that he'd like to give me a gift, but only if I wanted it. Inside the pendant, Henry had placed a lock of Zack's hair. It resembled a solid silver tear drop. Zack's hair was not visible so no one would know that this necklace contained Zack's hair except me. It was as if a piece of him had been hidden inside much like Zack was hidden inside my heart and soul. I stood motionless. I hesitated at first, but of course I wanted the gift. It was part of Zachary. How had Henry even thought of such a sweet gesture? My mind drifted away once more.

***

Zack was a little more than a year old when he had his first hair cut. Dan and I took him to an old-fashioned traditional barber shop complete with the candy cane striped pole. It was owned by two charming white-haired ladies. The shop had an aura of the shop run by Floyd the Barber on *The Andy Griffith Show.*

Each one explained to Zack precisely what she would be doing during the hair cutting process. One of the barbers placed Zack on a booster seat and draped the apron around his neck. They squirted his hair with water, combed it, and carefully took the scissors to begin trimming. Zack had one long curl which hung slightly in the back. Cutting this lock of blonde hair from his head seemed to signify the end of his babyhood. That particular curl was placed into a baggy for posterity. Those sweet lady barbers had put Zack at such ease that he never cried or even moved a muscle. Dan took several photos of this historic family event. I went home and placed the long blonde curl into his baby book.

***

Now, I thought, I have the first and last lock of his beautiful, blonde hair. I put the pendant around my neck immediately. Somehow, it helped me feel closer to Zack. I wore it for the next few days as sort of a way to connect with Zack.

The topic of the casket was the next item for consultation. Henry remained ever so kind, calm, and reassuring. We could do this. We'd do it together. All of us got up to follow Henry to the room containing an assortment of coffins. The closer we came to the room, the less I could breathe. We broached the door. I simply couldn't go through that door. How could I possibly select a "box" for my child?

I fell to the floor crying out, "I can't do this. Please don't make me!" Dan came over and reassured me that he and Joel would take care of it. The rest of us waited outside of the room. I felt so weak. I wondered if I would be able to see Zack's hand after all. I felt as if I had let Zachary down. Somehow, I needed to regain my strength. Zachary had always thought of me as a strong diligent protector, but now I just wanted to go home, curl up in a ball, and disappear.

Dan, Joel, and Henry returned to us after making the selection. They had selected a casket with the Lord's Supper imprinted on the front, removable corner pieces with music notes and praying hands, and a special drawer for notes or items we might want buried with him. I still felt inadequate… disappointed in myself for lacking strength. I knew I needed to muster up the courage to make it through these next few days. "Help me, Lord!" was my constant prayer.

Henry asked if I was ready to view Zachary's hand or if I wanted to come back another day. I responded that I was ready. Forcing myself to be strong, I drew in a long breath and left the room. Debby, David, and my mom were waiting for us outside one of the chapel rooms. I had asked them if they wanted to see his hand and their attendance told me of their intentions. Henry had placed Zachary's body on a gurney much like one he'd been placed on when he was a young boy of eight. He was covered from head to toe with a white sheet. The only part of him that was in view was his right hand. Debby, David, Brytni, Jason, Joel, Hillary, and Dan went up first. Dan stayed beside Henry while Jillian and I went up together.

I knew at once it was Zachary. Even though his hand was cut and bruised, I recognized his long, thin fingers, chapped knuckles, and chewed cuticles (He bit them like his father.) Henry's eyes locked with mine. I told him that I'd know that hand anywhere. That hand belonged to Zack.

Henry said, "Misty, I want to assure you that he didn't suffer. Those kids never knew pain. Their deaths were instantaneous."

I asked, "How can you be sure?"

"If he had suffered at all, his fingers would be swollen. If you look at those fingers, there is absolutely no sign of swelling. Zack felt no pain," he replied.

As I continued to stare at his hand, my mind went back to his Wurlitzer upright piano that he played since the age of five. Lord, how can this be happening to my talented son who made the piano come to life? Why? Just as I was thinking these thoughts, the sheet covering his arm slid back revealing his forearm. It was in the shape of the letter, "W." Gasping for air, I gently covered his arm as if to shield it from further exposure. "How bad was bad?" I asked myself once again. I held his hand and cried. Lord, how I miss you, Zachary Joseph! Dan helped me out of the room. Thanking Henry for all he and his staff had done for us, we left the funeral home with four empty bulletin boards to fill before we were to return in two days.

The nightly routine continued. More food had come and more people had stopped by to see if there was anything that they could do for our family. Alberta had stayed all day writing down names of well wishers and answering the telephone. Her daughters, Heather and Noelle, had helped as well as her husband, Todd and son, Matt.

As I looked at their family, memories of times our families had shared together – vacations, trick or treating, trips to Chicago, birthday parties, late night writing sessions for our teaching books, times full of fun and laughter – echoed in my mind. Todd had taught all of my kids to water ski. Once while we were houseboating, all five of the older kids skied around the lake. Matt was too young at the time, but the other kids were the talk of the lake: five skiers behind a single speed boat. What a sight! What fun! Where had the time gone? Kids grow up and we move on. I found myself wishing for days gone by.

***

"Nothing's gonna harm you, not while I'm around…" those words from the song resounded like a drum in my head. Memories continued to race through my mind as rapid as a subway train. I found myself longing to shelter my family and wishing I had protected Zack from the crash. I thought about his beautiful smile.

***

Zack didn't always have the bright, wonderful smile that is reflected in his latest headshot. We had taken him to an orthodontist when he was in junior high. The doctor recommended we wait to fix his teeth until he had finished growing because his dental repair would require surgery.

His sophomore year of college in 2001, Zachary took the first step toward fixing his teeth. He got braces. He wore the braces for two years before the oral surgeon came into the picture. The surgeon had to cut a quarter of an inch from each side of Zack's lower jaw. After the surgery, his mouth was wired shut (really, they used something like rubber bands) for a week.

After the surgery, Zachary was to spend the night in the Intensive Care Unit. Dan and I were told to go home and they would take care of him. Dan had to work the next day so I told him to go home, but I insisted on staying with Zack just in case he needed me.

At the ICU, the staff was very nice; but told me that the only place I could stay was on the one hard chair in the room. Thanking them, I settled in for the night. Around midnight or so, I woke up and looked at Zack, who had been sleeping earlier. He was looking right at me with his eyes opened wide as if he wanted to say something. I seemed to know the answer before I asked, "You're going to get sick, aren't you?" Zack nodded. I rushed out to get the nurse. She put something into his IV to prevent his getting sick and all was well. I stayed with him for the next three nights at the hospital.

Zachary's smile could light up a room. After the braces were off and he had his new smile, Zachary flashed those pearly whites as often as he could, something he had avoided before, even in his senior pictures. His self-esteem seemed to soar. He was proud of the fact he looked more like his dad and his brother, Joel. Some of the AU girls even called him the "new resident hotty."

***

I wished that I could whistle and he'd be there as in the song. No matter how much I longed to have helped him, I couldn't be there for him when that plane went down. I'm glad he had that beautiful smile to mirror his beauty within. Protecting your child is instinct for a mother, part of the territory, so to speak. I wanted to continue to do my job, to protect him. I just wanted to help him like I had always tried to do...I felt so helpless.

No One Is Alone

"Sometimes people leave you, half way through the wood." The plane that carried Zachary had crashed half way through the woods; yet, the words to the song meant so much more. Zack had left me when he was half my age.

***

Cards and letters arrived at the house daily. It was unbelievable. There was so much mail that on some days, the mail carrier had to place them in a bag to hang on the outside of our mailbox. The letters came with postmarks from all over the United States and some from overseas. Most of the letters, we put aside until we could have time to digest their contents. Zachary was only twenty-five. How could so many people have known him well enough to send messages to his home?

Not all the mail was uplifting. Large envelopes from attorneys were also received. What was this all about? Curiosity got the best of me so I opened the first big envelope. I couldn't believe what I was reading. They wanted us to pursue legal action against the pilot's parents. Were they serious? How could Dan and I even consider this? After all, Georgina's parents had just lost their child, too. Without opening any of the other envelopes, I threw them all away. Dan and I had found ourselves shaking our heads at the very thought of causing more pain to anyone else. My mind began to drift to thoughts of the other parents. Five families lost a child that night. I wondered what they were going through, but then again, I knew.

Another major jolting blow was opening the newspaper and being struck by Zachary's obituary. When did we write it? Things began to run together. Events, people, and activities seemed intertwined. Time seemed to mesh into mere moments. The constants in our lives became early morning conversations, walking, moments of panic, tears, and prayer.

This may sound odd but after Zachary passed, there was some confusion about whether or not Zachary wrote his name 'Zach' or 'Zack.' Dan and I even debated about it. How could we not know how our own son wrote his name? I had always written 'Zach,' but Dan used 'Zack.' His latest signature was 'Zack' so that was what we decided to use even though there are several documents where Zachary had written 'Zach.' I think Zachary wrote whatever he felt like signing at the time. Perhaps he liked being unpredictable.

Because time ran together, I am unclear which early morning Dan began the gruesome task of composing our son's obituary. (Writing that term, "obituary" even now seems out of place in a parent's life. How could anyone do that? You do what needs to be done.) I didn't want Dan to write this by himself so we opted to perform the dreaded task together. Dan had jotted down a few thoughts before he sat down at the computer. As strange as it sounds, the words seemed to spill out.

Our minds seemed to operate in tandem. There was so much that we both wanted to share about our son. My arms were wrapped around Dan's shoulders as the facts of Zachary's life were stretched over the computer screen. We wanted the world to know how special his life was to us.

Dan and I were keenly aware of the people who had each played an intricate role in Zack's life. We wanted to make sure we expressed the relevance of their contribution. When we thought of the person who laid the musical groundwork, Mona Jackson popped into our heads. I cried as I wondered if she knew about the plane crash.

***

As Dan typed Mona's name, my thoughts drifted back to his first desire to play. When he was only three, Zack asked, "Mommy, can I have a piano?" Odd that he would want a piano. No one in our immediate family owned or played the instrument. What made him want to play a piano?

Zack continued to make his plea for the piano for two years until we relented. Dan and I purchased the used upright for $1,000, which was a huge financial undertaking for us with three small children at home. We discussed the possibility that perhaps Zack, Joel, and Brytni might all learn to play. Even though only Zachary pursued the interest, it turned out to be one of the best investments we'd ever made. If we had never purchased that piano, oh, look what would have been missed.

I began to inquire around to locate a teacher for Zack. We were fortunate to happen upon a gentle, middle-aged woman named Mona Jackson. She told me that past students had always been at least seven years old, but she'd let him attempt one lesson; then she would let us know if she felt he was ready. After that first lesson, Mona expressed surprise at his innate ability to connect to those keys. "He's more mature than some of my older students. Let's give this a try," she responded with a light hearted chuckle. Mrs. Jackson was his teacher and friend for ten years; so many practices, so many recitals…memories.

He loved to play! As peculiar as it may sound, I didn't have to ask him to practice. Many times, I did have to make an appeal for Zachary to "call it a night" because he'd play all evening if permitted.

***

I thought about his hands…his right hand I had seen all bruised and cut. Now his hands would never grace piano keys again. I wanted to go back in time and allow him to play all night long.

After the obituary was complete, Dan and I knew we needed that familiar morning air. We needed to try to clear our heads. What had we done? How could we have just completed this gruesome task? God must have been there. Was Zack there, too?

At some time during this uncertainty, Joel and Brytni inquired as to what Zachary would be wearing. Dan and I were content to have him buried in whatever Zack had on when he was on the plane or even a sweat suit. My thoughts were that he needed to be comfortable. His brother and sister were shocked by our response. They proceeded to remind us of Zachary's impeccable appearance. Known for usually being overdressed, Zack had an assortment of dress pants, suits, jackets, and wide variety of ties, not to mention his three tuxedos with several matching pants. Joel and Brytni insisted on their well-dressed brother at least being in a suit. They selected his newest blue pinstriped suit. And so thanks to his brother and sister, Zachary remained the better-dressed sibling.

Planning the funeral was the next hurdle. Dan bookmarked a few scriptures in his Bible; then, we looked through our church hymnal to select songs Zack loved to sing. Between the tears, Dan and I chose a few songs. Looking around the room, we spotted an inspirational plaque. Zack loved the words written on it so much he had two of them. One plaque was kept in his room here at home; the other was in his apartment.

The plaques read, "God gave us music that we can pray without words." Music was his life, not his death.

Dan and I knew that music must fill Reardon auditorium where his funeral… no, Celebration of Life, was to be held. My mind went back to my small little boy singing so many Sandi Patty songs; then, I thought of my own amazing connection to Sandi.

***

Being a kindergarten teacher for most of my life, I have been blessed with many wonderful students and parents. I had the privilege of having all of Sandi's and her husband Don's girls in *our* classroom. (The classroom was not just mine, but ours. It belonged to all those who lived and learned inside that room.) Over the years, my life and Sandi's have connected and reconnected. Anna, Sandi's oldest, was a past kindergarten student of mine. The Novak family has vacationed with Anna and her husband's family, The Trent's, in Siesta Key, Florida. Sandi had sung at Joel and Hillary's wedding. Zack had listened to Sandi most of his life and loved her voice so much that he counted her among his favorite vocal performers.

***

Over the years, Sandi and I have become friends, so when Dan and I stopped by her home to ask her to sing, Sandi hugged me and cried. "Of course," she kindly and compassionately said. "I'd be honored." She would sing, "The Lord's Prayer". Good friends are pure blessings from God. I began to think of how odd life was: connecting the past to the present, years forging bonds that continue to grow.

Fritz Robertson had been Zack's voice instructor at AU as well as his future colleague. The two tenors sang together on many occasions including the last rehearsal in Lafayette. More importantly, Fritz and Zack were friends. Fritz and his wife, Patty, taught Zack and his college roommate, Doug, to play bridge. Many times on a Saturday evening, Zachary would tell us that he and Doug were off to Fritz and Patty's for a night of bridge. (Among his books, we found a book entitled, *Bridge for Dummies*. I feel sure that Zachary wouldn't want to lack understanding of the game, especially against his respected professor and friend.)

Dan and I asked Fritz to sing, "Ave Maria" at Zack's Celebration of Life and he graciously accepted. Zack strived for perfection and loved learning. We continue to thank his teachers, like Fritz, for being an inspiration. Thoughts of Zachary's voice and how it grew rang in my head.

***

After the first semester at Anderson University, Zachary came home for a visit. He always went into our living room, sat down at his piano, played and sang. He'd been able to sing all of his life, but something was different. His voice had developed a broader range and a robust power that seemed to make the room vibrate. Walking into the living room, I asked Zack, "What happened to you?"

Zack had not taken voice lessons prior to college. He relayed to me that his voice teacher, Fritz, had worked with him. Zack's eyes danced with excitement as he recanted some of the things he had learned. Zack said that Fritz had unusual techniques, like crawling on the floor, but Zack was already hearing some changes, too. He was so impressed by Fritz's voice and his teaching that he felt sure AU's professors would provide him with skills to help him grow vocally. I had to admit, as his parent, I was convinced that Zack was right. We were both extremely enthused at what the future might have in store! I wanted to go back to that day and stay…the future surely didn't mean this!

***

The music was almost finalized; Dr. Sowers and the AU Chorale were providing choral music; Sandi and Fritz were singing, but Dan and I still needed a pianist and we wanted violins, too. Unsure of who to call, we scanned Zachary's Rolodex for help. Zack had often mentioned a wonderful musician named Shirley Coolidge. We located her name in his file and gave her a call. We didn't know her but rather only heard of her and her abilities. I called her and requested her talent and help in recruiting a few violins. Her talent and her kindness proved to be fact not fiction for she was happy to fill both of our requests. The musical part of the ceremony seemed to have fallen into place almost effortlessly.

Gathering the courage to go on, Dan and I left for St. Ambrose to discuss funeral plans, a topic beyond my grasp. Unthinkable, but necessary detailed plans loomed ahead of us. How could we go on? We entered the rectory to meet with Father Dhondt, Connie Jo, and Joanne. Zachary loved Joanne, who was a good friend to our family, Jillian's mom, as well as a cantor at church. We knew that cantoring his funeral would be hard for her, but Joanne was willing to give her voice to help celebrate Zack's life. Cooperation just seemed to pour out to us from everyone, sort of like tributaries flowing into a large river. Looking back, it was pure harmony.

We also related to this planning group that two other priests had offered to help in any way that was needed. Father Bob had come to the house to pray with us and expressed his willingness to help. Father Bob had given First Communion to Joel and Brytni as well as playing an important role early in our married life. Dan and I felt that he should, if he could, assist in the Mass. Father Paul in Alexandria, Indiana had been a blessing to Dan's parents. He, too, had volunteered his services. The group felt that the service would warrant the support. Zachary would have a Mass with three priests? I couldn't help but think that Zachary would have been taken aback by all of this. Dan and I were grateful for guidance of this faithful group.

Jillian contacted FUMC in Bloomington to request Jimmy Moore to speak at the funeral. Jimmy had been the minister at the early services when the Wesley or the Children's Choirs sang. Zachary was the music coordinator for those church services and worked closely each week with Jimmy. Jillian advised us that having Jimmy would add a connection to his past two years in Bloomington. We had met Jimmy and knew him to be an inspired young man. Jillian made the arrangements and we were pleased to have blended both churches into one service.

We let the funeral planning committee know of two more speakers: my husband Dan and Zachary's Uncle Pat (Jodi's husband) wanted to speak. Pat had come over to the house earlier and expressed his need to speak about Zachary at the funeral. He had written out his speech to let us read it previous to the ceremony. We were touched. The prepared speech was heartfelt. I was unsure how Dan would be able to present his words at such an emotional event, but he insisted that he'd be fine. Dan conveyed to me that I shouldn't worry. "God will be with me," he said. I told Dan that when he spoke at the funeral, I wanted to stand by him. I knew that I wouldn't be able to speak coherently, but I could surely be strong enough to stand beside him. Here were two God-fearing men wanting to express their love of Zachary. I marveled at their strength when I had difficulty putting one foot in front of the other.

***

It was at this meeting that Father Dhondt reminisced about Zack: "The Maestro, as I often called him, was the only young person who ever had a key to the rectory and the church. I gave him a key to my house, that's how much I trusted him. One night, I heard the organ playing which was not unusual. Zachary came often to practice a few days prior to Mass. One particular night, the playing stopped. I usually heard his car start and would sometimes hear him drive away, but that was not the case. Growing concerned, I went over to the church only to find him fast asleep on a pew. I gently called his name and told him that it was time for him to go home to bed." Father Dhondt's story of Zack lifted the weight of sorrow, if only for a little while. Zachary and Father Dhondt shared a genuine love and commitment to God.

***

All the funeral pieces were secured for the day of celebration. Zachary's Mass of Christian Burial would be held on a Thursday, in Reardon Auditorium on the campus of Anderson University. Even in death, Zack had managed to be ecumenical; three divisions of Christian faith – Catholics, Methodists, and Church of God – fused together in one place, at one time, to celebrate the passing of Zachary's life here on Earth. Was God teaching us a lesson?

Dan and I had really wanted to capture the spirit of celebrating. Wanting to hear memories Zack had made with others, my sister helped us write a page to be displayed at the viewing asking people to write down some recollections for us. The framed sheet said: *We are compiling a scrapbook for Zachary. Please take a sheet and share a favorite memory (funny, fond, silly, best, etc.). When you are finished please drop it in the box. Thank you, Zachary's family.* Along with the note we also displayed a family photo. We placed a box nearby for the memories to be placed so that we could read them later.

Looking back on this, I was so glad to have recorded memories. Stories we hear now are our only new memories of Zack. At the showing, I had blocked out so much that I couldn't retain much of what people told me about Zack. With these written remembrances, I could read about Zachary's connection with others.

More visitors and family members came and went during those days. We were numb and confused; yet, we felt blessed by everyone's kindness.

The rest of Dan's immediate family arrived; Dan's youngest sister, Susie, her husband, Jim and their children, Jeannie and Patrick made the trip from Florida. They sat upstairs with us and cried. Dan's younger brother, Bob, and his children, Jessica, Heather, and Alexis, and his wife, LeDonna came from northern Indiana. LeDonna had been diagnosed with terminal cancer before Christmas of 2005. She'd even had the lower part of her arm amputated to try to prevent the spread of this disease. We didn't talk. We held onto each other and cried. There was nothing either of us could say.

It had been a long day already, but time went on. Food had not been a high priority for me over the course of these days. That evening, my faithful friend, Terri Ginder, arrived at the house. We had been close friends since before our babies were born. Drinking half-glasses of iced tea and eating chocolate chip cookie dough had been our trademark over the years. Terri's known for her cooking and baking.

With tears running down her face, forcing a smile, she said to me, "Well, I hear, my friend, you aren't eating. I made Shepherd's Pie and chocolate chip cookies for you – some are baked and then, of course, we have the dough. Please eat something." I sat down on the couch, hugged her, got a plate of Shepherd's Pie, and ate a cookie. How could I turn down my buddy? Terri had given me more than food. She had shared a piece of her heart.

Jerri and her husband, Dan brought over the video she had made. We all sat together and watched how brilliantly Jerri had blended Zach's musical recordings to his photos. She had captured his personality on film. What a blessing to have had someone who had known Zachary compile this video. The very fact that just days before we hadn't spoken and now, were together sharing this moment was nothing short of a marvel.

Sometime later, when most everyone had left except for our immediate family, we returned upstairs to the pool table covered with those sorted piles of photos. The funeral home had sent with us four bulletin boards to be filled with photographs reflecting our son's life. Assembling those visual reminders of the past would not be easy. Each photo represented a phase in Zachary's life...from birth to the last photo we had taken on Easter, a mere four days before the crash. Debby, David, Brytni, Joel, Hillary and I talked, smiled, and cried as we labored over each board. We filled three of those bulletin boards before it became too much to handle. (I just knew I would wake up any minute from this nightmare. I felt that none of this could be real.) Joel, so strong throughout this whole ordeal, was finally overcome with emotion as he saw a picture of Zack and him tubing together. We decided to just take the empty board back. It wasn't that we didn't have enough pictures, but we were all exhausted from the emotional undertaking.

Before leaving to go to his house, Joel had begun rummaging through some of Zachary's keepsake boxes. (I was thankful that I'd had them help me redo their boyhood room the year before and boxed up many keepsakes.) Joel rushed back into the game room with a shocked look on his face. He had discovered several copies of a poem with a profound message. As Joel read the poem, the room seemed to become perfectly still. We couldn't believe what we were hearing. At the time, we had no idea where or when Zachary had received the poem. It read:

What Is Success

To laugh often and to love much;
To win the respect of intelligent people
And the affection of children;
To earn the appreciation of honest critics
And endure the betrayal of false friends,
To fill "the niche" and accomplish "the task"
To appreciate beauty; to find the best in others;
And express both,
To leave the world better than it was,
Whether by a healthy child,
A garden of flowers,
A redeemed social condition
Or a rescued soul;
To know even one life has breathed easier
Because you have lived.
This is to have succeeded.
What I have possessed in this world
Will belong to someone else immediately…
On the day of my death,
What I am will be mine forever!
The purpose of my life is not just to be happy,
It must be useful, honorable, compassionate;
It must have made a difference
That I have lived!

The message filtered through the air. Was Zachary there with us? Finding this poem at this particular moment was a spiritual experience for all of us.

After everyone had left, Dan and I stayed up and tried to prepare ourselves for visitation the next day. We were to arrive at noon. Henry extended the offer of allowing family members a special viewing of his right hand, prior to the open viewing. We'd have to try to rest for the long day ahead. With each minuscule rest, those nightly panic attacks would cause me to sit straight up, and gasp for air. Finally, Dan and I took to the early morning streets again. How were we going to do this? I didn't want to see or talk to anyone else. I just wanted my world back! My mind was in such a state of bewilderment.

As the sun rose, we began to go through showering and dressing. Hillary's Grandma Tanner, who is my size, had given me a beautiful, pinstriped suit to wear. Hillary had told her that I didn't know what to wear so she sent over the suit. It fit like a glove. I could see why Hillary was so thoughtful. She had witnessed this generosity from her family. I put on the suit and thanked God for those who thought about the needs of others.

Before we left, a large vase containing an incredible bouquet of flowers arrived at our door. It was sent from Yatish and Louise Joshi. Dan and I paused and looked at each other. These flowers were from the pilot's parents. How thoughtful of them. I hadn't time to process my own life let alone think of someone else.

We had about an hour before we were to be at the funeral home when I decided to go into the boys' old bedroom. Dan followed me as I collapsed onto the floor into a pile of sobbing jelly. Through my tears, I told Dan that I just couldn't do this. I told him that he should go on without me. I simply didn't want to see anyone. Through my tears, I noticed that Zachary's closet door wasn't closed. Slowly, I stood up to shut it, but it wouldn't close all the way.

Then something phenomenal happened. As I opened Zack's closet door to clear the obstruction, a small photo album and a few papers fell out at our feet. What was all *this?* Chills ran down my arms as I reached down to pick up the contents on the floor. There were pictures that had fallen out of the album; some of them I'd not seen. The first two pictures we looked at showed Dan, Joel, Brytni, and me standing by a statue of Christ.

***

My mind flashed to a brief vacation we had taken in the summer of 2002. Dan and I planned the trip with a mission in mind. With all three kids in college, our trip must be inexpensive; yet, meaningful and fun. Before MapQuest or GPS systems, a typical road map listed scenic sites tourists might want to visit. Dan and I had selected a little known site written in fine print on the map as one of our destinations. We were trying to find, *The Christ of the Ohio* statue. It took us hours to finally locate the huge statue. It was Jesus Christ with his arms stretched as if to welcome anyone to draw near. The view from the top of the hill was amazing. The statue was lined with flowers, and the Ohio River flowed below. The location was extremely random. It wasn't near a park or any other tourist attractions. After all of the traveling, the statue was the end result? Needless to say, our children were less than thrilled.

***

Dan and I stared at the photographs. Zack was with us on that trip, but he wasn't in the picture. He must have been the one taking the pictures; yet, Dan and I don't remember ever having seen a picture of any of us at the statue. What could this mean? Did the photo signify Jesus was watching over us? We were mystified. Both of us recalled the trip and our kids' total lack of enjoyment about this particular outing, but here was this photo giving us an intense message. We continued to look through the stack of fallen objects.

Another photo seemed to jump out of the pile. This picture was of my dad outside his lake cottage petting two roaming basset hounds named Oscar and Roscoe. My parents usually went to the lakes for extended weekends and warm weather holidays. They fed these dogs their leftover table scraps and enjoyed the dogs' company whenever they were at the lake. Even though these dogs didn't belong to them, Mom and Dad knew their names because these dogs sort of belonged to everyone at the lake.

My dad was confused and frustrated upon hearing the news of the plane crash. He is a man of great faith. The idea that Zachary was gone seemed to discourage and irritate him. During one of the long days prior to the viewing, Dad was sitting in his car. I went out to him and expressed my concern for him. When we had finished our talk, Dad left for the lakes to mow the grass and reflect. Upon his return, Dad appeared to be at peace. He told me that he'd had a long talk with Oscar and Roscoe and he felt better. (Dan and I had not seen that picture before. Was this a sign? Where did Zack get this? When was it taken? Why had we not seen it before now?)

We came across other photos. Each group of pictures seemed to have special meaning:

- Zack at AU sitting on a bench outside of the music room being goofy while playing the clarinet. (He loved being silly and making others laugh. I'd never seen him with a clarinet.)

- Two photos of Zack with two of his college friends; one picture was with Doug, his roommate for three years, plus Doug's nieces and nephew; the next was of Zack and Leah, both all dressed up and acting goofy (He loved his friends and spoke of them often. Both of these friends had been to our home on several occasions. Both friends we loved, too.)

• Several photos of Zack in Europe with friends and one in his crazy Russian hat (As a joke, Joel had asked his brother to bring him back one of those furry Russian hats. Zack gave that hat to Joel as a souvenir after one of his AU Chorale trips.)

• Zack lying on the floor after practicing with the Highland Singers. (He was face down as if he had just collapsed, much like I wanted to do right then. Zack was notorious for sleep whenever and wherever he could catch some zzzz's.)

• Zack with a good friend, Leonard. (Zack was a year older than Leonard, and shared a mutual dislike of playing Little League. Leonard and Zack often collaborated on musical arrangements in high school. Even though they were very different, their lives crossed paths many times. We had become friends with his family. His family, especially his mom, Rita and I enjoyed many show choir competitions. She was pure class and great fun. We later found Leonard's business card in Zachary's Rolodex.)

• Many photographs of Zack with family from Illinois. (Dan was born in Joliet, Illinois, where most of his family still live. Dan's mom came from a family of nine children. All of us are very close. Several of them came to Anderson when Zack sang at the symphony and went to Carmel, California to hear him in the Bach Festival. Zack talked for days about how much he cherished them and appreciated their efforts to be there for him. I felt sure that we'd see all of them at the viewing.)

• Photos of Zachary with two different choirs: one was AU Chorale and the other was the St. Ambrose choir. (Zack directed Dan and me in the St. Ambrose choir for seven years.)

• Several pictures of Zack with Garth and the cast after the opera, *Little Women*. (There was Garth! I had seen similar photos that Dan had taken. I wasn't sure where Zachary had gotten these pictures, but what were these doing here and now? Garth had been a good friend at AU and was on the plane that fateful night.)

• A picture of Zack in high school with his arms draped across our shoulders, sporting his first attempt at facial hair –a mustache and goatee. In this photo, I was also holding his hand. (He had come home that last Easter, just four days before the crash, with the same, unshaven look. Zack was hopeful the new look would make him seem older. Oh, how my heart yearned to touch him!)

All of these photos took on their own message, so it seemed. The room, for me, began to take on its own sense of vitality. We kept gazing back and forth at one another as life emerged from each photo. I remember yearning for more.

Tucked away with the photos, we discovered a picture of Zack when he was in third grade mounted on a piece of yellow construction paper. Accompanying the snapshot was an autobiographical diamante poem. Written in his beautiful cursive writing, it read:

Zachary Novak
boy
funny quiet
run   play   eat
amusing walking talking sleeping
smile relate think
skinny joyful
kid

That poem applied to him still at age twenty-five. He maintained these attributes throughout his life. How odd that this poem was here and had fallen at our feet…how strange that he had it in his closet among all these other random things. Dan and I continued to shoot glances of disbelief back and forth at each other. This surely was the better part of my living nightmare. We continued to look through the small pile of artifacts.

Possibly the most amazing discovery found among the items was a torn out page from *The Upper Room Devotional* pamphlet. My mom provided copies of this bimonthly pamphlet for all of our family. "What was this and why was it torn out?" I asked. My knees began to shake. "Dan, look at this! Look at the date!" We read it together, *"April 29ᵗʰ, 1994."* It was entitled, "Peace for the Troubled Heart". The author, Violet Perera of Colombo, Sri Lanka, wrote from a grandmother's perspective, telling about her daughter, a mother who had lost her son and was in mental agony. (Yes, I thought. I, too, am in mental agony.)

The article began with a scripture from Jeremiah 17:7 (NRSV): "Blessed are those who trust in the Lord, whose trust is in the Lord." The article spoke of God's light shining in the darkness around us as well as being disillusioned about praying. (I had felt that way, too! Prayer, at times, seemed almost painful. I found myself often asking, "Why, Lord? Why these wonderful talented kids? They could have made the world a brighter place!") The small article concluded with comforting, enlightening, and uplifting words: "God's love and mercy can be seen in the midst of our suffering. The prayer focus: Those needing reassurance of God's wonderful love." We read this article on April 26ᵗʰ, 2006. Violet and I were separated by time; yet, not at all separated by emotions.

Why had Zack removed this from the booklet more than 10 years ago? What made him save it? I felt the need to hurry and get that last, blank bulletin board that we couldn't fill the night before. I told Dan that I needed to have these things with me at the viewing. These new discoveries gave me strength that I had not felt for days. Fervid urgings to share these findings with everyone had begun to surge through me. Dan and I quickly assembled the items onto the last bulletin board.

When we had completed the task, these new-found discoveries had been exactly enough to fill the bulletin board. I knew that I could go to the viewing and not fall down. We felt that God (and Zachary) would be there to hold us up.

As the song says, "No one is alone… truly. People make mistakes, fathers, mothers, people make mistakes, thinking they're alone, holding to their own… Things will come out right now. We can make it so…no one is alone." We were no longer *holding to our own*, but rather holding onto our faith, and the hope that we would see Zack again.

See You in a Minute

You'll Never Walk Alone
~
You Are My Home

A s Dan and I crossed the parking lot, we knew we were not walking alone – we felt Zachary. Henry greeted us at the door of the funeral home. Most of the extended family was also in the foyer. For the past few days, I had listened to Zack's music. In my mind, hearing him sing and play the piano brought Zachary's presence into the room with me. My first question to Henry was, "Do you have the CDs? They will be playing, won't they?" Henry reassured me that of course, the CDs of Zack's music that I had given him would be playing, and if I needed anything else, he'd be sure to get it for me or anyone else in the family.

Entrusting Henry with the newly completed bulletin board, I requested that it be placed right beside where Dan and I would be standing to greet well-wishers. Henry was agreeable to whatever we wished. An easel for the board was placed near the front of the room close to our destination inside the largest of the three viewing rooms. The two vacant viewing rooms would provide extra space for the line of people the funeral home was expecting to attend Zack's viewing. I was totally unaware of anything except that bulletin board. It had almost become an appendage to me.

I began to explain to our family what had happened in the boys' old bedroom before our arrival at the funeral home. Detailing the particulars of each item on that newly filled bulletin board, I relayed what Dan and I had experienced only a few moments ago. The family gawked at me as if I'd lost my mind. I didn't care about what anyone thought or said, I was still filled with the strength gained from that experience. I knew what happened and that I wasn't on my own now. I believed it even if no one else but Dan and I understood!

The lobby of the funeral home was crowded. Close relations from Illinois, California, New York, and Arizona were in attendance. They all loved Zack and he loved them. As I showed them the pictures that we'd discovered earlier, they, too, looked dismayed. I'm still unsure about what they thought as I recanted the episode. Our family is so close that I could feel the power of their love and support during our devastating hurt. I wasn't going to walk through this alone. From deep within me, I knew this to be a fact.

As we entered the viewing room; my mind and body seemed to separate. All of *this* was beyond my grasp. The sweet perfume of the flowers saturated the air. Potted plants of all shapes and sizes, blankets, books, and other similar items infused the room. A television with his DVD was playing as Zachary sang in the background. All of Dan's aunts and uncles were there. Having been in his family since I was eighteen, they had become my family, too. All of his aunts: Nancy, Pat, Lois (who had lost her son,) Judy, Ruby, and Joni were there. I cried and hugged all of these special people, too numerous to mention. Clinging to Aunt Joni, who had come from California for the funeral, and LeDonna, we stared at the photos as we watched Zachary's life move on film in front of us. I could truly feel the pain they felt for our family. We didn't say much as we watched the video. We just cried together.

At the far end of the room was Zachary's casket, closed at the foot and partially at the top. Henry had Zachary's hand available for family to touch, if they wanted to, before the actual viewing began. A shiny silver frame containing Zack's 8x10 photograph was positioned at the foot of the casket. I could hardly stand. I felt myself disconnecting from reality. Scanning the room for that bulletin board conveying the message of power and faith, I gravitated toward it to steady myself.

Dan and I waited for our family to have a chance to see his hand before Henry ushered them out. The immediate family would have the last view prior to the lid being closed for the rest of the crowd. Dan and I were the last to go. I really don't remember much about that. As the next two days went on, I found that to be the case about most of the events.

The casket came equipped with a special drawer for mementos that we might want to go with Zachary, so to speak. Dan and I had invited a few people to put in things that they thought epitomized a special memory between them and Zack. My nephew, Stephen, put in a bottle rocket. I realize how strange that sounded to everyone, but for those who knew Zack well, it made us smile.

***

Every Fourth of July for as long as I can remember, my sister and I take our families to our parents' lake cottage to celebrate the holiday. Zack and Steve could hardly wait until they were old enough to help light the fireworks. Zachary was several years older than Steve, but those two boys shared the title of our family pyromaniacs. For the first few years, Dan, Ervin, and my dad lit the fuses for the fireworks. Then the men allowed Zack to assist. The last few years before the funeral, Zack and Steve took turns setting off the celebratory display while the rest of us reacted with the appropriate, "Ooohs and Aaahs." Who would help Steve now?

***

Each family member added their own personal connection. I don't know what everyone put into that drawer. Only a few family members felt the need to share with me their personal unforgettable article. My sister gave him a key to her front door so that he could come to her house any time. Dan gave him his well used ring rosary. He placed it on one of Zack's fingers of the hand we were able to see. He also wrote Zack a letter. I, too, wrote him a letter telling him how I would miss him and detailing what an incredible gift he'd been to me. I wanted to seal myself in that envelope, too. How was I going to meet all these people?

Drawing in a deep breath and praying for God and Zack to be with me, I tried to compose myself for the day. Slightly before 2:00 p.m., Henry opened the doors allowing viewing to commence. I was told that the crowd was so large that the funeral home had to borrow extra chain barriers from AU to help the crowd weave in and out of the other viewing rooms and that the crowd wrapped around the building and down the road. Still focused on the last bulletin board, my mission was informing everyone that Zack would always be with us. I knew that from the depths of my soul.

Among the throngs of people we saw that day, Dan and I met numerous people for the first time. There were three particular meetings that I can recall as if they happened yesterday.

The first meeting was someone Zachary had wanted us to meet, but time had not permitted. Greeting us with a look of true loss and intense sorrow was Duane Diedrich. He was a thin gentleman with a soft spoken, gentle spirit. As we shook his hand, Duane introduced himself.

Dan and I reacted by excitedly saying his name almost in unison; "You're Duane! How very nice to meet you finally. Zack has told us so much about you!" I will never forget the look of astonishment on Duane's face. Zack and Duane were truly not divided by their age difference. They were kindred spirits who shared a variety of commonalities. (Since our meeting at the viewing, we have had the privilege of speaking with and visiting with Duane. We feel like he's always been part of our family. Zachary had an uncanny sense about people with big hearts and kind, spirit filled souls. Duane certainly falls into that category.)

Zack's work in Bloomington also introduced us to another family we had not met until that April 26th. Eric Behrman had come from Bloomington to introduce himself and tell us that he knew Zack through FUMC. Dan and I recognized his name from the news over the past few years. (Eric's daughter, Jill, had been abducted while riding her bike and murdered.) Eric's eyes spoke to us. They told us of the pain of the loss of a child. We knew and felt the connection instantly. Before he left, he gave us a hug along with his phone number and told us that he'd be there if we needed help. (An odd fact: Zack and Jill were both born on September 17, 1980.)

Eric's willingness to extend his hand to parents who have lost children will never be forgotten. How could my loss compare to his? My son died in a tragic accident while his child was …hurt so much more? Eric explained to me loss is loss, grief is grief. It doesn't diminish the fact that I, too lost my child. Somehow, I felt inadequate to stand in the same shadow of their tragic loss of Jill. Eric's strength of character and selflessness to stretch his hand across the miles to us left a deep imprint on our lives.

Another encounter involved a young man and his new wife. The couple told us that they had just gotten married the year before and Zachary had been the cantor at their wedding. They were Jewish and Zack had done such a marvelous job that their Rabbi had asked which Synagogue that Zack cantored so he could hear him sing again. His enunciation of the Hebrew language had been that flawless. They had waited for four hours in line to share that story with us. (We later found CDs of Hebrew diction among his things.)

Most of the encounters remain vague, but I do remember seeing Dr. Charles King and his wife, Pam. When I saw Dr. King, I hugged him tightly and cried, "You saw him first." Dr. King had delivered all three of our babies as well as being our family physician until he retired. Most of that day, I truly didn't cry. But the memories with Dr. King just couldn't be pushed away. I could even hear Zack's first cry. I could see Dr. King dancing around the delivery room holding our only baby girl, Brytni. How do you effectively thank someone who has been with you and your family in such earth-shattering occasions? All I could do is cry. His coming to be with us once more spoke volumes.

My high school friends came to the viewing, too. Cindy (Staley) Granger greeted Dan and me with a special box. Several of my high school classmates had established a scholarship in Zachary's name through Anderson Community Schools. The striking wooden box held cards with the names of contributors. We were both speechless. What a tremendous way to express compassion! I felt overwhelmed by their kindness. Old classmates with such character are invaluable.

Several teachers from Zack's past came to the visitation. One special teacher stood out to us: Ms. Julie Morse, Zachary, Joel, and Brytni's high school Honors English teacher. Her face was pale and wet with tears. Knowing how close Zack and Julie had become, I knew that this was hard for her. Zack really loved how she had made learning enjoyable while teaching him concepts that had enabled him to breeze through college English course work. Since graduating from high school, Julie and Zack had met to discuss his college and future career. Julie had even taken piano lessons from Zachary after he had graduated high school.

We also discovered that the page we had found in Zachary's belongings, "What Is Success," had been distributed by Julie to all of her students. She was one of two non-family members that we allowed to place something in that special casket drawer. Ms. Morse is a remarkable teacher who has left her mark on our lives.

Zachary's friends came. Some high school friends came from far away. Joel Crabtree came from New York to express his sorrow. (Zack and Joel had been the two top pianists during their days at Highland.) His college friends, Doug, Lee, Leah, and Marci, spent the entire day. Doug worried me the most. He seemed intensely grief stricken. Doug and Zack were like brothers in so many ways. (Dan and I prayed for him often over the next few years.)

Students from my classroom at East Side Middle School came to the funeral home with cards, flowers, books, and other gifts for me. I sensed that they were worried about me and wanted to make sure that I wasn't a total mess. I'm not sure what they thought. I did have trouble fighting back the tears when I saw their sweet faces. What blessings they were to me!

The number of people in attendance was astounding. Most of the day I can't recall. My friends, Alberta, Carolyn, Sylvia, Mary, and Terri worked out the food arrangements. Dan and I stood the entire day in the same area beside that bulletin board. Dan never left; not even to use the restroom. Occasionally, Alberta would come and stop whoever we were talking with, and tell them that she wasn't leaving until Dan and I took a few sips of a milkshake. She stated that since we refused food that a milkshake would be the next best thing. How great was that! We still don't know who came up with the milk shake idea, but it worked. Dan and I giggled slightly and took a swallow or two just to appease her.

During the viewing, our other two children, Joel and Brytni weaved in and out of the two viewing rooms trying to greet those who couldn't stay. We were told the wait was four hours. Jordan Hird told us that he'd been in Washington, D.C. and had been to Rosa Parks' viewing. He said, "I've waited longer to see Zack than Rosa Parks!" Dan and I did have to chuckle a little at that. Zack would have been embarrassed at the very thought of that comparison.

Henry told us later that Channel 8 News arrived. The news crew interviewed Joel and Brytni about the throngs of people and their big brother, Zack. We've not seen that newscast, but possibly someday, we might. Henry said that he'll always remember their interview because the crew seemed to be in a big rush to leave. Henry was curious because they seemed so relaxed when they arrived, so he inquired about their hurried departure. One of the news crew told him that they were leaving to find out about an accident involving a van carrying five Taylor University students. We found it odd that the Taylor incident had happened on the evening of Zachary's showing.

We had arrived at the funeral home at noon and left at around 12:30 a.m. the next day. We'd been there for more than twelve hours. Strange, we should have been spent, but we felt surprisingly not physically drained. Henry walked us out while instructing us to get some rest. He'd see us back at the funeral home the next day. Dan and I didn't talk much on the ride home. We had said so much during the day that there was nothing left to say.

You would think that we'd go right to sleep when we arrived home, but sleep just wasn't that easy for either one of us. Dan and I did go to bed. What loomed ahead kept us wide awake most of the night. My thoughts were focused on the never ending nightmare of what was now my life. Tomorrow was waiting and I did not want to meet it.

But the next day did come, of course. I don't remember walking that morning, which is unusual as we had walked every other morning that first week. We went to the funeral home and then caravanned to Reardon Auditorium for the Mass. I don't remember entering the auditorium. I felt as if I was being carried. I practically was... Dan wrapped his arm around me to keep me upright. Most of the funeral service is a total blank in my mind. I watched Joel, Hillary, Jason, and Brytni unfold the pall or white cloth that covered the casket. I placed Zachary's Bible on top of the pall and Dan added a gold crucifix which had hung in a hallway at home. Our immediate family sat in the front row surrounded by our extended family. Recollections of watching the Indiana University Choir join with the Anderson University Choir floated in my mind. Bits of the music, Father Dhondt's homily, Jimmy Moore's message, and Pat's tribute were fragmented in my psyche.

When Dan was ready to speak, I wanted so badly to stand next to him. He turned to me and said that I needed to stay here, at my seat. "Please listen to me. I need you to stay here. You simply aren't physically strong enough." So I did. I can't remember one word that Dan said, but I recall being amazed by his control and poise. He spoke with such authority and strength of character. I was proud to be his wife and thankful for God's power in the room. The details of the rest of the service remain sketchy in my mind even today. Perhaps that's God's way of keeping me from entirely losing my mind.

After the funeral, Henry had originally wanted us to ride in a limousine as is the funeral tradition. When we first discussed this I had expressed to Henry that I wanted to walk to the cemetery. I explained to Henry that I was a walker and after the service, a walk to Maplewood would be necessary for me and my family. The logistics were fitting with the cemetery being less than a mile from Reardon. Henry would have a limousine ready just in case I changed my mind. Father Bob led the procession. We followed, walking close behind the hearse. (My friend Jerri took pictures. I was told that it was a sight to behold: hundreds of people walking down the road to Maplewood Cemetery.) I do remember people coming out of their homes to inspect the great crowd.

The weather was picture perfect for spring; not too hot, not too cold, with a nice breeze blowing through the trees. As we approached the blue tent positioned over "the hole" with the casket placed over the top, I noticed the familiar chairs that I'd seen at other graveside services. My knees began to grow weak once more. Our walk from Reardon Auditorium had given me a breath of fresh air and renewed energy. Now I felt that unmistakable feeling of panic sweep over me once more. I couldn't breathe. I couldn't move. Thankful for a chair, I sat down and tried to collect my head. Not being a public crier, I found myself struggling to keep my feelings private. My grief felt extremely private. No one could possibly understand my pain nor did they know how much I loved my boy. How could they?

My mind was lost in thoughts of Zachary when Father Bob asked, "Do you want to watch the casket lowered?"

I snapped back to reality. "What?" I asked and Father Bob repeated the question. "NO!" I responded ardently. (This episode was a flashback that woke me for years and even today, I can see myself looking into the ground, thinking my baby gets so cold, how could I put him down into that hole? I thought that, even though I was very aware that *that* was no longer my son. His spirit was not in his "shell." My mind was just in another zone.)

At the grave site, Dean Richards handed Dan and me Zachary's Master of Music degree from IU. Our conversation was brief and thank yous and condolences were exchanged. Several of the IU choir members were present, but one girl left an impression. She was crying so hard that it made me stop to console her. She said that she had sung with Zack and would miss his voice, but more than that, she'd miss his wonderful sense of humor.

Wiping my tears, I said, "Oh, he told you Angus jokes."

She immediately paused from her tears and responded, "He told *you* Angus jokes?"

***

One evening after school, Zack met Brytni and me at a small coffee shop located close to AU. I treated both of the kids to a sweet roll and coffee. When we went out into the parking lot to get into our cars, Zack asked if we wanted to hear a joke. Now these jokes were told in a thick Irish accent and would not have been rated "G". Zachary acted out the entire joke with his touch of theatrics.

When we finished laughing hysterically, Brytni and I looked at each other and responded that we were shocked that he could tell such jokes. Zack simply gave us one of his sly smiles and hugged us both goodbye. Over the years, Zack occasionally shared with me from his repertoire of Angus jokes. How lucky was I!

***

I recanted to the young lady, "Yes. We were very close." The confused look on her face almost made me stop and smile for a split second. Was Zack trying to lighten the moment? I could feel him right there with us, telling us to relax and enjoy the day. How could I do that when we had just completed his burial?

Dan helped me to the limo which would take us to St. Ambrose for the funeral dinner. Dan, Joel, Hillary, Brytni, Jason, and I slowly got into the vehicle. Isn't it odd how after such an intense, life altering event, tradition dictates that we should get together and eat? I hadn't eaten much at all for days.

~ 103 ~

Why would I want to eat now? Food was the last thing that I wanted.

When the limo arrived at St. Ambrose, the family piled out and I went upstairs to the balcony. I wanted to be where Zachary loved to be: by the church organ. Wanting to have some private time, I told Dan that I was okay. He should go to the basement where the church had prepared a huge feast. Our family and other guests would be waiting and I just needed some more time. Waiting on the front of the organ was the song, "On Eagle's Wings." Gently, I felt my fingers touch the sheet music. We had just sung that song! Sobbing, I sat at the organ bench longing for Zachary to play.

***

Zachary had purchased organ shoes that he wore over the last few years. Joel and Brytni teased him mercilessly about the sound those shoes made when he went downstairs to receive communion. "Tap, tap, tap, tap," they'd say as they followed him down the stairs. Even when he got home, they'd rib him.

Sometimes a fellow parishioner, Terry McQuade, who had keys to everything, would hide things inside his organ shoes. Zachary was notorious for always pushing-the-bell, so to speak. He kept those special shoes locked inside the organ so he'd hurry upstairs and throw on the shoes just seconds before church began. When items were in his shoes, Zack would scan the room to find Terry laughing in the corner. He'd shoot him a look of disgust and shake his head. Zack was not above retaliating for Terry's orneriness. Zachary and Terry quite enjoyed being pranksters.

***

As I sat mesmerized by my thoughts and memories, Dan startled me. Requesting me to come downstairs, I obstinately refused. I was not hungry and did not want to eat. I simply wanted to stay where I could feel Zack. Appealing to my sense of duty, he told me that people had traveled a long way for us. We needed to try to be sociable. Reluctantly, I descended with him to the church basement, Ambrosian Hall.

The aroma of all kinds of food met me at the double door entrance. We had to pass the choir door first. I found walking past that doorway painful. Resisting the urge to go inside the choir room, Dan led me into the main hall.

Several tables filled with a large assortment of foods were located near the stage. Dan and I were so thankful for the generosity and kindness of our church. Other tables were arranged for our family and friends to dine. Dan had already filled his plate and was seated by out-of-town relatives. Slowly, I followed Dan's instructions by grabbing a plate and plopping spoonfuls of food onto it. I'm not sure who said what, but one of the ladies putting out food said to me, "I don't know how you can eat when you just buried your son."

Now, I feel like she didn't mean it as it sounded, but I went right over to a table, put my plate down, and told Dan that I was going home. Alberta knew something was wrong. She asked me if I wanted to go home. My quick answer was, "Yes. Please take me home. I just want to be alone." She told her husband, Todd, and we left. We didn't talk much on that ride that I remember, but I was so very grateful that she knew me well enough to help me when I was in need.

There are always lessons to be learned if we just listen. Walking through a storm, we must walk on through the wind and rain, speak only when necessary (sometimes less is more), and have hope in our hearts. Without hope, we are nothing. I left church that day, drained and exhausted; and yet, I had hope that I'd see Zachary again. This couldn't be the end, I just knew it.

Being Alive

The days that followed the funeral seemed to continue like all the previous days – one day running into the other. Sleepless nights, morning walks, sympathy and thinking-of-you cards filled our mailbox, and Dan added more things on our "Need to do" list. Somehow this list kept us going with small jobs or missions to accomplish. We just kept moving. We just kept on *being alive*.

I have often reflected on the CD Zachary made for my fiftieth birthday. It's almost eerie, the song titles he selected for the CD. Zack had written a list of my own personally requested selections along with his own individual favorites. Once he'd narrowed down the songs, Zack appropriately entitled the CD, *You Asked for It*, because of course I had practically nagged him into recording it.

***

"What do you want for your fiftieth birthday, Mom?" Zachary had asked.

"I want what I always want... for you to sing for me," I had replied. "Put your voice on tape so that I can hear you anytime that I want. Just put a tape recorder by the piano, play and sing. I'd be happy with that."

Of course, being the perfectionist, if Zack was actually going to do this for me, he would record in a studio so that his singing and playing would not be muffled or sound amateurish. My sister had pursued my request and urged him to select a studio and just do it. And he did.

How odd the first song on that CD is entitled, "Being Alive"? Is there some hidden message that only nine months after my fiftieth birthday, Zack was *not* alive? I often find myself listening and praying for some semblance of an answer to my millions of questions. While paying close attention to the lyrics of this expressive song, "Somebody, need me too much, Somebody know me too well... Make me alive," I found myself pondering the substance of the song.

I need him too much and *I* know him too well, but how can I make him alive? Oh, if I only could!

***

The funeral home had two vans deliver the flowers, planters, and other items including some beautiful Afghans to our house. We placed them all together in the living room. After everything was delivered, there wasn't even a place for us to walk. Our entire house reeked like the mortuary. I'd always loved the fragrance of flowers. Now the scent seemed to stab me like a dull knife, unable to cut out the pain. I wanted to distance myself from the past few days as quickly as possible. (I just knew that I must be dreaming.) My sister and I made a list of who sent what. After calling family and friends, we began the process of deciding what to keep or to distribute. Mostly, we just let people choose what they wanted. *Things* just weren't important.

The names of those persons who had sent such striking, inspirational Afghans were the only names that seemed unaccounted for after the list was completed. Without their names, I was unable to send the proper thank you. I'm sure that I put the tags somewhere, but couldn't find them. I knew several people had been listed on each tag. I found it fitting that we had been sent three of these blankets; just enough for each immediate family to have one for remembrance. I hoped that these people knew that we were appreciative.

Dan and I also felt the need to go back to the cemetery. As our van approached the new grave, the hefty mound of flowers on top of the grave was a remarkable site. The vision of the flowers in the shape of a G-clef and the bright scarlet sashes with the silver glittered words, *son* and *brother* inscribed on them remain etched in my brain.

Suddenly, a feeling of panic swept over me. What would mark his place when all the flowers were gone? We needed to go to make arrangements for a marker or stone or something to announce that Zachary was left here, at this particular location. A sense of urgency came into play at that moment. We decided to go to Wearly Monuments, located directly across the street from the cemetery entrance, to discuss Zachary's headstone.

Entering the office, I was surprised to see a friend of mine sitting behind the desk. Jackie was a friend from high school and parent of Amanda, a kindergarten student from long ago at Park Place Elementary. Jackie immediately got up from behind the desk to give me a big hug. She had read about Zachary and had attended the funeral. As we cried together, Jackie told me that I needed to take some time before deciding what kind of stone to buy or what should be written on the stone. Her husband, Jim came over to offer his condolences and to reiterate Jackie's suggestion of waiting. They stated that something this permanent needed a great deal of thought prior to acting on it. Dan and I agreed to go home and think it over. As we left the building, I shook my head thinking, "What are the odds that Jackie and I would meet here at this point in time?" Lives from my past continued to overlap my present.

Friday's events seemed to run together. Joel, Hillary, and Brytni decided to go with us to Bloomington for the day. We needed to clean out Zack's apartment as well as his office-with-the-door at FUMC. Dan removed one of the back seats from the van knowing we'd need as much space as we could get. He had called ahead to Bloomington to rent a U-Haul for us to use in hauling home his things. After having a week to think about the past events, our kids also thought that maybe now they could see the crash site. Dan and I were agreeable to whatever they felt they wanted to do. Grateful to have them near me, I was very willing to do anything. Knowing that our home was still full of flowers and visits from well-meaning friends, a couple of nights away while doing the unthinkable job of packing seemed almost like an escape. Escape to where? To Bloomington? To the crash site? How could that be a getaway of any sort? What we were broaching would be as hard as staying home; yet, I longed to flee from my new reality.

Later that Friday evening, Dan arrived at Hillary and Joel's home on West 8th Street. He returned home to our house to gather Brytni and me along with several empty boxes and some suitcases. Once we had gathered most items we thought were needed, we set off for Bloomington.

We spent the next two nights at Gloria (Glo) and Kevin's who lived in a nearby suburb of Bloomington and had invited us to come to stay with them on our visit. Joel was very reluctant and spoke openly about his objection. He didn't really know my friends from junior high and high school and he didn't want to have to socialize. I understood his concern, but I also knew that he didn't know the warmth of these friends. Dan and I knew. Between Kevin's easy manner and Gloria's sense of humor and kindness, I knew that their home would be the perfect safe haven for our family.

Our late arrival at Glo and Kevin's house allotted us time for a quick "hello" and "goodnight" with little time for conversation. Early Saturday morning, Dan went to rent a U-Haul that we would use to transport Zachary's belongings back to our house in Anderson.

Dan, Joel, Hillary, Brytni, and I stayed together throughout the next two days. The crash site was our first stop. None of us, not one, remember details of that visit. We know that we went, but that is where the specific pieces come to a halt. With the entire family there, all of us looking for Zack, the rest of the world disappeared. It was too deep an experience for us to keep in our active memories.

All through this grief journey, I have found that your mind will block out some of the painful steps. I just couldn't recall some things – almost as if the event didn't happen at all. Yet other moments are as clear as a freshly cleaned glass. That particular visit to the crash site is but a mere haze.

Our next stop was Zachary's apartment. Rachel, who was subletting a room from Zack, greeted us at the door. Rachel had sorted his VHS tapes and DVDs from hers and had acquired a few boxes for us. She looked so lost. How very hard this must have been for her. Not only had she lost Zack, her friend and landlord, so to speak, but four other friends. You could truly feel the sorrow as you entered the apartment. We each exchanged tears and hugs.

Walking though the living room, then rounding the corner into his bedroom, my body moved as if it had become detached from my mind. On top of the desk was a round, ruby colored ceramic covered dish holding his cufflinks. I picked up the cuff links and wondered if he'd worn them to his last big performance. My hands trembled as I touched Zack's tuxedo jacket he'd left draped over the corner of his free standing mirror. How could I touch his things, let alone pack them?

I couldn't breathe. The grief began to swallow me up. I don't remember if I even packed anything. I do recall leaving his room and rushing outside to the terrace to try to catch my breath. Dan met me outside and told me that he'd take care of everything. I didn't have to go back in; yet, I wanted to be wherever I could be close to Zachary. (This conflicting feeling of panic and fleeing became part of me and remains part of my life, even today.) We went back inside to begin the task of boxing and sorting.

While we were there, a lady arrived with another couple. The six of us were unsure how these people knew Zachary. We shared casual greetings and handshakes, and then the lady asked if they could come in. We asked how she knew Zack, but I don't recall her answer. As she began stepping over boxes to walk them around the apartment, we all shot glances of dismay and shock back and forth to each other. It actually took a few minutes for it to register what was truly taking place. Had she come to the apartment with future prospective tenants? Was she really *showing* the apartment? As the lady began to tell the couple about the dimensions of each room, her actions became crystal clear. She was indeed attempting to acquire new boarders. After gathering his thoughts, Dan told her that this was not a good time as he swiftly accompanied them out of the apartment. Always socially appropriate, Dan handled the issue almost before I could react to what had just transpired.

As peculiar as this may sound, I was almost grateful for the out-of-place event because it caused the heaviness of the room to shift. It was as if Zack was saying, "It's just stuff. Let it go." Our mood became that of getting on with the task at hand rather than being immersed in the sadness of our loss. The irritation of the rudeness of the intruders became the topic of our conversation. The packing took on a new dimension. We would take only the basic, memorable things and would leave items Rachel might be able to put to use.

Most of us returned to his bedroom to tackle the gruesome task of packing Zack's "stuff." I found the spiral striped notebook I had given to Zack during his days at AU. I had one like it and our mission was to share our journaling. I would write important notes into my journal while he was in school and Zack would write in his journal. Some of the items in his room gave me pause... particularly his big a** desk.

***

When Zack moved out of the dorm into the rented house, he felt the need to have a "work" space. Zachary loved office supplies that helped keep things organized. I would have to say that he was more than a tad bit obsessive compulsive when it came to orderliness. The desk he purchased was large enough to hold his electronic keyboard which he'd connect to his computer.

The computer program he used most often was called Sibelius. The program allowed him to arrange and compose music as he played on the keyboard as well as play his composition back to him. He could then make the necessary adjustments before printing his final composition.

The extra large desk was carefully placed in the lower level of the tri-level home Zachary rented from Fritz. His roommates expressed to Dan and me their opinion of the desk taking up more than its own fair share of Zack's allotted space. None of this banter diverted Zack from the thrill of finally achieving his own office space with, as he called it, *the big a** desk*. His cousin and friend, David helped Zack assemble and disassemble that desk numerous times when Zack moved which often resulted in the desk having other such similar names.

***

Running my hands across the front of that desk, I couldn't think about Zack not sitting behind it. Headsets on, his eyes closed, Zachary would arrange and compose music for hours on end. Joel asked if he could have the desk. Dan and I agreed that the desk would be a great fit in Joel's office. We knew that Zack would want his brother to have it.

One of us opened the long top drawer in the desk to find every single item in its proper place. Zack not only had several different sizes of paper clips, but several varieties of styles. He had assorted sizes of silver and black clamp clips and assorted colors and sizes of regular clips, all of which were held in their suitable containers. Pens and pencils, both regular and mechanical, rulers, and several pairs of scissors were placed in an orderly fashion in the top drawer. Markers of every shade and size were placed into boxes which were sorted into permanent and highlighters. The amount of office supplies was extraordinary. Zack could have opened his own supply store.

Zack also had a clear round dish containing loose change on top of his desk. It was full almost to the point of overflowing. I could envision Zack coming home each evening, emptying his pockets and placing his pennies, nickels, dimes, and quarters into this container. Nightly, his dad still empties his own pockets into a large container. (We placed both of Zack's containers with his old desk at home. The dish with the change remains as we found it.)

***

Zachary was always ahead of his time when it came to electronics. The Mac computers were the newest, top-of-the-line in the industry when he was at AU. Zack also had an iPod to accompany his computer and an ear piece or Bluetooth for his phone long before I was even aware that such things existed. Zack loved new ideas and gravitated toward having the best of whatever new gizmo was released. Technology agreed with him.

Next to his desk in the bedroom was a four-drawer filing cabinet. He had a variety of photos and phone numbers taped or placed with magnets on the side. He had Joel and Hillary's phone number, which Joel removed and kept. One thing I found particularly funny was a photograph of Dr. DooRiddle. Through my tears, I smiled, peeled off the picture, studied it for a moment, then placed it in my purse.

***

When teaching Academic Advancement, my friend, Alberta and I came up with what we thought was a fun way to involve students in associative, inductive, and divergent thinking skills to solve problems. We found a book entitled, *Dr. DooRiddles* by John H. Doolittle. Dividing the book into several different grade levels, I placed the riddles into a three ring binder. After a few minutes of brainstorming, we decided that we'd have a puppet dress up each week and ask the students the riddles. This puppet often acted as my alter-ego. The students would request his visits each week.

Zack came to school one day for a surprise visit. While making the puppet Dr. DooRiddle speak in a low, gravelly vocal manner, I happened to noticed Zack and my principal, Pat Cox watching through the window of the door, giggling while they watched. Red-faced, I rushed to the door, smacked him, and then gave him a big hug. I just never knew when Zack would come calling although it was always such a joy. He'd just pop in to say, "Hi."

Dr. DooRiddle had become such a vivid personality that our school photographer took his picture for the school yearbook. One Christmas, I put Dr. DooRiddle's school photo into a small box and wrapped it up for each family member. It was a standing joke that Christmas. How funny that Zachary had saved it and taped it to the side of his filing cabinet. I felt sure that Dr. DooRiddle's picture made him smile, too.

***

As if not to be upstaged by the office supplies, the black, three ring binders full of sheet music flooded the bedroom. Every binder had a label on the spine making the music inside clearly identifiable. Lining the bedroom wall were three book cases with four shelves. Each book case appeared to be bursting with these binders. There were thousands of pieces of sheet music and CDs Zack had purchased. We were in awe of the variety Zack had accumulated. His selections ranged from Bach to Bublé, although I must admit that Zack was definitely a connoisseur of the classics. The sheer volume and weight of music made for sore arms. He didn't or couldn't play or listen to all this music…or could he? (We had found a receipt in his car. One of the last purchases he made was to a music store on campus.) If music is your passion, I guess there can never be too much.

Next to his desk was Zack's four-drawer grey metal filing cabinet. I knew that I couldn't look inside of it, not yet. That would have to wait. Whatever was inside would hold great significance to Zachary and I just couldn't look at it while it was in his apartment. At that point, I wasn't sure if I could ever look inside.

***

Being organized was a lifestyle for Zack. At a young age, around his ninth birthday, he asked for a filing cabinet. "Are you sure that you want a filing cabinet?" I asked. "Are you sure that you know what you're going to do with it?"

Zachary told me that he needed to organize his piano music. I knew Zachary was different, but his request for a filing cabinet clearly set him apart from other kids his age. Looking back on it, I should have bought him the four-drawer cabinet then instead of a rather inexpensive beige two-drawer. Zack definitely utilized that filing cabinet until he moved on to a four-drawer.

***

Maps of locations around the world and photos of famous composers and conductors hung in his room. We also discovered three posters Zack had purchased from different locations he had enjoyed while vacationing or performing. Brytni and Joel loved the two Paris posters. Then there was the New York at night poster. Gazing at it, I could see him walking the busy city streets. My mind pushed the thoughts of New York away. I couldn't allow myself to lapse into memories of that trip just yet. It was just too much. I left the packing of that room to the others.

Moving into the kitchen, the task to sort and pack more of Zachary's possessions began to wear on all of us. How much can the mind absorb? Right on top of the counter was his round, light wooden spice rack with cooking utensils in the center. This item seemed to be calling to us to be used and remembered.

***

Zack loved to cook and had requested a variety of spices to enhance his cooking. His three roommates, Doug, Lee, and Nathan rotated the cooking and cleaning responsibilities. Zack sometimes tried trading the cooking for the cleaning. Being notorious as a bargain hunter, I surprised him with that spice rack as well as an assortment of knifes. Even though this rack wasn't new, you would have thought that I'd given him gold. Zachary hugged us and told Debby and I that he'd have to have us over for some of his home cooking. My sister and I stayed for a short visit and wrote "ZN" on the handle of each knife so that his would not become confused with the other knives shared by his roommates. Although the home cooked meal didn't take place, Debby and I did occasionally stop for a visit.

***

Brytni and I gathered his initialed knives, a rolling pin, and a skillet that I had purchased for him. Zachary also had an electric coffee grinder with a few packages of gourmet coffee beans. Brytni would be getting married in October. She told me that she'd like to have most of the cooking supplies like a few of his knifes, the coffee grinder, the spice rack, and his rolling pin.

Brytni recalled Zack and her discussing making Potica, a traditional Polish and Slovenian bread made by Dan each Christmas and Easter. The two had plans of making it with their dad the next Christmas. The rolling pin would make it feel as if Zachary would be with her. Of course, Brytni could have whatever she wanted, but she gave me the skillet. (When I use it today, I always pause a minute or two while envisioning Zack cooking breakfast or browning something for an evening meal.) We completed gathering the last few items, then told Rachel that she could keep the rest.

There were only a few large items Dan and Joel carried out to the U-Haul, but I did not watch: his bed frame, mattress, and box springs which he'd taken from his room at home, chest of drawers, book cases, desk, and clothes. If I did see them being removed from the apartment, I've blocked it out of my mind.

We left Zack's couch and entertainment center along with several odds and ends for Rachel, said our goodbyes and moved on. After some debate, we decided to continue the packing of Zachary's belongings at First United Methodist Church. Some of us just wanted the job to be completed that day. Others wanted to put it off and make a return effort to finish. The thought of extending the daunting task of packing more of his things to another weekend was just too much. Dan, Joel, and I decided it was best to just "get it over with" while we were there. Off we went to the FUMC.

Mary Beth, the person in charge of Adult and Family Ministries at FUMC, greeted us, and then led the way to Zachary's office. Everything was so neat and organized. She commented about his request to have matching light fixtures. The church didn't have a coordinating pair so Zack had gone out and made that purchase. (Those lamps are now a permanent part of our living room décor.) Zack had also created a drawer full of snack foods. He was known for "eating on the run" so it only stood to reason that he'd have an established place for a quick bite. Being his mother, I was impressed and relieved that it wasn't all junk food. He did have granola bars and other assorted foods from a nutrition store.

Dan, Joel, Hillary, Brytni and I gathered up a few items, but left most things for the church. Mary Beth and Jimmy, the associate pastor who had spoken at the funeral, told us how they confiscated something from Zack as a joke a few months ago.

***

A box had arrived at the church which required an adult signature. One of the secretaries signed for it, but expressed concern to Jimmy and Mary Beth about the requirement of the adult signature. What was Zack having sent to the church that would require an adult to sign for it? Was it something of ill repute? Chuckling, Jimmy and Mary Beth told the secretary that it was probably Zachary's wine shipment from California. Zack had told them that he belonged to a wine club, but they, too, were perplexed about his having this shipment sent to the church.

When Zachary arrived for choir practice, Jimmy and Mary Beth told Zachary that they had a suspicious package for him that they were holding for ransom. Zack explained that he had to have the shipment sent to the church because he was never home to sign for it and he didn't want it shipped back to Napa Valley. They all had a good laugh over that parcel. Jimmy and Mary Beth had a few conversations about quality wine with Zack so they were aware that this shipment contained some of the best.

After sharing the story, my mind floated back to our trip with Zack to Napa Valley. Debby, her husband, Ervin, David, Dan and I went to Carmel the summer of 2005 to hear Zack perform at the Carmel Bach Festival. Zack had a reprieve from his choral duties for two days so we ventured northward to Napa Valley. Zack had become a small scale wine connoisseur of sorts. Being a race car enthusiast, Ervin's only request on our outing was to visit the Andretti Winery. Zack made some snide comments about a race car driver's knowledge of wine. Debby recanted that Andretti *is* Italian so perhaps Zack might be pleasantly surprised.

Lining the counter of the winery, we paid our small fee for wine sampling. After tasting a few, Zack commented on the flavors of each wine having a true taste of quality and inquired if they had a club. As if synchronized, we turned and looked at Zachary, then back to the wine steward and said, "Yes, do you have a club?" All of us joined the wine club that day and remain members.

***

Mary Beth and Jimmy told us that his ransomed shipment was still at church. They wanted to return it to us right then. Dan and I looked at each other and said that Zack would want them to keep it. He'd want them to remember the fun times and to have a toast to him.

Drained from the day of endless packing, Joel, Hillary, Brytni, Dan and I called Gloria for Mass times. My family looked like we'd been through a war. When Mass was complete, we returned to Glo and Kev's place where we feasted on a scrumptious homemade meal complete with deep dish apple pie. Glo has a manner of selflessness and uncanny humor and for the first time in days, we all actually laughed. When dinner was over, I hugged both of them. How can you thank someone who has given you a smile when you were sure that you'd never be able to experience joy of any kind again?

Before going to bed, Glo walked me to the refrigerator. Tears were in her eyes as she opened the refrigerator to point out the cartons of milk. "I didn't know what kind of milk you drank, so I bought all three: whole, 2%, and skim." Some memories and acts of kindness will remain embedded in my heart. That was one of them. Who does that? Who thinks of others to that extent? My good friends had reached out and provided my family with comfort and joy, and it wasn't even Christmas. They are living examples of love.

When we arrived home, several family members had made arrangements to help us unload the U-Haul. We cleared out half of our garage for the large items and put his personal possessions upstairs. Our house seemed to be a maze of Zachary's things. Boxes of his clothing were stacked into one area while his computer, software, accessories, and other miscellaneous items were pushed under the pool table or stacked to the side. The feeling that all of these things belonged to just him had me questioning how much "stuff" do any of us really need. The words to the poem we found came rushing back like a whirlwind: "What I have possessed in this world will belong to someone else immediately…" This truly was immediately. It seemed as if we had barely had time to breathe before he left this world.

What were we going to do with all of his possessions? Certainly we'd keep several things, but after all, everything was functional and should be put to good use. Dan and I had Joel and Brytni go through some of the items first as well as having David and other family members take some memorable articles, too.

I called Doug, Zack's college roommate from AU and he contacted Marci, Leah, and Lee; all of these friends were close to Zack. After having a meal around our dining room table, we asked them to share Zack stories. It was so nice to hear them tell about good times they shared. We adjourned and went upstairs to show them some things.

Opening box after box of music, they were amazed by the massive quantity of music Zack had acquired since his undergrad years. Yes, they were very aware of his music collection, but it seemed as if the sum had doubled.

One box seemed to totally enthrall them. It contained "Blue Books." Marci, Lee, Leah, and Doug looked at Dan and me. They asked, "Do you know how much each one of these books is worth?" Of course, we didn't so they proceeded to tell us that each one was worth at least $100.00. Marci asked if we'd thought about what we were going to do with them. Everything was happening so fast. Dan and I just hadn't managed to think of so many things. AU had a real need for this music so a few months later, Marci cataloged each piece and we donated several thousands of dollars worth of music to AU. It was hard to let some of it go. Our thoughts were that perhaps others would grow to love and value music as much as Zachary. He would not have wanted to have the music just sitting in a box at our house.

As for his clothes, I selected some items that I just couldn't part with: shirts he wore to lounge around, old clothes he'd worn often, his tuxedoes, and a few other things. Doug is about Zack's size so he took a lot of clothing. I knew that my dad was also Zachary's size and I wanted him to have some of his jackets and a tuxedo. We bagged up the rest to donate to Operation Love. Dan's sister, Jodi worked there and knew several people who could use them. It was hard on all of us. How was I going to do this…live without my baby? When I came across his long black dress coat, I couldn't bear to look. My heart was in my throat again.

***

Christmas 2003, Zack expressed the need for a dress coat long enough to cover his suit coats. Because he was so thin, a sport coat just wasn't enough when he had to make long trips across campus. I met him at a quality store in town where we happened to find "the coat."

As he slipped it on over his sport jacket, Zack hurried over to the closest mirror to admire its look. It was expensive, but it was just what he wanted. Of course, he always was so appreciative and hugged me with great gusto. No one hugged quite like Zack. His sincerity was felt from his heart directly to mine. I miss his hugs more than I can say.

***

I hugged that long, black dress coat in the closet of his old bedroom. Some things I'm not sure that I can ever part with. That coat had the smell of his Tommy Hilfiger cologne. He'd worn that same scent since high school. We kept the partially used bottle of cologne in his room and another bottle in our bathroom because every once in a while, I needed to breathe him in.

Dan was off for about a month. We walked each night until the sun went down, and then I'd wake up in the early hours and we would walk again. After each early morning walk, we ate our cinnamon raisin toast and sipped tea as the sun rose. The night panics continued. Dan returned to work in half day increments. Not wanting him to leave, I would sit on the stairway and cry. Worrying about loved ones leaving was a source of anxiety.

I took off the last six weeks of the school year. I had a wonderful substitute named Deli who was also a friend. Because it was my first year in sixth grade, I knew that she would do a better job than me. Her experience in sixth grade was a genuine plus. I knew Deli as a master teacher and my gratitude for knowing she was in that classroom took the pressure off of me. My mind was not able to even think about school. I did think of the students... I love kids and watching them learn. I considered teaching a privilege and a joy. Now I couldn't bear the thought of even entering the building where I had found out about Zack's accident. How would I ever be able to go back?

Television and listening to the radio seemed like a waste of time. Most everything appeared to be trivial. My world had been altered permanently or was I dreaming? Reality was somewhere in the distance. I found myself searching for answers. I went to the Family Christian Bookstore near our home to look for books that might have answers. Surely there must be a book to help me understand what I'm supposed to do now? The funeral home had provided some lists about the stages of grief. For some reason, this just didn't seem to apply to me. Thoughts of being in a dream were constant for me.

I began to accumulate grief books. I'd read one after the other. Most of them discussed how God can be seen in everything. Well, at this point, I prayed, but felt I was really invisible. How could God have taken Zack? Didn't He know that I needed him more? I don't remember ever being angry with God, but I did want to know some answers. And so I continued to read.

We have an armoire in our bedroom containing a small television, drawers, and some shelves. I began stacking those grief books on a shelf directly in view from my bed. As ridiculous as it sounds, I made a deal with myself. When I woke up (the short amount of time I did sleep) in the morning, if those books were still there, I was still in this crazy dream. Each morning, I'd open my eyes slowly and look at that shelf. Upon seeing the books, I'd talk to myself and say, "Okay. The books are still there. You have to sit up, put your feet on the floor, and stand up. Zack would be disappointed in you if you just lie here. You can do it. One foot at a time now." Sometimes I said those words in my head. Sometimes I said them out loud. And so it went for more days than I could count.

I continued to buy books and would ask others who had lost children if they had any reference books they could recommend. Dan came home one day after discussing the topic with a colleague who had lost a young child. He gave Dan the title of a fiction book entitled *Room of Marvels* by James Bryan Smith. It was a quick and easy read, but this book did make me feel hope. Without that feeling, truly, what do we have? I knew that it was fiction, but as long as I felt that twinge of "perhaps I can stand up or maybe I can move my feet", well, that was a step forward for me. I purchased several copies and gave them to others I saw struggling. It may not help everyone, but it was worth a shot. Eventually, I had gathered more than thirty grief books.

While staying at home felt safe, I longed to escape. Each night, I'd read cards from people from everywhere. Some letters and cards were from people we had known for years... cherished friends, relatives, and acquaintances. Others came from people who had known Zachary and just wanted us to know what a marvelous person Zack was. The messages were from so many different persons; yet, they contained the same message. Zack had helped them in some way or had inspired them by his actions. All of these notes and letters gave me pause to reflect on my own life. Was I touching those around me, strangers or friends in a positive way?

One evening, as I sat on the sofa in the den, I turned on the lamp. Taking the pile of letters and cards from the day, I took the letter opener and began to read. The first envelope of the evening was post marked, 02 May 2006, Lafayette, Indiana. It was thicker than most, it piqued my curiosity. As I unfolded the four-and-a-half-page, hand-written letter, I instantaneously had cold chills. It was from the lady who had driven the kids to the airport that fateful night.

5/1/06

Dear Mr. & Mrs. Novak,

I have thought many times about how to write this letter and what I should say. After much prayer I decided it was best to just write to you from my heart.

I had the honor of knowing your precious Zach through his involvement with the Lafayette Bach Chorale. He brought so much to our group. He brought his wonderful voice, knowledge and training to share with us. More importantly, he brought himself.

Zach was never an outsider in our group – he was one of us. I have heard <u>many</u> people say that in the past.

I loved to hear Zach sing, though I always hated being behind him as I wanted to watch the emotion in his face as he sang. He was always "in" his music when he sang.

I was somewhat of a mother hen to some of the IU students – Zach & Garth especially. I was always making sure they had eaten, had enough sleep, offering words of encouragement etc.

At the end of rehearsal on April 20th, Maestro Gray had asked the soloists if they could arrive a little earlier the next night. At that point my mother hen radar went off. "These are busy college students – when will they eat – will they need water?" I approached the group and offered to bring them dinner the next night. It was at that time I was asked to drive them to the airport. Since it was on my way home I was glad to drop them off. We all _piled_ into my small SUV. Garth and I were in the front – all others were piled, squished and sandwiched in the back. (A Hyundai Santa Fe is not built for 6 people – especially two men who are at least 6 ft. tall) Needless to say, my back got a knee massage during the short drive to the airport. In the car there was much chit-chat and joking. It reminded me of my college days. I dropped them off – waving goodbye. Zach blew me a kiss as he walked away. I prayed for them as I drove the rest of the way to my house. As I pulled into my drive way I could see that they were in the air. (My home is about 15 miles west of the airport – so I could see the lights of the plane) I continued to pray for them and their safety.

On my way into the school parking lot on Friday morning I heard the devastating news. I sought out a colleague here at school who also sings in the Chorale. I began to pray that the Lord be with the parents and families of each person on board.

I did not know what to expect when I went to Zach's funeral. Thinking back now, I knew! I knew we would celebrate the life of an amazing young man. A man who touched the lives of so many.

Mr. Novak, the words you read from the paper in Zach's bag… wow – what an amazing principle to live by and I know – from my experience – that Zach did just that.

I have often struggled with the idea of whether or not I am using the talents given to me by God in the way that He wants them used. Zach and I had talked briefly on this – he had amazing insight for someone so young. I have been truly blessed to have known him and to have called him a friend.

As a parent I felt the need to write you and let you know your son's last moments here on earth were happy and doing what he loved – singing. While I am very sad that I will not see Zach anymore, I find comfort in knowing that one day I will see him again when we are *both walking the streets of gold in Heaven. Until then I will listen to my recording of a concert he did with the chorale. And when I hear his sweet voice, I will say a prayer for you and your family and know that Zach is in heaven singing a most glorious song.*

In His loving care,

Lesli Hansen

After reading the letter, I wanted to talk to her right away. Then again, what would I say? My mind was discombobulated. I just couldn't process thoughts. It was so very thoughtful of her to take the time to write to us about Zack. She was incredibly reassuring that the trip to the airport had been full of joy and laughter. My thoughts turned to sorrow for her, too. I prayed that she too would receive comfort from God. She'd known all of those students and had been the last to see them alive. That would shock anyone's life and leave an indelible mark. I prayed that I'd have the opportunity to meet her when the time was right for both of us.

It was May and Mother's Day was right around the corner...another hurdle to jump. As the song says, "Somebody make me come through, I'll always be there as frightened as you to help us survive, Being alive, Being alive, Being alive!"

Mama A Rainbow

Today is Mother's Day. As I write this chapter, six years have passed since my last Mother's Day when all three of my children were here to celebrate this day with me. With each passing family event, I realized I was so fortunate to have had three remarkably different and incredibly wonderful children. Getting to watch them begin their adult lives has been a special blessing, one not to be taken lightly. Zack was twenty-four on my last Mother's Day with him. He made his last gift one I'll never forget.

***

He was running late... not unusual as Zack spent his life darting in and out of places. Rushing into the house, he yelled for me. "Mommy, I'm home! Come here! I have something for you." Zack grabbed my arm and pulled me into the living room. "I didn't buy you anything, but I brought something. I brought you a song," he exclaimed enthusiastically. Ushering me to the piano, I sat down beside him. He asked if I'd ever heard of this song entitled, "Mama, A Rainbow." I told him that I hadn't. Zack told me that he'd heard it last year and thought of me right away. (I was curious and a little worried at that remark.) He unfurled the sheet music and began to play and sing, "Mama, A Rainbow."

Of course, I cried most of the way through the song; but, when the song had ended, I looked at Zack, and he was crying, too. There was nothing left to say. I felt immersed with the blessing of *real* love, God's greatest gift. What can be said after receiving a present that has no tactile form but touches you so deeply? Gifts that come from within are truly the best. A present that had no monetary value, but a message that continues to be priceless! I felt so unworthy of such a tribute. Zack was a remarkable giver.

***

How lucky am I to have that memory? Really…who does that for someone? Many times I've told friends and strangers that *I* am the lucky one. I was blessed with twenty-five years of knowing one of the most selfless, kindest people I've ever met. I was just lucky enough to be his mom.

That first Mother's Day without Zack rolled around. I was dreading it. How could I celebrate with Joel and Brytni without Zachary? I knew that life must go on, but my world had stopped. For twenty-five years, Mother's Day had been such a special day. School handprints, homemade cards and pictures, handfuls of fresh picked dandelions, wet kisses and gooey hugs had been a part of the early years. Later the gifts had progressed to funny and sweet greeting cards, gift cards to pamper myself, sandals, beach towels, and other special, thoughtful surprises.

And then there was the last year with the song. What a twist of fate! How could Zack have known to sing that song for his last Mother's Day gift? What a blessing that Zack had recorded it so that I could play it when I wanted. Somehow, even though it would be excruciatingly difficult, I knew that I'd want to hear it each Mother's Day.

It was a tradition to go to my sister's house for Mother's Day. (For Father's Day, everyone comes to my house.) That first Mother's Day, the atmosphere was thick with gloom. No one spoke of Zachary's absence so it was almost, as the saying goes, as if an elephant was in the room.

When the grief began to get too heavy for me, I'd have to leave the room. My M.O. (Mode of Operation) was more like M.I.A. (Missing in Action). I am not a public crier so whenever I felt the need, I'd dash out of the room, hurry to the restroom or some other place away from the crowd, push myself into the furthest corner and try to let loose of the pain.

It is difficult to articulate these "letting loose" occurrences. My body would tremble almost to the state of convulsing, my breathing quickens, tears begin to flow while I'd make those high pitched funny noises like an animal makes before death. Sometimes, I've actually gotten sick to my stomach, although that hasn't occurred too often. These episodes I later learned from my grief counselor have a proper name: *grief attacks*. The attacks would last for various lengths of time.

After each one, I'd regain composure and try to slip back into the room acting as if nothing had happened. My thoughts were so extremely private that I felt that no one would be able to relate to my ache. My family knew I was in deep pain and didn't know what to do or say to console me. I wanted to disappear from everyone and everything… including the agony. I wanted to spend those moments of intense pain alone.

Although those attacks happen less frequently, I still experience them. The intensity has tapered somewhat; however, the assaults still do strike. I'm never really sure what will ignite the attack so there is no way to prepare myself prior to the occurrence. I've often thought that life might be easier if I'd have a little advance warning. Perhaps I could prepare and brace myself for the moment of impact.

***

That first Mother's Day without Zack was piercing. Don't misunderstand; I was happy to be with my family, as happy as I could be with one third of my children not being there to join in the festivities. I was oblivious to everything; rather, I was just going through the motions of the day; eating some, making light conversation, distributing and receiving Mother's Day gifts and cards, etc. It was overcast that day with no hint of sunshine. Dan kept going in and out of Debby's house. Suddenly, Dan re-entered and called for me to go outside. He beckoned for everyone else to come too, and to please grab their sunglasses.

As we gathered outside, Dan pointed skyward. There was a rainbow. Not just a regular rainbow but one that went around the sun... not all the way around, but only half way, and only around the bottom half of the sun as if the rainbow was smiling. WOW! A smiling rainbow! I'd never seen anything like that before. We all stood as statues wearing sunglasses gazing at this wonder. As we gazed with awestruck faces, the rainbow suddenly, as if it were saying, "Watch this," burst around the sun totally encircling it. Were we dreaming? Was this actually happening? Then, as quickly as it had appeared, the rainbow vanished. We were all totally mesmerized. No one spoke for a few seconds. What could be said?

My family and I had witnessed a spectacular display of God's reaffirming promise to the world. Was it also a sign of Zachary's confirmation that he was alright? No, I knew that he was more than just all right, especially after seeing that special rainbow. I know that common sense would tell you that this was nothing more than a coincidence. Personally, I did not want to question or challenge the extraordinary occurrence. I just wanted to soak it in. Faith believes when common sense tells you not to. I heard that line in a movie once... no matter.

I just know what I believe. I have faith in the Lord and His ability to do anything. My family and I chose to believe that rainbow was a sign… hope in the future.

A year later, we were again blessed to see a rainbow on Mother's Day. Amazingly, the second, third, fourth and fifth Mother's Day after the crash we were again given the gift of a rainbow sighting.

After that first Mother's Day, I began thinking about the other mothers who lost their child in the crash. What they must be going through? But then again, I did know; pain and longing to see their child. Did they have hope? Should I call them? Had they received letters about their children, too? How did they find out about the crash? Would they even want to talk to me? Had they, too, had signs? Perhaps I would wait to share about the rainbow. So many questions…would I ever know the answers or would I continue to be tormented by confusion?

While I pondered on the assortment of questions and continued to debate whether or not to place a phone call to the other moms, I began to clean. As abnormal as it sounds, whenever I'm upset, cleaning seems to ground my senses and help me focus on the problem at hand.

After vacuuming the den, I put the sweeper away as usual. Upon re-entering the den, I noticed something shining in the middle of the room. How odd! I had just vacuumed the entire carpet. What could this object be? There, in the center of the room was a bright, copper penny. I hadn't any pockets so I couldn't have dropped it. My dad had talked to me about the correlation between angels and pennies. He called them, "Pennies from Heaven," like the song. Yes, I did believe that there was a connection, but this was really bizarre! I called Dan at work and told him. He was excited for me and felt sure that this was another sign.

I wondered who might know something about this kind of thing. People would think that I was crazy if I began inquiring about such things or telling about this finding. Who did I know who dealt with death?

Dan and I knew we needed to pay another visit to Wearly Monuments. Neither one of us could wait until a month had passed before deciding on a marker for Zachary. Jackie had told us that it takes a few months to create a headstone. Zack must have one before Christmas. How would we find his place in the snow?

Jackie was surprised to see us so soon, but she was willing to do whatever we asked. She took out some books containing photos of stones already made. Jim also took out another book with more stone selections.

Dan and I asked if they had any stones other than the ones outside the building. Jackie led us to a room containing additional stones. We looked around the room before happening upon a unique brown granite stone. It had a polished look with an asymmetrical shape. Because of its unusual shape and clean look, the stone appeared to apply to Zachary. Strange as it sounds, this particular stone was slightly discounted. (Not that it was cheap, by any means, but it was being sold at a modestly reduced price.) Dan and I decided to purchase this stone for Zack and have a smaller scale brown granite stone made for both of us. We would work on the design and wording to be engraved on the stone we had selected. Jim and Jackie were so gracious and patient. They would draw up a computer printout of the stone then we'd work on the details.

Before leaving, I casually mentioned finding the penny to Jackie and Jim. To my surprise, Jim's response was matter-of-fact, almost as if he was talking about the weather forecast. "Finding money, any form, is just *their* way of letting you know that they're around." Jim continued, "What you're saying is not uncommon. Just be thankful for them and keep looking. We find money all the time at the cemetery. I'll be cleaning off a stone, turn to leave and find a penny, nickel, whatever, just laying there. Sometimes the coins are foreign. I could tell you lots of stories. Some people find cemeteries creepy, but I find them peaceful."

I was amazed and rather excited. Maybe I wasn't going crazy. Was Zachary that close? This was the point when my opinion about Heaven's location began to change. Maybe it wasn't "over the rainbow" as I had always believed. Heaven, as I had always pictured it, was perhaps not what I'd thought. Possibly Heaven's location was more *horizontal* than vertical. Could Heaven be here on Earth beyond an invisible veil?

Comforted by the fact that Zack might be near, earnestly looking for pennies became my new secret activity. Sharing this information cautiously, Dan and I began witnessing what I'd call, "small miracles."

I wasn't alone with the discovery of pennies and other coins. Our family began finding money in arbitrary places. My sister once found a small pile of change in her bed. My nephew, David, discovered a penny stuck to his leg when he woke up one morning. We continue to share penny stories to this day.

Dan and I decided to place the coins or "angels" as we began calling them, into a special container. When Zack was a small boy, we'd given him a small tin bank with a toy soldier on the front and he'd saved it. This became the yearly collecting canister for these "angels." At the end of each year, we put the money into a small plastic baggy. We label each baggy with total amount and the year. Particularly special "angels" were taped to an index card listing the memories associated with finding them. Those first few months after the funeral, Dan and I were in such a survival mode that we didn't think about recording where or when the coin was found. We simply put the coins into the tin.

These "angels" don't always appear everywhere we have gone. Dan seems to have a special flair for finding them in most places. I have to admit that I'm disappointed when I don't see them, but find myself smiling and excited when I do.

One morning, the thought of the other mothers of the victims of the crash just would not leave me. I prayed for each one of the parents, but prayed for Robert's mom more than the rest. After all, she'd lost her only child. Joel and Brytni had often been my motivation for getting up. They sort of pushed me to keep on going. I couldn't fathom her loss.

IU had given us a list of the addresses and phone numbers of most of the parents. Drawing up the courage, the first mother I called was Laura Eppley. Garth Eppley and Zack had gone to AU and IU together as well as being in an assortment of choral and opera activities. Garth had been to our home a few times and I'd met Laura once when the boys had been together at AU. We'd even gone out to supper together with a large group of people. Perhaps she would remember me, too.

I was relieved to find that Laura had similar experiences. I hadn't broached the subject of rainbows or pennies. I shared my feeling of despair, grief attacks, and inquired into how she was told about the plane crash and about Garth. Talking things over with her was almost like a pressure valve being released. We spoke at length about details and experiences. Laura and I made a connection and a confirmation of our state of mind. If we were losing our mind at least we weren't alone. We made a pact to call each other whenever we needed to cry (or just explode) before we hung up.

Garth's parents met with Dan and me a few days later at a concert dedicated to the five victims. Dan and Bill had not met and Laura and I had only met that once. I wondered how we'd recognize each other. Locating her was simple. I just looked for the saddest eyes in the room. I looked for eyes that held the look of realizing your worst fear and expressing your deepest sorrow. As it turned out, Laura had taken the same approach, and after the concert our eyes met and we knew one another instantly. Something about the eyes being the window to the soul holds true for me today.

I waited a few days before feeling the nudge to call another one of the parents. I had felt reassured that Laura had felt a connection, so I decided to muster up the courage to call Chris Carducci's mom, Rainelle. My heart pounded as the phone rang. How would she react? Had she experienced the same emotions? Rainelle answered and at first, I could tell that she was shocked. We discussed the same things that Laura and I had chatted about during our conversation. Not knowing or having met her, our opening channel of communication had only a few moments containing some pauses. Hoping that I wasn't intruding, I continued to speak. I wanted to tell her that I had met her son Chris, and he had left a definite impression on me.

***

Chris and Zachary had been hired to sing at the Bach Festival in Carmel, California. The summer of 2005, Dan, Debby, Ervin, David, and I decided to visit Zack while he was in Carmel. Several of Dan's aunts and uncles made the journey for the concert, too. The entire family crew took up a few rows. Chris and Zack along with two other handsome young men entered the back of Old Mission Church in Carmel. Before the quartet's performance began, I remember how proud I was… Zack had a slight tan because we had been out touring San Francisco with him the day before this concert. He looked so good! All of these singers looked so grand in their tuxedos. Zack was eager to introduce us to one particular singer, Chris. Zack had told me once that if he were a baritone, he'd want to sing like Chris Carducci, emphasizing the name with gesturing fingers in exaggerated imitation of an Italian speaker.

Chris was so charming. As Zachary introduced him, Chris took my hand as if to shake it, and then gently placed his other hand over mine. "So very nice to meet you, Mrs. Novak," Chris said. "How proud you must be of your son, Zachary." I'm sure that he spoke some other words, but I distinctly recall the first part of our interaction. Chris left such a profound effect on me. He was so handsome and polite. I could see why the girls especially were enthralled by this young man. The demeanor in which Chris conducted himself was captivating. He had a way of making you feel important. As he sang, I understood why Zack admired Chris' voice and I admired his manner, too.

***

Rainelle was so pleased that Chris had been polite and left such a favorable impression. As we spoke, we discovered that we had much in common. We were both sixth grade teachers in a middle school setting and both Catholic. The more we talked, the more we learned our lives were alike. It was as if we'd known each other forever. Rainelle and I decided that we would have been friends even if this terrible accident had not brought us together. Before ending our conversation, we made a promise to call one another whenever we needed to talk about anything.

Feeling an instant bond seemed to become the norm with each parent who had lost their child that night. The fact that we shared the loss of our child became our common ground. Even though most of us had never met, once we had become acquainted, we knew our common experience would link us together forever.

A chain of events began in mid-May. Pat Wieche from North Central High School contacted Dan and me about a program on May 13th. Zachary had completed his student teaching at North Central where Mrs. Wieche had been his supervising teacher. Zack loved the time there and greatly admired Pat. Expressing genuine caring as well as being a philanthropic teacher, Pat created a $1,000 scholarship in Zachary's name to be awarded that evening. A song Zack had conducted with one of the choirs, "Weep No More," was sung in his memory that evening. Again, there was that twinge of irony of the title of the song. I wondered when or if I'd weep no more. Leaving at intermission, Dan and I thanked Pat for all she had done for Zachary. Zack had been blessed to have had Pat as a mentor.

***

While leaving a doctor's appointment in Indianapolis, my friend, Mary Jo and I decided to stop by North Central to surprise Zachary. Knowing he might be too busy, I was a little skeptical about interrupting Zachary while he was learning to be a high school educator. Pat greeted Mary Jo and me with a warm smile and enthusiastic comments about Zachary's innate ability to teach. She told us about how he was teaching her as well as being an eager learner.

Upon seeing us, Zack flashed his wide smile and gave me a great big hug. Zack shared his excitement of the students' progress and his enjoyment of the classroom experience. I was glad that Mary Jo and I hadn't missed the opportunity to see Zachary in action.

***

In the mail, we had received notes dated May 23, 2006 from the Congressional Record-Extensions of Remarks. The honorable Peter J. Visclosky of the Indiana House of Representatives had addressed the House. He expressed his feelings concerning the plane crash and the great loss to the community resulting from the deaths of the five students. Mr. Visclosky's remarks included eight paragraphs describing each victim and the lives they had led. Zack had made it into the minutes of the House of Representatives… Wow!

For us, it seemed the ceremonies and acknowledgements in Zachary's memory went on and on. Dan and I weren't complaining, only mesmerized by the outpouring of attention. Zachary's life was kept in the forefront of lots of people. It was quite an honor… it was overwhelming!

The Anderson Community School Foundation Scholarship program for the high school was held at the end of May. Dan and I were contacted about the award ceremony. We wanted to get the scholarship started right away even though Zack had only been gone for a month.

Making the trip into Highland High School was ever-so-difficult. Zachary had graduated in that same gymnasium where we were to present the scholarship. As Dan presented the award, my eyes panned the room blankly staring at the students seated in the bleachers; my mind went back in time.

***

It was May 1999, Zachary was graduating from Highland High School and the ceremony was held in the gym. Our family sat as close to the stage as we could to get the best view of Zack's singing and conducting. The seniors from Highland Singers would be performing. It was so hot that I remember sweat rolling off my face.

Zachary wore the gold honors cords with a silver cap and gown. Zack had the distinguished honor of conducting the piece he had arranged for his choir director, Debbie Andis. He was the first and last student to conduct the choir at a graduation ceremony. Perhaps it was that moment in time that inspired Zack to pursue conducting. I thought that he would be pleased that we were able to come back into the gym.

***

Unable to stay past the first few awards, Dan and I left Highland. I raced outside to try to catch my breath. A grief attack was already washing over me. My poor friend, Cindy tried earnestly to console me. My only thought was to get home as quickly as Dan could drive. Thanking Cindy for all she and the Foundation had done for our family, Dan and I left. We knew that we had one more high school scholarship to present at Anderson High School.

The Anderson High ceremony was held in the evening. I remember being numb while Dan spoke about the crash. After the recipient was named and presentation made, my eyes looked across the stage and locked on a kindergarten student of mine from twelve years ago – Sandi's middle daughter, Jennifer. Now, here she was, graduating high school. Although Jennifer was clapping for the winner, her tearful gaze touched my heart. How fast the years had gone! In a way, Jennifer and I were both graduating into a new chapter in our lives. Dan has no recollection of that night at all. Grief continues to block out some things.

The First United Methodist had a memorial service remembering the life of Zachary. So many members of the church wanted to commemorate Zachary. Our friends, Glo and Kev came to be with us as well as much of our extended family. The service included the two adult choirs and the children's choir. The huge cross Zachary had sketched on a napkin was also presented to the congregation at that service. The cross was consecrated to the glory of God and for the service at FUMC in loving memory of Zachary. The dedication Zachary had for the church had been extended to him, too. You could feel their warmth and love.

It wasn't any wonder why Zachary loved these people and the church. In some ways, that ceremony was harder than Zachary's funeral. Perhaps because the service was June 4th and I'd had time to truly feel some of the reality of Zachary's loss or maybe it was the tears the people shed at the service…the children's sorrow was the hardest. Their hearts were so pure.

The children's choir members struggled with the shock of losing their director so suddenly. The children of FUMC were working on a musical with Zachary that had a camp in one of the scenes. The children renamed it "Camp Novak" in honor of Zachary. They even painted t-shirts inscribed with "Camp Novak" across the front. Photographs of the children wearing those special shirts appeared in the church directory later that year.

The church continued to express their affection for Zachary. Mary Beth presented Dan and me with a very special gift. Children, ages ranging from preschool to high school, had written letters or drawn pictures which they had compiled into a black scrapbook. They told of their love for Zachary and the impact he had made on each of their lives. One student wrote, "I think that this anonymous quote describes Zack perfectly: *Some people come into our lives and leave footprints on our hearts and we are never the same.* Zack was a very special person in my life and I will always remember his kind personality and what a great friend he was." I still cry when I read the book of their memories.

When we left the church that evening, I was speechless. What a tribute to someone who had been attending and working at the church for less than two years.

My thoughts began to turn to all of the wonderful things that friends and relatives had done for our family. The funeral home had provided us with thank you notes, but I wanted to do more. I talked it over with my friend, Jerri, who had made the video for Zack's showing. She had an idea to put Zack's photo along with a scripture that we had found written in his journal on the outside of a note card: "To God, a minute is an eternity, and eternity is but a minute." I thought how profound it was that Zachary had written this on one of those two pages. I couldn't bring myself to read both of those pages at that time, but those words had seemed to jump off of the page as I scanned the journal. How fitting to incorporate that message onto the thank you notes.

The card would give everyone a black and white picture of Zack to keep should they choose to do so. Then I could put a personal note inside each card. Jerri took care of all of the details. All I had to do was go to the printer, pay for them and bring them home. As oblivious as I was of the world surrounding me at that time, I felt capable of being able to accomplish that task.

Taking the lists that Alberta and Debby had kept, I began writing cards to those persons who had extended kindness to our family. The lists seemed endless. How long I worked on those notes, I really don't know. For days, I would sit at the computer and pound out one thank you after another. My sister and mom came over to help me on some days. Dan would mail them out after the notes were completed, stamped, and addressed.

One day, late in afternoon, Joel stopped by the house. I was upstairs at the computer pounding away. He calmly walked over to where I was sitting behind the desk on Zachary's swivel desk chair and asked me what I was doing. I told him that I was writing thank you notes to all the people who had been so kind to us. He responded, "No, Mom, what are you doing?" He spun me around and pointed to the room.

I have always prided myself on being a tidy house keeper for the most part. I blinked as I began panning around the upstairs room. The room was askew! Boxes and boxes of Zachary's possession were littered about the room. The pool table was almost non-discernible. It was covered both on the top and underneath with notes, sheet music, newspaper articles, CDs, and other such items.

Joel said, "Mom, you can't keep this up. Debby, David, Hillary, and I are going to help you box up some of this and put it aside for now. " Had I been so consumed with my mission of writing those notes that I hadn't even noticed my surroundings?

I agreed that something must be done, but I didn't want to throw anything away just yet. Joel understood my desire to keep everything until I could go through it. His plan was to box things up, label as much as they could, and stack it neatly in the corner of the room.

Soon after Joel had finished explaining the plan, Debby, David, and Hillary arrived. As I watched them descend on the task at hand, I felt sure that there had been much discussion about my state of mind as well as the condition of the room. Debby took all the cards and notes along with their envelopes and placed them into a box. She explained to me that she and I would work together to put these items into binders and sheet protectors. We would compile them into commemorative scrapbooks of sorts. Maybe I wouldn't need to save everything, but she promised to help put each note and article into some form of order that we would agree upon.

Creating scrapbooks for family members was certainly not a novelty for my sister and me. We had made many scrapbooks for all of our children for their high school graduations and for our parents for their 50th wedding anniversary. Our last scrapbooking project had been for our trip to the big city of New York.

***

Debby, David, Zachary, and I were fortunate to be able to do lots of outings. Our schedules just seemed to merge and blend together. We would go out to lunch or meet with my mom and other family members at the swimming pool.

On one of these swim excursions, David and Zack were planning their next big trip to New York. David and Zachary took many vacations together, usually to Florida to spend a few days with my parents after Christmas or summer trips to New York City. While each of them floated on a raft in the pool, they proceeded in detailing the trip. Debby and I mocked them with comments such as, "must be nice to have money" or "too bad we can't join you, but of course, we weren't invited," etc.

That evening, Zachary called me and invited Debby and me to join David and him on their trip to New York. I told him that we were just fooling around and he shouldn't feel pressured to take us. He and David had discussed it and both felt that nothing would be funnier than watching our reactions to the charm and grandeur that is New York City.

Debby and I talked it over and even though the money would be tight, how could we afford NOT to go. After all, when do adult children invite their moms to go with them on an outing such as this? Long story short, Debby and I went with David and Zachary for a five day, four night trip to New York. Rather than expounding on the roast we carted with us and plans of cooking it in our rented room (to save some money, of course) or the extended driving times in my new van, I'll simply say that those were some of the funniest and most exciting times of my life. Debby and I, of course, made each of us a scrapbook detailing the adventure.

***

Putting away all of Zachary's possessions gave me pause. I actually began to take hold of the concept written in the poem Zack had kept, "What Is Success" : "What I have possessed in this world will belong to someone else immediately…" That reality was staring me in the face. All the Earthly possessions Zachary had accumulated over his lifetime were now here at our home. With the touching of each of Zachary's things came the flood of questions. Why did he save this? Where did he get this? Did each item have value or some deep seated memory? What is this? Some of his possessions were completely foreign to me. They related to his future livelihood, conducting. Also Zachary was so much more gifted and intelligent than me. Some of his writing was well beyond my intellectual capacity. Planning to learn more in the future, I pushed on to accomplish the task of merely putting things into boxes for future examination.

Not everything could be done that particular evening. The job was simply too much to take in. Debby came over one day with the goal of reassembling Zachary's music CDs onto his old high school shelving units. Zack had the CDs categorized in his own style with plain white index card dividers. It took her most of the morning to complete the task. Debby had placed the last few CDs in place when the entire shelving unit fell forward onto her head. The CDs spewed out everywhere. Gasping and almost laughing, I asked Debby if she was all right. Looking around the room, her response was, "Okay, Zachary, I'll try to put them in the order that you had them in." It was so clear to us that Zack was present in this situation.

It's difficult to explain the feeling of someone being there when reality tells you otherwise. There were other unusual situations that made me wonder about the distance between those we lose and our normal everyday lives. Can some of God's creatures see beyond what humans are capable of seeing with our naked eye?

***

Brytni has a beagle named Bailey that often visits our home. Bailey spent most of the first year of her life with us because the dog was a gift from Jason for Brytni's birthday. Since Brytni didn't have a home of her own, the dog stayed at our house.

All three of our children are close and Zack was one of the first people to meet Bailey. He was actually with Garth in Lafayette for a Bach Festival performance. Brytni was at her apartment while finishing Finals Week at Purdue. She couldn't wait to show her big brother her new best buddy, little Bailey. Zachary loved that dog. We had a beagle named Arfie when the kids were growing up, so I think they all have a deep love for the breed.

***

After Zack passed, whenever we couldn't find Bailey, she would be in our living room by the piano. Prior to the loss of Zack, Bailey seldom ventured into that room. She's too much of a people dog to ever want to be alone and we had rarely been in that room. The family found Bailey's new affinity to that room odd. We'd practically have to drag her out of the living room.

Once while Debby and I were reminiscing in our living room, Bailey was also with us. The phone had rung and I was busy talking. Bailey had been resting on the floor when all of a sudden she stood up and began wagging her tail excitedly. With her eyes looking upward, Bailey continued to wag her tail at full excitement speed which included her entire back side. Bailey only did this when she was really happy to see someone. I stood up and got off the phone right away.

"Bailey, what is it? What do you see?" I asked. Bailey just looked at us then turned her attention back toward the air, all the while wagging excitedly. Debby and I looked at each other in amazement. Bailey trotted to the landing of our stairway as if she were following someone. She looked at me as if to say, "Don't you see him?" Bailey stood on the first step never taking her eyes off the stairway. Finally, she turned back toward me, then back to the stairway, and finally back to me. Looked dejected, Bailey walked back into the living room and lay down.

I ran upstairs to see if I could see anything. Of course my mind felt that Zachary might...no, must be there. Why would Bailey have acted so strangely unless she could see something that I couldn't? Straining my eyes, I looked around the entire upstairs, but to no avail. I could not see anything out of the ordinary. Debby and I couldn't believe our eyes. We both knew that Bailey had reacted as if she was seeing a friend. Zack had been the dog's friend...what else could we believe?

After telling Dan and the rest of the family about the incident, we discussed Bailey wandering into the living room, but this...well, I'm not really sure what they thought. I only knew what I had watched with Bailey. Again, I found myself pondering on the same questions: "How far away is Heaven? How far away are those who leave our world?" Wishing I had experienced what Bailey had seen, my thoughts turned toward the mess in the game room. The situation would be a hard chore to complete.

The room held boxes neatly labeled according to the contents, but the pool table remained covered. Sifting through the piles of material, I noticed a large, unopened manila envelope. It had no stamps. How did we get this? Why had I not noticed this before? Ripping it open, the contents spilled onto the pool table. My heart almost stopped. Three pages of Zachary's school work fell out along with a typed letter and a concert program. His school work was dated. The last quiz was taken on April 18th, a mere two days before the crash. I wondered how he felt in that class on that day.

Reading the letter, I spread out Zachary's three graded quizzes. The letter explained that his associate instructor, Andy, had not had the opportunity to return the papers to Zack. His letter spoke of his friendship and commonalities with Zachary. He and Zack were practicing Catholics working for Protestant churches, both as music leaders. Zachary had conducted a piece on April 7th for Andy's organ recital. His conducting might have been his last official performance. (I wished I'd been there to have seen Zack conduct that piece.)

To have taken the time to write and put these items together for Dan and me was a conscientious gesture! My fingers traced Zack's writing. Looking at his cursive handwriting on the quizzes made me smile. Zack and I have extremely similar handwriting – so close in fact that sometimes the difference could go undetected.

Looking at Zack's signature again, I loved that we both put a special little flare to our autographs.

***

One day, I had already left for school when it dawned on me that I had forgotten to write a note excusing Brytni from school. She had been sick the day before and needed a note to allow her to return to class. My mind raced trying to arrive at a solution to the problem. It was too late for me to return home to write the note. Then it occurred to me that Zachary could write it for me. I went over the fact that this was a "one time deal" and that he must use my exact words so that essentially it was my letter, not his. After talking it through with him, the letter was ready to go, and Brytni made it back to class without incident.

I found out later that this wasn't a "one-time" occurrence. Joel and Brytni had used his writing skills to their advantage a few times, such as when they had forgotten to have permission slips signed. Luckily, the use of Zachary's skillful replication of my signature was more for convenience than to truly get away with something inappropriate. They really were well-behaved!

***

During the afternoon and evenings, Debby and I began putting cards and notes into scrapbooks. Debby took great care placing the items sequentially by the date the article was received.

At some stage in a sorting and organizing session, a student from my sixth grade class rang the doorbell. The young girl expressed her worries for me and my family. She stated that the sixth period class had selected her to come to my house since she lived in my neighborhood to inquire as to when I'd be returning. I explained to the young girl my need to be home, but was doing okay and appreciated everyone's concern. My request was if she would please carry that message back to the class.

After she left, I began to think about school and the students I had left behind. My love for teaching had always been a huge part of my life. It seemed so foreign to me that school had not been even a flicker of a thought for weeks now. Rushing upstairs, I began discussing the student's visit with Debby. I knew that going back to teaching now would be a mistake; yet, there must be something I could do for those students.

How could I possibly talk to each class when I could barely move or think each day? I didn't want to disrupt my substitute's day nor did I want to interfere with the schedules of my sixth grade teammates. All of them had lent a hand in helping me through my first year in sixth grade. Then the solution seemed to pop into my head. (I truly think that the Lord put the thought there.) If the Little Theater wasn't being used during homeroom, I could meet with all 167 students at one time. Homeroom lasts only about 30 minutes. Surely I could handle it.

Debby was a bit skeptical, but applauded my willingness to give it a try. She and I knew that I would need to go back to the place where I had first heard the news before the beginning of the next school year. Confronting my fear of that building, my own classroom, and the overall memory of the worst day of my life had to be done sooner or later. Perhaps I could go back on the last day of school as well as a thirty minute period to face the students. A lot of prayer would need to be said before this decision could be reached.

Later that evening, I explained the plan to Dan. He insisted that he'd go with me just in case I needed him. He could fill in the gaps for me. How blessed I am to have such a wonderful partner in life. I called school the next day and discussed my plan with the principal. She was gracious and in agreement with whatever I thought I could handle. Dan and I would come in the week before the last day of school. After the large student meeting, she and I could discuss further plans.

I recall waiting outside the principal's office and hearing the announcement for my students to assemble in the Little Theater. My mind filled with the pain of being told about the plane crash. Her office was where my world changed. Bits of flashbacks obstructed my thoughts. My mind began to choke my concentration. Many times I have felt like Scarlet O'Hara in *Gone with the Wind* when she says, "I'll think about that tomorrow." (I've even said that statement aloud.) Shaking my head and shutting my eyes, I walked down the entrance hall and into the Little Theater.

My sixth grade students were assembled as planned during the homeroom period. Dan stood off in the corner like a sentinel ready to protect if needed. As I looked at each face, I saw the future and it was full of questions much like my own. The meeting began with me telling the students about Zachary and the accident. Amazingly, I was able to remove myself and emotions from the picture and focus on the students. I told them that they could ask me anything that they wanted to know that day, but when I came back on the next school day, I would not answer anything but school related material.

The students' hands shot up. They were so full of questions. Where did the plane crash? Where was he going? What caused the crash? Were there any survivors? And many more... but the question I found the most provocative was, "Among his belongings, what did I find the most interesting?" Wow! I even think that was my first response out loud. I answered with, "his journal." I still stand by that answer. After all, his two page jottings in his notebook gave me a glimpse inside Zack's thoughts, if only for a little while. Of course, they all wanted to know what Zachary had written in his short journal. Luckily, the bell rang for the students to move to their first period class. Many came and hugged me goodbye before leaving the theater. Breathing a sigh of relief, Dan and I walked to the office, bid our farewell, and exited the building.

I was glad to see the students and felt that issues had been averted because of the meeting. Feeling dizzy, I knew I was ready to get home. Dan left for work after making sure that I was going to be all right. Rest was the first thing on my agenda. The meeting had depleted my energy.

After making a cup of tea, I decided to watch television. For weeks, the TV and radio had seemed like an insignificant waste of time. How could I do such mundane things when my world was crashing?

I settled onto the sofa, steaming cup of tea in hand, and pushed the once familiar remote. What should come on but, *Little House on the Prairie*. My first instinct was to change the channel. I certainly didn't need to hear any more sad news and this show was usually what I would call a tear jerker. Something made me keep it on that station, so I watched. The scene was a tearful Laura confiding in her mother about the woes of her unfair world. Her mother held her and responded, "Oh, Laura, don't you know that the best way to stop hurting is to start doing for others?" As I watched and let those words seep into my brain, I grabbed a pencil and paper to jot down those words. Had the Lord put this show in front of me to ease my pain? How strange that I would hear those words at that time?

I called my mother to tell her what I thought was a revelation. She reassured me that I could do all things through Christ who strengthens me. I knew I had to move forward even if it meant dragging myself out of the pits of grief. God and my family would give me strength. I had always believed that and now I would put myself to that test. More of life, holidays, birthdays, and school days were looming ahead. I had to move…little steps at a time. Maybe I could help someone else along the way.

***

Six Mother's Days have passed since Zack was here with us. As this day drew to a close, I had more than a little sadness well up from deep inside. Mother's Day without Zack was hard enough, but somehow viewing a rainbow was like a sign that Zack was truly not that far away from me. This year, I hadn't seen a rainbow. It had been a beautiful sunny day which was not the norm over the course of these past few months. Rain had been in the forecast, but our family felt fortunate to be able to spend the day playing outside in the warm sunshine. What if this year, for the first time, the rainbow phenomenon would not happen for me?

On the ride home from my sister's house where we had celebrated Mother's Day, I expressed to Dan how disheartened I'd become about not experiencing a rainbow sighting. The sun was beginning to set as it was around 8:00 in the evening. I had begun to lose faith that I'd see a rainbow so I had stopped looking skyward. Dan said "Just look over there. I see your rainbow! Keep your sunglasses on and it'll appear more clearly." Looking toward the west, there was a small, bright piece of a rainbow arching through the clouds.

"Oh, there you are! Thanks for remembering me on Mother's Day," I responded aloud. I must learn to keep faith and trust in the miracles that happen all around us. That was the lesson learned that day.

Cousins and first babies, Barb, me & Mary Kay.
October, September, and July babies.

Zack as Santa. He created the costume
complete with an old diaper for the beard.

The Wicked Witch of the West. Even
good guys like to be bad sometimes.
(Notice the blanket and the crochet
hat-once used by my grandma as a towel
tissue holder.)

Always acting with a make shift costume, Zachary, the spy. (Notice the blanket once again that is safety pinned as a cape.)

Riding on high. Zachary in the top bunk of the motor home where we shared many discussions...including the Easter Bunny.

Sandi's Biggest Fan.
Zachary with Sandi after a concert.

Three Blind Mice-my homemade costumes.
(I used socks for the paws.)

Bubbles and camping...nothing is more fun than the simple pleasures in life.

Joel, Brytni, and Zachary in the Smokey Mountains.

Brytni, Zack, and Joel in the Badlands. Notice they still struck the same pose.

Oh that sweet smile, Zachary in the third grade.

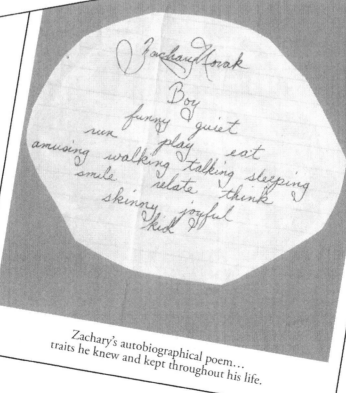

Zachary Horak
Boy
funny quiet
run play eat
amusing walking talking sleeping
smile relate think
skinny joyful
kid

Zachary's autobiographical poem...
traits he knew and kept throughout his life.

Trying to stay dry on a family vacation at Niagara Falls.

Zachary, Joel and Brytni with my crafty crewel creations Christmas stockings.
We still hang them on the mantel every year.

Zachary and I after a junior high
awards ceremony.

Going to the high school prom, Zachary, a senior,
Joel, a junior, and Brytni, a sophomore. This was
the only prom they <u>all</u> attended.

Me, Joel, Brytni, Zachary, and Dan on our vacation out west.

Unshaven and looking quite grown up, Dan, Zack, and me.
I was holding his hand.

One of the phenomenal photos found before the
funeral showing : The Christ of the Ohio Statue,
Brytni, me, Joel, and Dan.

Standing outside the studio of the Today Show in NYC with my sister Debby,
her son David, me, and Zachary.

Blessed with a beautiful daughter-in-law.
Me, Dan, Zachary (as best man), Brytni, Hillary, and Joel

In Grand Irish Style, Zachary was the featured tenor in the Paramount Theater April 2005. Pictured with Dr. Richard Sowers and some of the extended family.

Zachary and me at Shadyside Park, the day I found out about his "Zack O'Novak" performance with the Anderson Symphony.

Our last Christmas with Zachary.
Zachary, Brytni, Hillary, Joel, me, Dan, and Bailey (our granddog).

The family that keeps growing. Grandbabies are the best!

Always thinking while reflecting on the music, Zachary at the studio recording songs for my surprise 50th birthday CD.

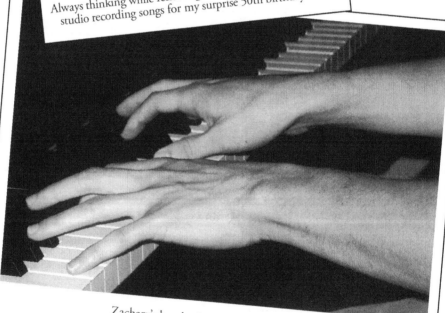

Zachary's hands...Making the piano sing.

The Birthday Song

Our family truly loves to get together! Each member's birthday and other monumental occasions have always been huge celebrations for our family. When my parents' Golden Wedding Anniversary arrived, it would of course be a total family affair.

***

As a gift for my parent's fiftieth wedding anniversary, the grandkids created a CD entitled, *We Remember When*. Debby and I encouraged (more like pushed) our children into creating the CD. As David, Steve, Zachary, Joel, and Brytni sat around our dining room table, it was obvious that the CD would consist of more than a couple songs. The finished product turned out to be eighteen selections. Debby and I listened from the kitchen as the memories of their childhood flowed.

Each of the grandchildren took a special family event, wrote about that memory and then followed it with a song. Being the family perfectionist, Zack labored over the entire CD, both editing and filling in some rough spots with his voice. The final song wasn't the way he felt it should be so Zack created a voice-over which he sang a range of parts to form the harmony. The finale had to be just right in Zachary's eyes.

Reflecting back to that time, it's almost prophetic that Zachary's part of the CD gift for my parents would be about birthdays. Our family birthday song blends tradition from both Dan's heritage and mine. This makes the birthday song so long that the candles on the cake almost melt down before the birthday recipient can make the wish and blow them out. As we sing the song, many members of our family seem to not be able to recall which individual is having the birthday *or* the birth date *or* day of the week of that person's birth (all of which are mentioned in our version). We often just muddle through the song so the wishing time won't be delayed too much. The last chorus would always have Zachary and my mom or sister harmonizing.

After the accident, it took me five years to sing the birthday song without leaving the room or crying. Maybe it was so hard because I kept waiting on Zack's voice to fill in the empty piece of the song's melody or it could be that having these events felt vacant without Zack. I don't have the answers. I only know that the song remains a tough song to hear, let alone to sing.

Having his speaking voice and reflections is priceless. On the *We Remember When* CD, Zack tells his earnest love of birthdays as well as reflecting on my parents and their impact on our family. When I hear his voice, I shut my eyes and float to that moment in time. Life seemed so carefree and complete when Zachary was here. What a great treasure to have a studio recording of his voice!

***

School was out and the summer appeared to be flying by. Debby and I put the scrapbooks together holding the cards with notes or special memorabilia received after the accident. The books began to fill up quickly until we'd assembled four large binders and still had more items to file. Debby and I concluded that the task would not be completed prior to the beginning of school, but at least we'd made a dent in the undertaking.

Knowing school was just around the corner, Dan and I longed to get away from all the sadness. We had even talked of selling the house and moving to a lake or someplace where we might find peace. Dan was so stressed at work and I still wasn't sleeping. We longed to go away…to run away from home. Where would we go? How would we go?

While taking a pontoon boat ride one evening with Dan's sister, Jodi and her husband, Pat, they made us an offer. Pat and Jodi had a week's stay at a hotel in Clearwater Beach and would love for us to take it. Their schedule wouldn't permit them to go; at least that's what they told us. At first, we refused but they kept insisting we needed the break and that week's trip was just going to go to waste unless Dan and I used it. Their daughter, Amy, even aided in the plan. The Lord had opened a door just when we were ready to jump out of a window, or so it felt.

The trip was a week spent with reflection, reading and sharing without the interruptions of everyday life, like work for Dan or the starting of the school year for me. We still were surrounded by the strong sense of loss; yet, Dan and I reconnected in ways when at home we were miles apart. I had heard it said that many marriages don't survive a tragedy like the loss of a child. Dan and I had been married for twenty-nine years before the plane crash. He was and continues to be my partner for life. I'm thankful that we didn't lose each other, too. The trip was a bridge back to our future.

The future we faced together would have some difficult moments, even in times that are typically cause for celebration. Dan had to celebrate his fiftieth birthday without Zack. I'm 364 days older than my husband. We often joked about being the same age for one day a year. I felt a little guilty for having had such a spectacular fiftieth birthday when Dan's special fiftieth birthday would feel somewhat empty with Zack being gone. Just the year before, the family had thrown a big bash in honor of my arrival at what some call, life's midpoint.

***

My big 5-0 party had been set to be held at Joel and Hillary's, unbeknownst to me. My dad had just purchased the house next door to theirs. We often joke that my dad's trying to remodel West 8th Street, one house at a time. (He has refurbished six homes to date.) Debby and I were taking the tour with dad and debating on whether or not this one of a kind place was even salvageable. While looking around at the dilapidated home, I fell through a hole in the floor, really scraping my left leg. Joel and Hillary had gone out of town for a small vacation, but we had their front door key for emergencies. My sister tried valiantly to persuade me to go home and take care of the injury. I was insistent about simply going to Joel and Hillary's to handle it.

Debby accompanied me hoping to steer clear of any party paraphernalia we might bump into as we walked though the house. My focus was totally on washing off the blood and putting ice on my leg to stop the swelling. Being my usual oblivious self, I walked right past the huge amount of party supplies. Debby said that she was holding her breath the whole time. Again, I was unaware.

The next day, Dan told me we were invited to Joel and Hillary's to see photos of their recent vacation. A red flag should have gone up for me as Dan thought I was dressed a little too casually and I might want to change. Puzzled but not alarmed, I changed and we left for the visit. Opening the large wooden gate leading into Joel and Hillary's backyard, I was startled by voices of forty family members ringing through the air with shouts of, "Surprise!"

Much to my delight, Jason and Brytni were there. They had told me that they needed to pay a visit to Jason's family and would be out of town for a while. They were now a mere three months from their impending wedding date. Everyone had a big part in the arrangement of this surprise.

The yard looked as if it belonged in an advertisement for the perfect garden party – five eight-foot-long tables draped in white pressed linen table cloths, sparkling wine glasses flanking the brightly colored china plates adorned by hand crafted floral napkin rings, and several large floral center pieces.

As if not to be outdone by the decorations, the food tasted as if it could have been prepared by Rachel Ray. Hillary had made roasted pork tenderloin, twice baked potatoes, fresh garden grown corn, and assorted hors d'oeuvres.

Stacked neatly in a pile beside my assigned chair were several gifts. After each one had been unwrapped and thank yous extended, I came to the last gift. It was a compact disc Zachary had appropriately titled, *You Asked for It*. Zack shared behind the scenes information about certain songs on the CD and his inserting a piano break here and there. Zack had prerecorded the piano background for most of the songs; however, for a select few, he played the piano and sang the song in the studio. "Mama, A Rainbow" was one he had recorded vocals and piano together.

Joel took the CD inside his house to play through the computer. He opened the window and the sound drifted through the air. Zachary swept me up into the moment with a spontaneous dance. I recall smiling and laughing so much that my face hurt. Zachary put his arms around me and gave me a huge hug, and a resounding, "Happy Birthday, Mom!" Of course, I stifled the tears. What an incredible gift and memory of a birthday!

Later, I inquired as to how he could afford to have this CD recorded. Zack explained how my mom's sister, Aunt Naomi "Ruthie" York, had approached him after hearing him sing at Joel's wedding. If Zachary had the time, she would love to help him financially with creating a professional CD. Zachary had simply disregarded the conversation until the topic of my birthday present arose. Aunt Ruthie was more than willing to advance the cash with the stipulation that he include "The Lord's Prayer" on the CD for her. Of course, her request would be granted, but it sparked some thoughts concerning other songs on the CD.

Even though the CD was a gift for me, Zack could include favorite song selections for other family members. Zachary decided to add some of their songs to the recording: "Ave Maria" which was dedicated to Grandma "Rory" Novak, and "Danny Boy" dedicated to his dad. How like Zack was that: continually thinking of others while making the most of each opportunity.

***

During the first few months after Zack passed, I played that CD non-stop. It had been an anchor for me during the funeral visitation. I would also play music from operas and plays which had his voice. Then, all of a sudden, his voice was too painful to hear. I'm not sure why. Maybe it was because Zachary wasn't here and my heart couldn't stand the pain of not being able to reach him. I simply stopped listening to his music.

Around that time, two friends, Melvin and Phyllis Shaul from Bethel United Methodist called wanting to meet with Dan and me. Zachary had been choir director at Bethel for seven years. They had an idea about using Zack's music as a fund raiser for his scholarships. Melvin and Phyllis loved Zachary's voice and felt that everyone should have the chance to enjoy listening to him sing anytime and a CD would do just that.

Melvin and Phyllis spoke of families that may have recordings of Zachary when he sang at a family wedding or funeral. Perhaps we could compile some of this music along with the CD that he had made for me. Maybe we could ask the Anderson Symphony if it would be possible to use a song or two from Zachary's performance in 2005. I began to think about the opportunity to stumble onto music Zack had sung that I had not heard. Now that would be quite a discovery. Finding myself refreshed and excited about the possibility of increasing Zachary's Scholarship amount, we agreed to pursue the CD.

An exciting chain of events began to unfold. I approached a local musician, Rick Vale, about helping with the CD jacket. Zachary had worked with Rick on a few projects and Zack had admired Rick's abundant musical talent. I also knew Rick, and had worked with him as a judge at Highland High School's Singsational, a program showcasing high school choirs throughout the country. Rick was more than willing to help.

Rick also provided us with an original song he had written. It was titled, "Come Away," a duet Zack had sang with Erin, a soprano from his AU Chorale group. Dan and I had not heard Zachary sing this song before. It was an incredible find! Rick's help was invaluable with all the little and big details, particularly with obtaining the correct information about each song.

The Anderson Symphony released Zachary's performance of "A Medley of Irish Song" to be used on the not-for-profit CD which we titled *Reflections of Zachary Novak*.

***

Saturday, April 30, 2005 at 8 p.m., Zachary was the featured tenor for the Anderson Symphony Orchestra. Zack was so modest that he would often not tell us about upcoming events in his life. He would refer to the events as "no big deal." My finding out about the symphony program was unique to say the least.

Dan and I had taken his parents to watch the fireworks display held on July 4th, 2004. His parents had trouble negotiating the Shadyside terrain so we parked at the top of one of the hills closest to the orchestra. I happened to pick up a program announcing the coming events for the Anderson Symphony. I noticed that they had a concert scheduled for April, 2005, entitled *Irish Eyes are Smiling*, listing Zack O'Novak as the featured tenor, adding an Irish twist to our Polish surname. I was elated of course, but upset to have discovered this exciting news in an advertisement.

Zachary had the position of cuing the fireworks with the music for a few years prior to that evening. Dan and I knew Zack would be there so I tracked him down, program in hand. Walking at a brisk pace, Zachary saw me approaching and met me at the bottom of the hill.

Before I could open my mouth, Zack said, "I really meant to tell you and Dad about this before it officially was announced. Sorry about that, but really, it's no big deal." In no uncertain terms, I told him that it *was* a big deal. He gave me one of those fabulous hugs and all was forgiven. Dan took a picture of Zack and me at that moment. It is part of a photo collage displayed in our kitchen and remains one of my favorite photographs.

The Anderson Symphony performs at the historic Paramount Theater in downtown Anderson. The theater opened its doors in 1929 and has been restored to the grandeur of its day. That April evening, Zachary sang to a sold out crowd. Family had come from Illinois for the event and his brother, Joel was about to hear his big brother, Zack sing for the first time since high school. Joel had gone to Nashville,

Tennessee to play baseball for Belmont University and had not made it to Zachary's performances. Likewise, Zack had not made it to Joel's baseball games. Scheduling and time had always interfered with their plans to see one another.

Most of our family was seated in the mezzanine, section A. Joel was seated right beside me in the front row. His palms were so sweaty that he continually rubbed them on his pants. "Look at me," Joel said, "I'm a nervous wreck!"

The orchestra opened with a few songs but soon after, Zack entered the stage. Clad in his black tuxedo with tails accented with a green satin hanky in his breast pocket , crisply pressed white shirt, white vest and coordinating bow tie, Zack began to let his tenor voice bounce off the walls of the theater. His first number was "A Medley of Irish Songs." When Zachary had finished, there was thundering applause. At the end of the performance, Zachary received a standing ovation from the audience that beckoned for an encore. Zack re-entered and sang, "When Irish Eyes Are Smiling," inviting the crowd, "Would you sing this with me?" And we all did. My chest couldn't puff up any more than it already was; I was so proud of Zack and his ability to remain humble.

Joel leaned over to me and whispered in a metaphor that only a baseball player would use, "I do believe that he hit it out of the park!" I smiled, agreeing. It was one of those moments when a mom feels extremely proud of both of her children simultaneously. The boys still had that connection that had made them so close throughout their lives despite the distance of time and space.

After the concert, Joel took a pen and the program to his big brother. Joel asked Zack for his autograph. After much brotherly banter, Zack sarcastically took the pen and wrote, "To the only brother I have, Love Zack." (Joel had a shadow box made with photos of Zack and him doing various activities together. The program is encased inside that box that is displayed in Joel's house today.)

***

Other songs for the CD just fell into place. One unusual featured song gave me the feeling that Zack simply wanted to "do it again." Brytni video recorded Christmas Mass in 2005. Zack had asked his father to sing a duet with him entitled, "See Amid the Winter Snow." The choir, including myself, sang the chorus. When we played the video back, we could hear Zack's voice beautifully, but not Dan's voice. Dan decided to go to the studio to fill in his missing part. The finished product played as if Dan and Zack recorded the song together.

Another song had an extra voice added. Laura, a fellow friend and choir member who attended Bethel, lent her beautiful voice in tribute to Zachary's memory of the many duets they had sung together in church.

After months of collating all the pieces to the process, Melvin, Phyllis, Dan, Debby, and I began to see the full picture. Debby, Dan, and I made several trips to the studio asking help and advice. We were so grateful to the sound engineer, Darrell Powell, who was very helpful and extremely patient with us. The *Reflections of Zachary Novak* CD was complete and ready at the beginning of December.

Marketing was another issue. Where would we sell these CDs and how would we gather the money to deposit into the scholarship fund? Another answer to prayer seemed to appear: Moneyhun's Fine Gifts and Furnishings, Notre Dame Book Shelf, and Gaither Family Resources agreed to have displays at their shops. The sales of the CD helped put our scholarships into perpetual standing! We divided the proceeds between the two scholarships. Watching God's hand in this work was and continues to be another miracle.

***

To Joel, Hillary, Brytni, and Jason's credit, a birthday party for Dan's fiftieth was planned. Once more, Joel and Hillary's backyard was transformed into the faultless garden-party-like setting, complete with gifts and family members. Everyone put on their best party face and tried to go on as if it were a normal festivity for our family. Birthdays have always been a time of fun and family. This day should have been a huge event just like the year before on my fiftieth. Marking this special day like this for Dan seemed so unfair. The valiant attempt by the kids to make it a celebration was commendable. I remained in an elusive state for most of the summer…perhaps more like the first year or two. Coping with life was almost all I could do. I thanked God each day for the strength of my husband and family.

Prior to the party, Dan kept insisting that there needn't be a celebration. He'd rather take in a Cub's game at Wrigley Field. We did just that. The weather cooperated which sometimes isn't the case, especially in windy Chicago. Our kids made the arrangements and once again our family tried to act as if our lives were normal. Looking back on that day, I was the thorn in everyone's side. I even had a grief attack at the ballpark. They ate the traditional hot dogs and I just couldn't eat. Zack was gone and I wanted to go, too. It doesn't work that way.

Shortly after Dan's party, Joel's birthday came next, in August. That year, he would be twenty-five just like Zack. The boys would find humor in the fact that they were the same age for three weeks every year. I had Joel, Hillary, Jason, and Brytni to our house to celebrate Joel's special day. He didn't talk about it much but I could feel his sadness. How could he ever be older than Zack? Zachary was the oldest child, but now the title would fall on Joel's shoulders. In my heart, I knew that the next birthday for Joel would be harder. He'd be twenty-six.

I made Joel's traditional favorite of double layer chocolate cake with homemade chocolate butter cream frosting. Making that cake was hard. So many memories of past birthdays came pouring in. We somehow managed to muddle through; although I tried to make it fun for Joel. Birthdays are supposed to be fun. That sentence I repeated loudly in my head, hoping I could convince myself to have fun.

***

Joel was born only twenty minutes after I arrived at the hospital. To this day, he's always early even though he was in reality three weeks late by the doctor's predicted due date. I have a photo of eleven month old Zachary attempting to hold newborn Joel. Having the boys so close was almost like having twins. Their personalities meshed perfectly together. Zack and Joel rarely, if ever, fought. When they played, Zack was the villain and Joel was the hero. Zack was a night owl while Joel was an early riser. Both boys possessed a competitive spirit. Joel thrived on athletic competition, but Zack loathed it, fulfilling his passion in artistic endeavors. They both also strived for perfection in school work. I often felt that both boys were right about competition as sometimes it's a good thing and other times, not so much.

They shared a room until Zack went to college. Memories of telling them to just go to sleep and to stop talking or laughing remain fixed in my mind. They could always talk or laugh together even when they hadn't seen one another in a while, the boys would pick up where they had left off...never missing a beat. Maybe that was what made them such good friends. Zachary was Joel's best man at his wedding and I was sure that Joel would have been Zack's. They were both *my* best men.

***

In the middle of all this CD adventure and three weeks after Joel's birthday was Zachary's... the first birthday without Zack in twenty-five years. How do you celebrate without the guest of honor? Of course being the mother means that you knew him before anyone else. You felt the kicks and those hiccups from the inside. You felt the pains of labor and held those tiny little fingers that sweetly grasped your touch. All the years of watching your baby grow. Kissing for each boo-boo, helping when needed and trying to back off when you weren't...simply watching time go by with each marked point of another year gone; yet, anticipating many more birthdays to come. Zachary will forever be twenty-five in my mind. We will all grow older but he will remain no older than twenty-five.

On Zachary's birthday, I went to the cemetery and cried. There wasn't a stone there yet to mark where we had last laid him. Dan and I had given the final diagram to Jackie and Jim at Wearly Monuments. The plans for his monument and ours had been completed.

Wanting to have light at the cemetery, we didn't know what to do. While visiting the cemetery one day, I met a lady who had lost two children. She had a special candle holder in between her two daughter's headstones. She spoke of leaving a light to shine for their lives. I loved the thought so Dan and I incorporated the candle into Zachary's stone, too. Jackie and Jim located the holder and provided the mounting of the candle as well.

Zachary's headstone represented three faiths that fall under the same belief. Zachary was very ecumenical so it stood to reason that his stone should represent his beliefs. Catholics,

Church of God, and Methodists all believe in God the Father, Jesus the Son, and the Holy Spirit. The candle represented letting our inner light shine for the world to see our love for one another. Zachary's life was like that candle. Hopefully, his final place would be marked before the holidays.

Even though I was busy working on the CD and had now returned to teaching, sleep remained an obstacle. Morning walks with Nancy, my next door neighbor and college friend, began where we had left off before the accident. We walked with the morning stars and sunrise. Sometimes, I felt like I was walking in my sleep. Each morning, I would look up and say, "Good Morning, Zack." Sometimes I could hear him respond as if he were right next to me, "Morning, Mom." I would find myself constantly wondering about Heaven's location.

Nancy listened as I talked about not wanting to be seen in public and the crazy comments people would say. I knew that others have your best interest at heart but they simply don't know what to say to someone in grief. My best advice is to say that you really don't know how that person feels because no one has really walked that exact path. We can only offer our best wishes and pray for that person.

Then there are people avoiding you because they don't know what to say. Once, while doing my weekly grocery shopping, I noticed someone who knew me almost run away down another aisle to avoid speaking to me. To my knowledge, that had never happened before the accident. Dragging myself to the store was enough of a challenge. I didn't want to see anyone, but to actually watch them flee from you as if you had something contagious was hurtful.

I also had a good friend send a card every week at first, then once a month for the first year. The cards from everyone else tapered off, but Carol kept those cards coming to the house. She didn't say much, just that she was thinking of Dan and me. She and her husband, Ron, were keeping us in their prayers. I was always glad to go through the mail to find Carol's card. This act of kindness encouraged me to keep going forward.

My next door neighbor at school was remarkable as well. Dan Alexander had been in the principal's office when I was told about the plane crash. He had watched me and literally helped me stand during my weakest hour. When I returned to school, my mind still was whirling. One day during the first six weeks grading period, Dan took a snapshot of each member of our sixth grade staff. The sixth grade teachers often took our lunch break in Dan's classroom. One day at lunch, he projected our photos onto the screen in the room. I saw myself for the first time in months. My eyes looked vacant and my face seemed drawn. My appearance was more like an empty shell.

After the rest of our staff left, I asked Dan if that is how I really looked each day. His reply was simple, "Yes." He also told me that he was glad I noticed. He said that my Dan and I were always in his prayers.

My principal had arranged my schedule so that my prep time and lunch backed up with one another giving me a break in the middle of the day. Living so close allowed me to go home and "breathe," then return to work. The schedule worked as a means of survival for me. I was going to try to fix that empty shell that my friend and colleague had revealed to me. Lucinda, my principal, and I were also becoming friends. We met a few times after school and sometimes I would just sit in her office to talk. The bond we had forged in the midst of the tragedy had formed a common thread.

Debby was really concerned about my "empty-eyed look." She had contacted a friend who knew a grief counselor. Debby really thought that I should go to talk to someone about my pain. I had never sought outside help for problems and felt unsure about the counseling process. She convinced me to give it a try.

Three days after Zachary's birthday, I went to my new friend and counselor, Connie. Having a husband as funeral director, she had witnessed several parents who had lost their children. Her description of me at our first meeting was: broken, trembling, with every part of me seeking to survive. I have since asked Connie for her first impression of my mental health. Her response was that she knew that I would survive because she saw a spark from within.

Connie felt that adjusting to my "new normal" would take a long time. She was comforting without being smothering at each session, and was glad that I was exercising by walking daily. Drinking water was another area emphasized as well as taking one moment at a time. Getting away if I could to just have some "me time" was another suggestion gleaned from the sessions. Her advice was valuable and I took her words to heart.

I once asked her if she released patients when she felt they were "cured." Her response was that there is no magic cure for grief. Patients leave when *they* are ready. One comment that I made during one of my sessions was that I wanted her to just reach inside me and pull the grief out. In a way, I think Connie did that. She worked with me for two years and let me release a lot of pent up pain. My thought on the pain of grief is that it is more like an enduring internal bleeding that no one can see, with symptoms that a pill can't cure. Talking over my invisible internal bleeding with someone I trusted was a helpful step for me.

We turned the calendar page to October, Brytni's birthday… and wedding. Being the baby of the family and the only girl had its advantages. Brytni loved learning how to play ball with Joel and sing with Zachary. She is a blend of both of the major talents her brothers possessed.

Brytni was the "go-fer" for Zack. She would do whatever he said to be part of his elaborate playing. If he was the mad scientist; she was Igor. Zack even went so far as to have Brytni hunch over while she stirred the mud potion. If he was the Wicked Witch of the West; she was Dorothy and her stuffed toy dog was Toto. And so it went. Not having her big brother to give her advice or guide her through life's play was almost too much for her.

After Zachary's funeral, Brytni moved north to Elkhart for the summer. I knew she wanted and needed to escape much like I longed to do. Brytni had shown Zack her wedding dress on Easter. I was so glad Brytni and I had found it before the accident. We'd had such fun shopping for it with Debby and Hillary. Her dress would not be clouded with the loss of Zack not having seen it.

Brytni was home for her birthday. We sang (I made it through some of the song), had gifts, and the usual birthday traditions. She was now twenty-four, just a year younger than her oldest brother…that was something new for her. Zack had always been two years older. I'm sure that weighed heavily on her. Her wedding day was only twenty days away. Brytni was totally focused on her future and I was so glad for her. That's the way it should be, I knew, but inside, I was hoping I could smile and be happy again, especially when her big day arrived.

Now our family had experienced our birthdays without Zachary, and Brytni's wedding was waiting in the wings; could we ever really celebrate? I was determined to make it through, but my mind remained focused on what was missing… our Zachary. Family celebrations had been and must somehow continue to be in the forefront of our lives. I'd try to dig deep and make it work. As strange as it sounds, I could feel others in the community praying for our family. Dan and I spoke about feeling those prayers… especially when occasions like birthdays and weddings seemed insurmountable.

See You in a Minute

Ave Maria ~ The Lord's Prayer

Jason and Brytni's wedding plans were in full swing. Even though Zachary wouldn't be at the wedding, his voice could be since we had his recordings of "Ave Maria" and "The Lord's Prayer." Music was still an issue for Brytni. After all, she and Zachary had already discussed some music, but he was going to take care of that part of the service. Brytni didn't want anyone but Zack.

Finding ourselves in uncharted territory, Brytni and I decided to talk to Zachary's AU roommate, Doug Beam. Doug had many of Zachary's attributes along with a similar work ethic. Without hesitation, Doug expressed his willingness to fill in for his good friend and roommate. Upon entering the house, he began going through Zack's file box of piano music. Zachary had put this box together to ease in the client music selection process. As Doug opened the carrying case, I envisioned Zachary opening it, too.

***

"It's taken me several years to finally compile the music into a condensed and organized fashion, but I think I've finally achieved my goal," Zachary told me one day at the house. He was preparing to leave for a wedding consultation with a prospective client. In front of him was a sturdy two-toned grey plastic filing box about a foot in height and seven inches in width. I asked if I could see it before he left. Although Zack was known for "pushing the bell" on time, I think his excitement to show it to me outweighed the time constraint.

As he opened the box, Zack explained how helpful this mobile file box would be for him. He had organ preludes and postludes, miscellaneous accompaniments, and other such items. Zack had even included organ registrations to assist him in remembering specific details about each church's organ.

The one item Zack was the most pleased with was his blank information sheet that detailed facts about the couple and their musical wedding wishes. "You have no idea how much of a time saver this little sheet will be for me and the prospective bride and groom. You see, Mom, no one seems to recall specifics when we get together to work on music. This will help me and everyone else stay on track…be on the same page, so to speak." Since it was just one page, we smiled at each other as he said the pun. Zack had an uncanny ability to interject humor and organize materials. Now the file would help keep some needed items at his fingertips.

***

Reaching into the file, Doug pulled out some sheet music, uncovered the keys and began to play. No one had played Zachary's piano since the accident. I had trouble looking at the keys let alone touching them. Brytni and I just sat there as still as statues. We couldn't even make eye contact for fear of losing control. When Doug was finished, he asked us what we thought.

Speechless and dazed, I said nothing. Quickly, Brytni replied that anything Doug felt was good was fine with her. She just wanted some music that her big brother would have suggested. Brytni also emphasized that she wanted no singing, only the songs "Ave Maria" and "The Lord's Prayer" that

Zachary had previously recorded. Finally coming to my senses, I told Doug that Brytni had also really wanted a violin or two.

Doug said that he'd do his best to make her wedding everything that her big brother would have put into the service. He also explained that Catholic ceremonies require some solo parts when the cantor participates. Doug explained that he'd have to work on those issues, but perhaps he could call on some of Zack's musical friends to give of their time and talents.

After Doug left, Brytni ran upstairs. I knew that her wedding would seem empty but that was just how our lives had become. Our family wasn't complete. That hole inside me was as wide as ever. How would I get through my daughter's special day? Somehow, I'd just have to draw on inner strength. I also knew that Zachary had incredible friends who possessed great musical talent. I must believe that the service would be filled with Zachary's spirit and love for his little sister.

That was exactly what would happen: Doug recruited Marci Wagnon to cantor and Melissa Walsh to play the violin. Doug would orchestrate the music for the ceremony as well as accompanying Marci as she cantored. He even provided his MP3 player for Zachary's prerecorded solos.

I'm not sure what we would have done without Zachary's friends. God took care of the one part of the service which our family was ill-prepared in accomplishing: music. I've often thought about how Zachary could have so much musical ability when his immediate family had none. Zack had made talented friends with good hearts who cared for him even after his departure from this world. Can anyone ask for more in life?

***

Preceding the wedding were bridal showers for Brytni. My sister helped to host two, one being at her home. It was a warm autumn afternoon and my mind continued to flip back and forth with emotions. These events should be full of fun for Brytni's future and I knew that I'd put on my happy face and go on with the show.

LeDonna, my sister-in-law who had been diagnosed with terminal cancer, was at the shower despite her own real life drama. Her forearm had been amputated in hopes of stopping the cancer. She could have been the poster person for strength and courage. I don't recall ever hearing her complain about the missing limb. LeDonna just figured out a new way to work without it.

While the crew was cleaning up after the shower, LeDonna asked if she and I could take a walk. My sister insisted that I take a break and go with her. As we walked up and down the dead-end street, LeDonna expressed her sorrow for my loss. She loved Zack and had such special memories of the little boy Zack singing, with his broken arm at her wedding. We talked about her future and the length of time the doctors at the clinic had given her: eighteen months since the date of diagnosis. The longest anyone with her cancer had lived was five years. She was determined to be another record setter and surpass the odds.

I remember telling her that I would trade her places if I could. Her children were still young. (At the time of our walk, Jessica was sixteen, Heather was thirteen, and Alexis was only three.) My children were grown and now both would be married. LeDonna knew my pain of missing Zack was strong. She wished that I could trade her places, too. She wanted so badly to watch her girls grow up. I recall her stating, "If I could just live a few more years. I'm so afraid that Lexi won't even remember me." It was an earnest walk full of topics most people don't have the misfortune to share. We were both experiencing deep pain that enabled us to cut through barriers that prohibited many people from embarking into conversations of such frankness and honesty. That walk kept us close during her fight.

***

October 24, 2006, AU planned the awarding of Zachary's first memorial scholarship for the university. It would be held in the music building with a luncheon to follow at the Olt Student Center. I had not been inside these buildings without Zachary. Dan and I took the day off from work. My parents and sister also attended.

It was a beautiful fall day with crisp leaves crunching underfoot. Brytni had selected an October wedding for just that reason. She loved the sights, sounds, smells, and feel of autumn. Joel and Brytni had bowed out of the awards service due to job conflicts, although I suspected it was that they did not want to hear their brother's name attached to something as final as a memorial scholarship.

When we entered the music building, I began to feel a grief attack coming on. My heart was racing and my stomach turned. Dr. Wright, the Dean of Music, came to escort us in, but the feeling was too much for me. Excusing myself, I bolted for the front entrance and rushed outside. I found myself almost in front of the student center when I momentarily looked across the street. Were my eyes playing tricks on me? Right in front of me, I watched as the truck lift was backing up with Zachary's headstone.

At that moment, I experienced what I'd call an "out-of-body" feeling. The world seemed to spin around me as if I were not moving. It was as if I were an inanimate object looking at a television show going on across the street from me. I felt as if *I* was not real. Dan came to the door and called for me to come inside the performance room. My body seemed to float above the scene. As my head whirled, I felt as if I was watching the activities around me rather than being involved in the action. I stood pointing at what was taking place in the cemetery. Dan called to me from the doorway again. He looked over at the cemetery, too, but told me that they needed us inside. We'd go after the service and look at the headstone. My feet felt as weights, stuck to the sidewalk, and my legs seemed rubbery and disconnected from my body. I wondered if I was going to faint. Taking deep breaths, I forced my feet to move, continued down the walk to the music building.

Just as I was about to re-enter the building, I glanced down and saw a bright shiny penny reflecting the sun. Wiping my eyes, I bent down and picked up the penny. A penny, right in front of me, how could this be? That penny was a small miracle in a much-needed place. I made it through the ceremony with that penny clutched tightly in my hand. That penny made me feel as if Zack was with me.

AU had an exquisite luncheon following the musical performances. Zachary's first AU scholarship went to Theo Hicks. He would be one of the recipients for the next four years. He had tried out for the AU music program on April 21st. I recall Fritz Robertson and Laurel Goetzinger, both remarkable professors at AU, commenting to Dan and me about the irony of having to conduct those try-outs the day after the crash. Both of these teachers had left a profound mark on Zachary's voice and his life. We felt blessed and honored to be with them at the performance and luncheon.

When the events at AU were complete, Dan and I rushed over to the cemetery. There stood Zack's headstone, the polished Dakota Mahogany granite with asymmetrical shapes that we'd selected just a few weeks earlier. Dan and I had combined Zachary's single memorial with our double memorial sharing the same base stone. That extraordinary candle holder was placed between our stone and Zachary's. Our two stones projected distinctly different shapes but felt drawn together through the use of the same lettering style and inscription panels. It was beautiful, especially with the replica of the FUMC gold cross reflecting the sun.

I stood for a few minutes just trying to take the moment into my reality...my son's tombstone.

***

I used to think that the most dreadful thing in the world would be to see your name in print on a headstone. The closest comparison I can make is to the book, *A Christmas Carol*, by Charles Dickens. I had always envisioned my worst nightmare much like the scene showing Scrooge seeing his name on his tombstone. My view couldn't be more wrong. Seeing your child's name is beyond appalling, past dreadful...further than shocking. I could and did look at my name, but not... no, never the name of my child. None of this could possibly be happening.

Later, my sister visited the cemetery. Having been a secretary for the court system for years, Debby had to proof read it to make sure that everything was accurate. It took me one year to even look at Zachary's name on that stone. I trembled as I touched the letters for the first time. I still have trouble looking at the headstone. A name in stone – that is permanent – it made it real.

Life plunged forward. In mid-October, a second cousin from Joliet, Illinois was getting married. Jake was a few months older than Zachary. Attending this wedding would be arduous, but we loved Jake and knew we didn't want to miss his special day.

The drive from Anderson to Joliet was around four hours, so we decided to get ready for the wedding at the hotel. Somehow, Joel and Hillary had snuck into our hotel bathroom with a 4x6 framed message. Unaware that good news was in the air, Dan and I went about the business of getting dressed. Ready to leave, we hurried out the door when Joel stated that we needed to go back inside our room and take a good hard look around the bathroom. Dan and I objected at first, but the twinkle in their eyes said that there must be something special about the hotel bathroom décor. Back inside we went.

Noticing the framed note, Dan picked it up and said, "What's this?" It was a picture of a positive pregnancy test. Being confused and out of step with such things, Dan and I didn't know what was in the photo. Joel explained that this meant that they were going to have a baby in June! Dan and I were, of course, elated.

New life was coming into the family…our first grandchild! (If you do the math, this meant this baby was conceived sometime mid-September… maybe even September 17th, Zachary's birthday.)

Here we were, about to attend the wedding of a cousin, only a few months older than Zachary. What happened? Shouldn't Zachary be here to congratulate his cousin? Dan and I were going to Jake's wedding with our chests puffed out like proud peacocks, but my mind was conflicted, and continued drifting back to my first pregnancy.

***

It was 1980 and three cousins were pregnant that same year with their first child, with one of them being me. Even though Mary Kay and Dave are Dan's cousins, we are all so close that I felt they were my cousins, too. Whenever Dan and I went to visit in Joliet, we stayed with Dan's cousin, Dave and his wife, Barb. Mary Kay, one of Dan's other cousins, and her husband, Tom lived across the street from Dave and Barb so the entire crew got together every time we made it back to Dan's hometown of Joliet, Illinois. Mary Kay had Jacob first, and then Barb had Kristy a little less than a month after Zachary was born. All of our children grew up together. We have some funny pictures of the three big bellies in the year of 1980.

***

We have several photos but it's the memories that I can still envision, one day in particular – a clear memory of Dan, me, and the kids riding in our motor home to Joliet after Easter.

Zack and I were lying down on the top bed located over the cab of the motor home looking out the window. Zachary was no more than five years old. Brytni and Joel were down below talking to Dan about the surprises each one had received from the Easter Bunny.

Zack turned to me and stated emphatically, "About this big bunny, I don't think so."

I quickly turned to him and responded, "What are you talking about?"

"Give me a break, Mom… really, a big Easter Bunny? And the Tooth Fairy? I just don't think so." Zack paused and tapped his index finger to his lips. "I'm not sure about Santa. After all, he *is* a man." I had to turn away for a minute to keep from laughing, but I had to admit that I was shocked by his reasoning skills at such a young age.

"Tell me the truth, Mom, what about the big bunny? He's not real now, is he?" implored Zack.

Looking into his bright greenish-blue eyes, I could see that he really *did* need to know. If I didn't talk with him now, he'd never believe me again. I stated to Zack that if I told him the truth, he could never, ever let it slip to his younger brother and sister. It would ruin the fun and excitement of the holiday. He crossed his heart and promised, but told me that he just had to know. I told Zack that, yes, he was right about the "big bunny" as he had put it, and the Tooth Fairy as well.

The rest of the ride home, he told me how he had figured it out (perhaps putting socks and underwear in their baskets was not such a good move on my part), but he, too, enjoyed pretending and promised that he would continue to act like he believed to everyone except me. Over the next few years, Zack and I passed the occasional knowing glance back and forth whenever the subject of the Easter Bunny or the Tooth Fairy came up.

Later, Brytni told me how Zack would spin elaborate tales of seeing the Easter Bunnies because each child had their own special Easter Bunny. He'd seen Brytni's and it was pink. Even when Zachary found out about Santa, he didn't divulge the information. Zachary loved pretending, but he liked to be in control of the adventure. He had incredible insight for someone so young. I miss our talks.

***

Jake's mom, Mary Kay, and I had many talks about our boys over the years. Being a good friend and relative, she was very sensitive to my feelings that day. Going to the wedding and seeing our encouraging extended family had been the right thing to do. Life just kept pushing me along-one step at a time. After all, I was about to become a grandparent. It seemed that birth and death were walking side by side.

Sometime during those early fall months; Dan's older brother, Mike and his wife, Diane, paid us a visit. They had the idea to have Zachary's design for the cross at FUMC in Bloomington printed on shirts. Under the design would be the words, "The Gift," the same words inscribed on the plaque at FUMC. What a wonderful way to remember Jesus' sacrifice for us as well as remember our Zachary.

Mike had already paid a visit to a local embroider who had given him a catalogue containing numerous other items that could be embroidered with the design, such as towels and jackets. How remarkable that Mike had helped create something tangible to project faith and family! We took the catalogue to our next family get-together to allow them to select sizes, items, and colors. Mike, in turn, took the orders to the shop. We'd have the shirts prior to Brytni's wedding. How the tragedy continued to take a positive turn purely amazed us.

The wedding approached at a fast pace. Jason and Brytni had decided months ago to get married in Noblesville. The church was located at the half way point for Jason's parents and Dan and me. In reality, I think that it was a comfort to Brytni knowing that this church held no past memories. This day was going to be "a fresh start for her future" and back in time wasn't where she was going. Brytni was forging ahead.

Life continued to go around in a circle as the priest at Our Lady of Grace had been in Anderson at St. Mary's. Zachary, Joel, and Brytni had gone to St. Mary's School for their early school years. Father Tom remembered Brytni and the rest of us Novaks, too. It was a great comfort knowing that our priest knew us and understood our loss.

The big day came; October 28th. The girls in the wedding and I met at the salon to get our hair styled. My beautician Nicole and her co-workers Chrissy and Adrienne at the Shaggy Chic Salon were so great. Natalie, Hillary's big sis, did everyone's make-up as well as serving as Brytni's bridal assistant. The room was full of laughter and excitement. Brytni was definitely the vision of a radiant bride.

Friends and family filled the church. I suppose everyone was speculating if I would stay for the complete service since I had trouble remaining anywhere for the entire time. Flowers were placed by the grand piano in the sanctuary in honor of Zachary and Jason's grandmother who had also passed that same year. Glancing sporadically at those flowers during the ceremony helped me in some ways and made it painful in other ways.

The service began with some piano music and then Zachary's recorded solo of "The Lord's Prayer." During that song, I vanished out the front door of the church, had a brief "moment," uttered a brief prayer for strength, and returned. Collecting myself, I walked down the aisle to Zachary's rendition of "Ave Maria." Doug had the equipment set up so well, it seemed as if Zachary was really there.

The bride's maids entered the sanctuary to "Pachelbel: Cannon in D." Stating that Zachary wouldn't want his sister to walk down the aisle to any ordinary piece; Doug had opted to play "Prince of Denmark's March." Holding onto the arm of her proud father, Brytni made her grand entrance as the soft sounds of piano and violin soared through the air.

The ceremony went off without a hitch except perhaps for some of the comic relief from Brytni and the priest. Brytni was nearly jumping up and down during the service. When the scripture was being read, she and Jason were seated behind the altar. Brytni was bouncing in her seat like a jack-in-the-box. Throughout the reading, there was an undercurrent of giggling. When Father Tom began to speak, he turned around to Brytni, who continued to bounce up and down and asked her to calm down stating that he'd never seen a more anxious bride. The guests roared with laughter. Brytni was determined to bring joy back to all of us. It had been six months since the crash and she, so it appeared, had had enough of sadness.

On the way to the reception in Anderson, the limousine carrying the entire bridal party broke down. At first, Brytni was understandably upset, but then something remarkable happened. George Abiad, the photographer, saw a picture perfect opportunity. Tapping on the window of the limo, George said, "I know that this looks bad but look! Look at this light! Get out! Look where we are! This is a perfect chance to take some wonderful pictures!"

The limo had a flat tire right in front of a field of horses. The photo of Brytni standing in the field, bouquet in hand over her head, wearing her two-toned champagne and ivory wedding gown that billowed in the breeze… and horses running in the background… was a vision. It was almost as if Zack was saying, look around at what you are missing. The world really is a beautiful picture despite what could be construed as a catastrophe.

***

George is a remarkable artist. We first met him when he photographed Joel and Hillary's wedding. The photograph we had placed on Zack's casket had been taken by George. Dan and I didn't know that until George told us at the visitation. He had photographed each of Zachary's head shots for Anderson University during his college performance days. As he shook ours hands that day, I saw true love and compassion for our Zachary. "I took each of his photos including the one over there," he told us motioning his head toward the casket. "I didn't know him well, but your son was a nice, polite young man."

George looks at things with his heart and that love projects through his photographs. He has the ability to look beyond what everyone else sees around them and turn what others see as a negative into a positive.

***

The crowd was waiting for the featured guests when we received the news of the limousine's flat tire. A posse of people gathered to round up the bride, groom, and the rest of the party to bring them to the reception. Forming a caravan of vehicles the rescue mission ensued. The pictures resulting from the breakdown were accidental, humorous, and beautiful which told the true picture of the mood of the day. Of course there was more beauty around than anything else.

As the new bride and groom were being announced at the reception hall, the halter strap holding her dress up broke! The rest of the wedding party had already been introduced and then, *pop* went the strap. The guests had turned to see Jason and her, the light shining directly on the pair. Instead of having a meltdown, Brytni held up her strap and laughingly called for some help. In an attempt to be helpful, Jason tried to fix the strap, but to no avail. Aunt Debby was standing nearby and safety-pinned the strap to Brytni's expensive wedding dress. Not taking any chances, Debby followed behind her, holding the strap, just in case. Brytni and Debby smiled and laughed the entire time.

Brytni left the dance floor only to eat her dinner and cut the wedding cake. (Zachary and Brytni had danced together the entire night of Joel and Hillary's wedding. They were often dance partners at such events.) Brytni had her brother, Joel do the Macarena as a joke because he had often expressed his dislike of that dance. In the spirit of being a good sport, Joel did it anyway as it was, after all his little sister's wedding day. We even were able to have a family dance before the night ended when I was sure that I would never dance again.

Now, I'm not saying that I didn't have my moments. Many of my friends were there: Beth, Glo, Betty, Terri, Alberta, and more. They would go outside with me and listen to my cries of longing to see Zack. After each time (and there were more than just a few), I'd return to the reception and carry on as if nothing had happened. This was another pattern I'd begun to develop. I often felt schizophrenic; one way in private another way in public.

Brytni's determination to be happy, as our family had always been, shown in her face throughout the evening. I'd have to say that she succeeded because the day really was uplifting. It proved that we were still a family. Zachary's spirit was present even if his body wasn't.

Halloween was two days after Brytni's wedding. When thinking of holidays that might impact the mind, I don't usually think of Halloween. It's just a fun night of dressing up and gathering candy for kids, right? At the last minute I ran out to get candy. Our neighborhood is not full of trick-or-treaters but we've been known to have more than a few ring our front doorbell. After the first couple of children came, I couldn't answer the door any more. It was too much of a reminder of days gone by.

***

Growing up, my parents didn't buy Debby and me our costumes. Store bought ones, my mom felt, just weren't original enough so we made them. One year, I went as a television that my dad had made out of a large cardboard box, complete with rabbit ear shaped foil antenna and channel changing knobs. I wanted to continue the tradition and enjoyed being creative which is why I made most of Zack, Joel, and Brytni's costumes over the years. In the early years, I had the kids dress alike…three white rabbits, three bears, and three blind mice (complete with sunglasses that they wouldn't wear because it was dark outside). I am not a seamstress by any stretch of the imagination so a glue gun, pinking shears, and stapler were the tools of my trade.

As they grew, Zachary loved being the scoundrel. He was the Big, Bad Wolf to Brytni's Little Red Riding Hood, a ghost with chains, Dracula, and The Joker; although one year Zachary opted to play the superhero and dressed as Batman, mainly because he loved wearing a cape. Zachary was big into acting out whatever character he was portraying.

We also had All Saints Day at church. I loved that celebration because the kids learned so much about the saints in the Bible. Taking a white bed sheet, I'd drape it over each of their heads and use a few yards of gold rope I'd purchased at a craft store for the belt. After deciding on the saint they would portray, I'd cut a sash out of the sheet scraps, write the name in glue and sprinkle on gold glitter. Each head would be topped with a coordinating gold crown or an aluminum foil facsimile. They appeared to feel quite regal, even though the costumes looked a little rough around the edges.

One year, my friend Alberta and I decided to take our families to a state park over Fall Break. Break fell during Halloween that year, which meant our children would miss being able to go trick-or-treating. Most of our children were really too old to participate in the holiday, but Noelle and especially her youngest, Matt, would really miss that evening of fun. Matt really loved costumes. We didn't want them to miss out on the fun of dressing up.

Really wanting to get in a little vacation, Alberta and I came up with a plan to solve the predicament: our kids could trick-or-treat each other. The kids could change costumes and go back and forth between cabins which were located right next door. At first, our kids were a little skeptical of the solution to the holiday dilemma, but the idea of being many different characters in the same night outweighed the problem.

Zachary, who was always highly organized, held a meeting with Joel and Brytni to brainstorm costume ideas. He began listing all the characters that he, Joel, and Brytni could become for this adventure. Some of the basic elements of the costumes could be easily interchanged to make a completely different look. I enjoyed listening in on their inventive ideas for creating a wide array of characters.

The excitement for the get-away began to build. Zachary began finger weaving three multicolored ropes which could be used in a variety of ways. When the costumes off the list had been exhausted, the kids began to improvise with things they discovered in the cabins. The "going back and forth" went on long past the preplanned list of costumes. It was hysterical! The adults enjoyed the inventive costumes as much as the kids.

***

Turning the focus to November, I looked over the calendar to see what other activities besides Thanksgiving were coming. On November 5th, the FUMC in Bloomington had invited us back for an All Saints Sunday Worship Service at 9:30 a.m. At the service, Zachary's name would be mentioned and the family would light a candle in "remembrance of those who have joined the cloud of witnesses."

Later that evening, Anderson University Chorale would be singing "Brandenburg Concerto No.1" by J.S. Bach and "Ein Deutsches Requiem" by Johannes Brahms in the sanctuary of Park Place Church of God. The concert would be performed in loving memory of the five students on the plane, but especially for Garth and Zack since they were AU graduates.

Dan and I felt the need to attend both services. We arrived at FUMC a few minutes before the service. Greeted warmly by several of the members, we proceeded into the church. Not knowing how much of the service I could complete, I sat at the end of the pew. My sister and friend, Glo, came to be there for support. My heart pounded as Zachary's name was read. Fearing having a grief attack in the church, I lit the candle and darted out.

Dan and Debby knew that I wanted to be alone during these times so they did not attempt to follow me. Outside the church, I had a full blown grief attack. All of a sudden, I felt a warm hand patting me on the back. "Are you all right?" It was Gwyn Richards, the Dean of Music at IU, who attended FUMC. Extending his white handkerchief to me, I wiped my eyes and nose, thanked him while replying that I'd be all right – I'd just needed to breathe. Eric Behrman came out to see if he could help, too. He offered his hug and I clung to him crying intensely. After a few minutes, Eric and I stood for a moment, looking at each other when he said with tears in his eyes, "Oh, I can feel your grief. It's so fresh."

Both gentlemen asked what they could do to help. My reply was the one solution I had come to know: "I just need to walk." And so we did. We walked several blocks east on Kirkwood then turned around and walked back west on the same street toward the church. I'm not sure how many blocks we walked. All I knew was I could feel the breeze and walking served as an outlet for my pain. For the duration of the walk, Eric and I spoke of the pain of losing a child.

I asked for help as to what to do to survive. He and his wife, Marilyn, seemed so strong and they had been through much more than Dan and me. I felt unworthy to even talk about my pain – mine was a shadow of what they had endured. We spoke of the terror of missing your child. I couldn't fathom not knowing where Zachary was for three years. How had they done it? Eric's answer was simple, "We didn't have a choice."

Both of our families had sought ways to honor our children's lives. Dan and I had worked to establish scholarships for future musicians, both at the high school and collegiate levels. The Behrman's co-founded "Jill's House" which is a place established in response to a need for affordable, temporary housing for out-of-town patients receiving cancer treatment at the Indiana University Health Proton Therapy Center. Eric spoke of his excitement about Jill's House and how it would serve as a way to benefit others. Just as they had shared birthdates, Zack and Jill would have a common legacy of continuing to help others.

I explained to Eric about my alarming reaction to Halloween. Now my biggest worry became the ability to handle the approaching holidays which were all the more memorable. Eric's first suggestion was to "change it up." He told me that if Zachary had a regular seat at Thanksgiving or Christmas, mix it up. Have people sit in different places than usual so it wouldn't be like, "there's that empty space where Zack used to be." Eric mentioned perhaps going away for the holiday or making a new tradition. He told me not to try to make things the way they used to be because things just weren't that way anymore.

We spoke like old friends who had not seen one another in a long time, but friends with the common bond of grief. Gwyn was so supportive and listened while we shared. God's hand was on us and I was thankful for the breath of fresh air and restored hope. If the Behrman's could endure their tragedy, maybe there would be a light shining in our tunnel, too.

Returning to the church, we were greeted by my family members who had been frantically looking for me. The service had ended and after looking inside and outside of FUMC, I was nowhere to be found. I apologized for such thoughtless behavior. Next time, I promised to tell someone where I was going to be. Adding more stress to my family was not part of my agenda.

Before leaving the church, one particular member of the Wesley Choir, Beth Wininger, introduced herself. I immediately recognized the name. She had written to us after the accident with a heartfelt note. More than that, Zachary had told me of Beth and her family.

***

The phone rang late at the house one evening. It was Zack on the other end. "Hey, Mom, I'm at the house of my dreams. Right now, I am house-sitting for a member of FUMC while she and her family are away. Mom, you just wouldn't believe this house. It even has a wine cellar! One day, I hope to have a house like this."

I could hear giggling while we were talking. I asked who was with him, expressing my dismay about bringing someone else into the home when the proprietors weren't there. Zack told me that it was another member of the Wesley choir, Janet, and she was Beth's good friend. He was certain that Beth wouldn't mind their popping open a bottle of wine while they sat on the back patio enjoying the evening – she had left some bottles earmarked just for him. Zack went on and on about Beth's generosity toward all of her friends in the Wesley Choir.

The conversation was full of descriptive details about the baby grand piano and the many amenities the impressive house possessed. He told of singing with Beth and her husband, Tim, around the piano while he accompanied on their splendid baby grand.

Zachary had a way of smoothing everything over and stretching out his stories. Being a stickler for details, when he described things, it was effortless to envision whatever he was trying to convey. Zack was a great conversationalist with the ability to begin a chat with just about anybody. I liked it best when he let me in on the details of his life. It was great to be included. I was always glad when he called.

***

Beth invited Dan, me, and our kids to her home. As we pulled up the brick driveway, I could understand why Zachary was impressed. It was a stately home located in the woods. Beth gave us the tour which included the room where Zachary stayed while he house-sat and of course, the wine cellar.

Beth and Tim were so gracious. They even gave us two bottles of wine. I could feel the love and respect that Beth had for Zack. Telling her of the phone call and Zachary's mutual admiration, we stood outside and cried. (Beth was instrumental in establishing a scholarship at FUMC in Zachary's name. How can you repay someone who loved your child that much?)

Hurrying back for the concert in honor of Zachary and Garth beginning at 5:00 p.m. in Anderson, Dan and I were about out of steam. Dan always seemed to have more stamina than me. Whenever I was ready to back away, Dan would somehow add enough fuel to my fire that I could go pull myself along to the next event. Doug and Marci were at the concert. Doug had Zachary's copy of the Requiem so he could follow along with the performance.

After the concert, Doug was showing Dan and me Zachary's noted copy when Dr. Sowers walked up to us. He carefully looked over Zachary's copy. Dr. Sowers commented on the thorough manner which Zachary had earmarked certain details of the requiem. He turned to Dan and me, and stated that in some ways, Zack's copy was better than his. He then requested to keep Zack's copy. Since Dan and I were donating much of Zachary's music to AU, we, of course granted his request. Exhausted, yet, extremely proud of all the accolades bestowed on Zachary, Dan and I left AU and went home to rest.

Some nights, I just couldn't sleep at all. I'd creep out of bed and grab my cell phone. I'd call my friend, Beth who lived over an hour away in Greensburg or Glo who lived in Bloomington, also more than an hour away. I think that part of the ease of our talks were that they lived far away; yet, we were such close friends it let me feel free to say anything I needed to get out.

With the help of God, family, and many, many calls to Beth and Glo, I made it through many sleepless nights and crazy days. Bless their hearts; I'd call just sobbing, sometimes even when I was driving. Once I remember Beth requesting that it might be a good idea to pull over. Somehow, she would calm me down enough to focus on the road. As I have said before, I'm not a public crier so I'd cry where I couldn't be seen and sometimes that meant the car. Praying for me on their own and listening to me rattle on about my pain and the hole in my soul, my friends were there for me. I am thankful for listening ears and kind hearts.

The wedding was a success and I'd made it through the month of October as well as the beginning of November. The upcoming holidays were the ones that I feared the most.

See Amid the Winter Snow

Our biggest family celebrations were within striking distance. Shuddering to think of how I could keep from melting down, I prayed for the strength to forge ahead. My grief counseling sessions continued weekly. My counselor was always amazed at the diversity of the events: weddings, memorials, holiday parties, and …teaching school. She encouraged me to take some time off, perhaps half days, just for me to relax and process some of my emotions. There were a couple of times that I did take off from school, but life does go on whether we want it to or not.

Thanksgiving was a blur. My mom and dad hosted it as usual with my mom cooking homemade noodles, eight different homemade pies, and much more food than I care to list. We do eat extremely well at our family feasts. She makes the best noodles in the world, I believe and our full tummies revealed the truth. My appetite wasn't as usual. I found my weight fluctuating over the first year. I'd always looked forward to each family get together. Now, it seemed as if these events were more of a hurdle to jump as the year raced on.

***

One particular Thanksgiving, our family decided to take the feast to the lakes. My parents have a nice cottage at a lake in northern Indiana. It's not a big lake but it has family history.

My grandfather had built a block home on this lake. When my parents were in high school, they went there after prom. Mom even had a bass jump into their boat! My grandfather sold that cottage when my sister Debby was little. Later, when my parents were in their fifties, they purchased a fixer-upper home on that same lake. After a great deal of remodeling, the little yellow cottage became a family retreat. (All of our children caught their first fish from that lake.) Some years later, they built a brick home on a double lot where we go at least four times a year.

Hauling the turkey, sweet and mashed potatoes, green beans, relish tray, other assorted goodies plus all those pies was a sight to behold. Zack, Joel, and Brytni were in their early teens. The view of the snow on the lake as we ate was a scene from a Norman Rockwell painting. Gazing out of the large picture window, we watched a beaver swim back and forth smacking his tail on the water. You should have heard the sighs of pure joy as we all enjoyed the splendor that was experienced that Thanksgiving. Looking back on it, I'm not sure that my mom was thrilled about all of the extra labor involved in transporting the feast.

***

Thanksgiving was also a day spent mapping out our holiday shopping plans for Black Friday. We had established a tradition. After eating that huge feast, we'd prepare for the crowded adventure-in-shopping. Taking the thick stack of advertisements from the newspaper, we would plot our course of attack to get the best bargains for our Christmas shopping. (Funny, but we even wrote our names on the ads so there wasn't confusion as to whose ad was whose.) Each family member would make their Christmas wish list and we'd locate the store possessing the lowest price for the choice purchase.

Several years, I persuaded Dan to accompany me. As the children grew, the day belonged to Debby, Brytni and me. It was the thrill of the hunt for the great bargain that we loved. But now, how could I shop with all that Christmas music playing in each store?

***

Growing up in the '70s, the Carpenters were one of my favorite singing groups. When they released their Christmas album, I immediately added it to my Christmas song collection. Throughout the years, it has remained my favorite. Zack, Joel, and Brytni grew to appreciate their classic style, too...especially Zack. He'd sing along with the record as we'd decorate the house for the holiday.

When Zack went to college, I knew I could count on him to call me and sing, "I'll be home for Christmas, You can plan on me..." He'd sometimes sing the entire song. Zack was known for leaving singing telegrams, as I called them. I still can't listen to that song without breaking down.

***

After we finished our Thanksgiving meal, I approached the subject of our regular Christmas traditions with my family. Our family usually sits in the same places. Acting on the advice Eric had given me concerning holidays, I suggested that we change things up a bit this year.

The answer about Black Friday was not to shop too early. We'd go in the mid-morning hours and if it became too hard, we'd go home. I wanted to try to make it. Rationally speaking, I still needed to shop for Christmas.

Dan and I ventured out the next day, lists in hand. Sometimes I found myself covering my ears so that I wouldn't hear the music. Dan would tell me when I could uncover them.

We didn't stay out shopping nearly as long as we had in the past. It was just too emotionally draining. At least we had managed to mark some items off the list. Shopping, which I'd always loved, had become a dreaded chore.

It had become a custom at our house to start some decorating the weekend after Thanksgiving. This may sound strange, but Zachary was in charge of putting the tree together. When the kids were little, I discovered that I was allergic to live Christmas trees. After several years of sinus infections during the holidays, the doctor and I had put two and two together. Although we loved real trees, the next year Dan and I bought an artificial tree and voilà, no more sinus infections.

***

The Christmas of 2005 was no different than the rest as far as the decorating weekend was concerned. Zack stayed home that Saturday evening and put that old tree together. It was starting to show some wear and tear, to the point of falling apart. This caused Zachary to exclaim that we must invest in a new tree next year. He suggested a pre-lit one with clear lights as he felt they gave "an elegant feel to the room." We'd always had red lights and Zack also stated that he'd miss the traditional red glow, but he really disliked stringing the lights on those weakening branches.

Each year after the tree was up and the lights were on, the rest of the family joined in with the decorating. We had three favorite Christmas records playing during our trimming the tree festivities.

One Christmas when Zachary, Joel, and Brytni were teens, Brytni put on our traditional childhood Christmas albums. The boys protested, requesting more contemporary Christmas music. Brytni told them not to worry. Her plan was to take those three children's records with her when she had a home of her own. This news did not set well with her brothers who were not willing to abide by her plan.

It was at this point that each of them declared which was their favorite: Brytni claimed her favorite album first: *Christopher the Christmas Tree*. This was to be Brytni's because of her love for wildlife especially the owl named Hooty (and I think because it annoyed the boys.) Joel voiced his selection next: *The Chipmunk's Christmas*. Joel liked it because of its funny antics involving that crazy little chipmunk named Alvin, and that left *Christmas on Sesame Street* for Zachary. Although Zachary was impressed by the album's sweet message, he proclaimed that *The Carpenters' Christmas* mirrored his style more closely. I managed to put in my two cents announcing that all of this debate was worthless: the records would remain in this home with me, the one who had purchased them. Of course, my logic did not stop the continuing dispute. (We gave CDs of all three albums to each of them when they left for college. Dan and I found them among Zack's massive CD collection.)

Dan would fix the hot cocoa complete with whipped cream. Our ornaments were a mix of traditional, homemade, and school made. Each year, Santa would bring them a new ornament in their Christmas stocking. (I'm not Susie Homemaker by any means, but I've always been proud of the fact that I used crewel stitching to make each of their detailed stockings.) Zack, Joel, and Brytni had accumulated several ornaments of their own by the time they were ready for college. When they left home, I'd give them their ornaments to place on their own Christmas tree. Perhaps, they could hand them down to their own children someday.

Over the years, the kids had enjoyed hanging their own ornaments on the tree. One Christmas when Zack, Joel, and Brytni were in high school, they decided to place all of their ornaments in their own sections on the tree. Each declared his or her own space. Brytni claimed the front of the tree and to my surprise, the boys didn't protest. After the tree was completely finished and all the decorations were in place, Zack and Joel looked at each other and without saying a word, the boys lifted the tree, turned it around so that Brytni's ornaments were now facing the back of the room. Zack and Joel roared with laughter while giving each other high fives in celebration of their unified work. Brytni loudly voiced her protest to their action and I, of course, had them put the tree back to its original position. (I have to admit that I did laugh along with them at first. How had they done that without talking to each other first?)

The Sugar Bear ornament was another tale of siblings annoying each other. The Sugar Bear ornament came free in the Sugar Crisp box one year and it played the Sugar Crisp jingle over and over again when squeezed. Joel would push its tummy to the point of us pleading with him to leave the ornament alone.

Zachary made many a threat to put an end to the ornament when no one was looking. One tree decorating time, Joel pushed the jingle beyond Zack's limits. Zachary grabbed Sugar Bear off the tree and raced into the garage. When he returned a few moments later, Zachary held the ornament over his head and with a gleam of satisfaction in his eyes declared that he had put an end to Sugar Bear. He had squeezed the song out of him by putting Sugar Bear in his dad's vise. Zack threw him into the garbage stating that he was glad to be rid of him. Each of us knew Zack was frustrated, but using the vise? We were amazed by this unorthodox means of destruction.

After Christmas when we were out shopping, Joel spotted a bear ornament that resembled Sugar Bear. The ornament didn't play music but it would stand as a reminder that Sugar Bear was still around. We still hang the Sugar Bear facsimile on our tree each year. It's funny how something so small can leave such a lasting impression.

***

Decorating for the holiday had been such a joy and something I'd looked forward to each year. Zack was always such a big help. He had such a creative flare and I loved getting his point of view on where to place the Christmas decorations. Once Zack had done such a wonderful job of decorating the dining room chandelier, it had become his job permanently. I didn't trim the light fixture for many Christmas seasons; partially because I didn't think I could duplicate his style, but mainly because it was just too painful. After all, it was Zachary's job.

The house usually takes a few days to adorn with all the Christmas lights, both inside and out, the villages, the mantel, nativity, and so much more. Dan and I opted not to do much; however, we wanted to put up a tree for Joel and Brytni. It wouldn't be fair to them not to try. We'd do what we could to make Christmas feel like the holiday we'd always enjoyed at home.

Recalling the conversation Zack and I had the Christmas before, Dan and I purchased a new pre-lit tree with clear lights. Dan really wanted to keep our traditional all-red lights, too, so he strung those as well. Much to our surprise, the pre-lit tree had a button that when pushed, the clear lights went off and the red lights remained on. We were amazed that the Christmas tree could be lit red and clear, or with just a push of the button have that soft red glow which had become part of our family tradition. Dan and I felt that it was our own little Christmas miracle.

That Saturday, Brytni had promised to help me hang all those ornaments that held so many memories. Dan hauled the two large crates holding the ornaments down from our upstairs closet. Brytni whipped off the lid. There, staring right at us, was a beautiful red and gold wrapped box with a printed label that read, "Merry Christmas, Brytti. Love, Zack." (Zack's nickname for Brytni was Brytti.) I felt as if I'd been struck by lightning. The year before, the box broke that contained my grandma's red glass bulb. I'd forgotten that that box had been replaced by one of Zachary's pre-wrapped boxes. It was one of those boxes that had the lid wrapped separately from the box. (Zack was always running short on time so wrapping his purchases for the holiday was something he'd chosen to let the store undertake. Printing the labels for each person made his gift look neat and saved him time, too. His presents to us were impeccably wrapped when he did have the time.)

Pausing just briefly, Brytni said, "Well then, let's get on with it, Zachary." She said it as if Zack were there to help with the task. I was stunned by her response and impressed by her strength. I'd wanted to raise strong, independent children who could help lead others when confronted with a problem. Brytni led me that day. If she hadn't reacted with such vigor, I would have retreated to my usual corner of some room and probably collapsed into a grief attack. Instead, Brytni and I placed all those ornaments on the tree without much ado.

Trying my hardest not to internalize each ornament, I went about the job of putting them on the tree. If Brytni saw that the photographed ornaments or other memorable ones became a stumbling block for me, she would take it from me and hang it herself. She was totally fixed on the mission.

Dan and I had found a box at Zachary's apartment in Bloomington labeled "Christmas ornaments." We had placed his boxed ornaments with ours so that we could put a piece of him back with us. Brytni and I didn't open that box. Dan and I would put those on the tree later.

When the job was complete, Dan took the crates upstairs and back into the closet. Brytni left fairly quickly after we'd finished. I felt sure she needed some time alone. When she left, I began to put some of the gifts that I'd wrapped under the tree. Out of the corner of my eye, I glanced at the antique arched glass case that displayed cherished items... items like my Snowbabies.

***

Zachary had established a tradition with me. Each year since he'd been in college, Zachary would buy me a Snowbaby. Snowbabies are cream colored ceramic statues with cute subtitles to match their actions. In some scenes, there is more than one baby and some even have arctic animals. Snowbabies can only be purchased in select stores thus making them collectable. Zack began my collection and he was the only person to ever buy them for me. He'd go to an upscale store called Moneyhun's to find the new Snowbaby. Zack also liked the fact that they wrapped it for me, too. Most Christmases, I'd scoot the others around in the hutch to make room for the new one. I just knew that I'd never want anyone else to buy them for me.

***

Debby and I had begun a tradition of our own, decorating Zachary's tombstone. This action may sound morbid, but actually I've found it comforting. It feels kind of like, hey, I can still do something for Zachary. Debby and I selected poinsettias that were dark crimson rather than bright red to fill each of the two vases. We mixed in white poinsettias to add contrast. Dan and I would light the candle each week to be placed in the middle between our stone and Zack's.

As the snow began to fall, I worried about the grave. I know this sounds crazy, but I didn't want him to be cold. Zachary hated being cold and had always liked extra blankets or comforters. Yes, I was aware that he wasn't really there, but as I said, I still felt the need to take care of my child. Darlene, a friend of ours, volunteered to make a grave blanket for him. She had made one out of artificial greenery a few years prior for a past high school friend buried near the entrance of Maplewood Cemetery.

Dan and I had met with friends at the cemetery plot of the high school friend. Each person brought an ornament expressing something meaningful about their relationship or the personality of the deceased person. The ornament was wired to the blanket so that it became a permanent fixture. When winter was over, the blanket was rolled up and stored until the next Christmas season.

After talking it over, Dan and I decided that this was a tradition we wanted to begin for Zachary. It would be a way to keep his memory and love of Christmas alive with our family and friends, too. Our family has found this way of decorating Zack's place at the cemetery moving and peaceful. That first year, we made more than one trip to add a decoration to the grave blanket. It never ceases to amaze me what has given our family comfort.

On Christmas Eve of 2006, it had snowed. Dan and I made a trip to the cemetery only to find Ervin had shoveled for us. This gesture of kindness didn't cost any money, but I count it as one of the best presents we received that Christmas. Debby's husband, Ervin is a man of few words. He speaks with his actions. What a great way to be remembered…actions do speak louder than words.

Music had been a huge part of our Christmas Eve Celebration. Before my dad read from the Bible about the birth of Jesus, Mom would pass out small song books for us. Zack would accompany us at the organ while we sang Christmas carols. The opening of the presents came after we had reflected on the real meaning of the holiday. Zachary, Brytni, Mom, and

Debby would add harmony. As Zack got older, we'd sometimes sing a little softer so we could enjoy his voice. I wanted to skip the singing that first year without Zack. This was really hard for my mom. She especially loved the family sing-a-long, but we all agreed to omit the music…just until the whole family could handle singing together.

***

For Zachary, Christmas had always been a grand production. When he was around seven, Zack began creating plays for Joel, Brytni, and of course, himself. One year, he had Brytni bring one of her baby dolls to be the pretend Jesus while she was Mary and Joel would portray Joseph. Zack would narrate the action. Things didn't go quite the way Zachary had envisioned because Joel announced in the middle of the play that he was not going to be married to his little sister, even for pretend. Brytni, of course, was devastated and left the room crying. That was the first and last play about the true meaning of Christmas.

Most of Zack's productions from that point on involved the lighter side of Christmas…Santa. Joel would almost always be an elf because he could carry a wooden hammer. Brytni's character would change from year to year: an elf, Rudolph, Frosty, or Mrs. Claus (Zack didn't share Joel's concern, stating that he knew he could never marry his sister and that it was only acting after all.)

Zack was always the big man himself, Santa. He had fashioned a beard out of an old cloth diaper with a hole cut out for the mouth, and safety pinned it to a Santa hat. His first Santa hat was a red crochet toilet paper cover. Now *that* was creative and very comical, too. It was a struggle to keep a straight face. Later, I actually purchased him a Santa hat. Zachary used an old red robe he'd received for Christmas one year, stuffed it with a pillow to add the extra pounds to his thin frame, and held it together with the robe's coordinating belt. I can still hear his, "Ho, Ho, Ho-ing" while practicing around the house.

***

As we began to seat ourselves around mom's large dining room table, I suggested we sit in different places to try to make it less obvious that Zachary wasn't there. We always sat in the dining room while the plays were performed in the adjoining living room. Everyone was gracious and complied with my wishes. It would be difficult no matter what changes we made, but it did make it a little less, in-your-face, so to speak. I found myself sitting back during most of the merriment. I just couldn't "make merry."

Usually we would leave my parent's house and head straight to church. Midnight Mass played an enormous part of the holiday for our family. Dan and I began dating in high school. Our first date was Midnight Mass. I wasn't Catholic at the time, but there was a real peace that I felt on that date; one that continues to this day. Dan and I discussed whether or not to attend that year. I knew that if I went, my thoughts would be on the memories of past Midnight Mass services. Instead, we attended Mass on Christmas Day.

***

Zachary had been choir director for Dan and me for many Midnight Mass services. Wanting to announce the birth of Jesus in a glorious way, Zack would recruit fellow musicians to be a part of the service. Several years, he rounded up instrumentalists to play the trumpet, guitar, drums, flute, clarinet, oboe, and violins. Sometimes, Zachary was able to persuade a harpist or two adding that angelic touch to the celebratory service. Zachary put so much of himself into the Mass.

Being under his direction for seven years, I learned a great deal about singing. We'd spend a great deal of time warming up. It was always interesting to see what new ways of warming up Zack had learned in college. He'd impart that knowledge to us with the stipulation of never singing before preparing the voice prior to an actual performance.

There were times that Zack would forget we were novices rather than professionals. We just wanted to get on with the music. I have to admit that I could be a thorn in his side; always asking questions or making silly comments. I have a tendency to be a practical joker.

Zachary was a great teacher. He taught me to shut my eyes and really listen to the lyrics. Put myself into the song and sing the words from my soul. When the entire choir did as he asked, we sounded almost like certified performers. I was always amazed at what he could do with a group of untrained volunteers. Zack had a remarkable gift of bringing the best out of people, including me. I'm forever grateful that he was my teacher, too.

The Midnight Mass of 2005 was most unique. Zack had asked Dan to sing a duet with him, "See Amid the Winter Snow." Feeling honored that Zachary wanted to sing with him, Dan wanted to make sure that he hit all the right notes. Once while Zack was home, Dan sat a small tape recorder by our piano at home and had Zack talk him through it. Dan took that tape with him everywhere and sang the part over and over again to prepare. (Luckily, Dan saved that tape containing Zachary's instructions.) I was thankful to have witnessed this beautiful moment between father and son.

With his three-ring director's binder in hand, Zack organized that final Midnight Mass with precision and grace. We should have known years ago that his place was directing and conducting a production. Zack created the programs, played the organ and clavinova, conducted the choir, and sang a duet with his father. It was fun watching to see where Zack was going to be or what he was going to do. It was quite a treat. Zachary spoke often to the choir of how important it was to put your heart into God's service. As I watched him over the years, I was proud that Zachary had used his talents for the glory of the Lord.

***

After we left my parents' house, Christmas 2006, I cried all the way home. I missed the Christmases I'd loved. Saying that I missed Zachary was an understatement. There just aren't words written to express the longing in my soul. Nothing could be said. My faith must be in the future. God, I knew, must be listening. I longed to be back in time – to be in the past.

***

Christmas morning would find Zachary, Joel, and Brytni anxiously waiting to see what surprises Santa had brought them. They knew that we had a rule about coming into the den before Dad and Mom were ready for them. Dan and I wanted to capture their expressions on film as their faces often told the true story of how each one really felt.

As Zachary grew older, he would have to hurry because he had to play for Christmas morning services. I can still see him rushing out the door. Dan and I always kept the tradition of Santa alive. We still fill their stockings.

One Christmas when the kids were young, Dan and I had a cash flow problem. Dan had changed jobs and we were living primarily on my teaching salary which wasn't a lot. That summer, I shopped at rummage sales gathering items that could be construed as new or could be cleaned up to look good-as-new. Two of the items were large and could be for all three of the kids. I wanted the room to look full. One item was a hobby horse with springs. Another was a wooden tunnel with a slide at one end. Dan and I worked so hard to clean and polish the two so that our children would never know that those were used items. Some years later, when asked about their favorite Christmas mornings, Zack, Joel, and Brytni agreed that the rummage-sale Christmas was a standout. Maybe it was the size of the items but I'd like to think that they could feel the extra care and love put into them.

After Santa's gifts had been seen, Dan, Zachary, Joel, Brytni, and I would proceed to the living room for our own family gift exchange. Lots of coffee mugs and homemade gifts were given and received. I know that each Christmas wasn't a fairy tale. We had the occasional battle of wills over items meant to be shared. Most of my memories are about the love and laughter we gained from the day.

Each Christmas morning, my mom and dad would come to see what Santa or Dan and I had bought for them as well as a yummy breakfast. No one cooks eggs like Dan. I'd assist with the toast, bacon or sausage, and the table setting. The highlight of the breakfast was Potica.

Dan's specialty is bread called Potica, a family recipe passed on to him by his Grandma Legan. It is a lengthy process that takes most of the day. My job has been to clean up and help Dan stretch the dough. Dan spends hours making Potica for my family and his.

***

Zachary and Brytni were planning to learn the time honored process. Both of them shared in the love of cooking with their Dad. They made a pact that the next year, 2006, to join their father for a Potica lesson. Although that didn't happen with

Zachary, Brytni did come to the house for those special instructions.

Dan's side of the family gathers on Christmas Day usually at his parents' home. He comes from a large loving family of seven siblings. This Christmas, Dan's sister, Jodi had offered to take over the responsibility. Being relieved that Christmas wouldn't be held at the same location, we went to Jodi and Pat's for the day. Several family members wore the shirt with the cross design. To me, it was a silent way to honor Zack.

Dan had sent some of the rose petals from the funeral away to have beads made for medallions and rosaries. I remember boxing the rose petals for Dan, but he took care of the rest. There wasn't a dry eye when Dan passed out the boxes and explained what he'd done. Most of the family have the medallions hanging from our cars' rearview mirrors. I've found myself touching it as it swings back and forth. Each time, I say a prayer for Zack.

I knew that we couldn't skip Christmas all together, but how could Christmas ever be good again? Dan and I continued to pray and hope for peace in our lives. We felt blessed to have family supporting us and praying for us, too.

***

For many years, the day after Christmas was a day our family had named "Game Day." Dan and I began the tradition after not wanting the games to stop one Christmas. On Dan's side of the family, after the presents were opened and the meal was over, we played games.

Sounds of laughter and sometimes lighthearted yelling would echo off the walls. Playing the game *Pit* was the loudest. Sometimes participants would get so tickled that they couldn't play. They would just sit and laugh.

Game Day was always at our house. Friends and family would bring the Christmas leftovers into the house and the feasting and playing would continue into the night. The kids would take their crowd upstairs to the game room while the remaining adults would party in the dining and living rooms. Occasionally the crowd would extend into the den area, too. The house smelled of Christmas and felt overflowing with love.

***

After thinking it over and discussing it with Brytni and Joel, I called Jodi to explain that I wouldn't have Game Day that year. Our family was going to take a trip instead. Getting away seemed like the right plan of action. We'd leave the day after Christmas.

Dan and I would take our now-married kids to Gatlinburg for a three day vacation. Getting away from the holiday would be a new change for us. We rented a chalet in the Smokey Mountains large enough to accommodate the six of us. I was hoping to see a bear while we were there. Dan and I had made the trip to Gatlinburg over my school's Fall Break for the past few years and had a few close encounters with the furry friends. The last time we had visited was just a month before the crash. I tried to push that out of my head. Dan and I were here to share the splendor of the mountains with our family as well as relax for a few days.

On the way down to Tennessee, we'd make a brief stop in Nashville. Joel had attended college at Belmont University and had shared an apartment during his junior and senior year with three great friends. One of them, Jason, lived in Nashville. His family, including his Nana, had taken Joel under their wing. Joel had spent many Easters with them. Due to his baseball games, Joel didn't make it home for several assorted holidays.

Dan and I had gotten to be good friends with Jason's parents and extended family, too. When we heard the news that Nana had passed away, Dan and I knew we wanted to stop to express our sorrow at her passing. Joel was glad to see Jason and his family. He'd been like a brother in many ways while Joel was in Tennessee.

When we arrived at our destination, it was later in the evening. The kids were amazed at Dan's ability to maneuver through the mountains at night. It was a long trip, over the usual seven hours due to our stop in Nashville. We selected bedrooms and turned in for the night. For the first time in weeks, I began to feel myself relax and rest. Getting away felt like an answer to prayer.

Our family loves to play games so in the evenings and sometimes during the day, that's what we did. *Guitar Hero* was the game of the day. As I recall, there were many late night challenges between Jason and Joel. I even think they had Hillary and Brytni compete with the boys. Dan joined in, too. Most of the time, I just watched. We also played other games like *Canasta* and *Would You Rather*. We actually laughed and relaxed together.

Dan and I treated them to an extended trip to the Biltmore Mansion in Asheville, NC. It was being decorated for Christmas so we were able to enjoy watching the hanging of the greens. One of the restaurants was a refurbished old horse stable which added to the adventure. It was a delightful experience even though my heart still felt the ache of missing Zack.

Our getting away proved to be helpful in dealing with the holiday. It was almost like an escape from the reality of the accident. I found myself pretending that Zachary was away on tour and just couldn't make the trip. Sometimes I found myself using that pretense as a coping mechanism. I knew it wasn't real but it made life make sense for me. After all, how could Zack be gone from me?

It was lightly raining when Dan and I returned home. It had been our first family vacation without Zachary, the unmentionable void. When the rain had stopped, a full blown rainbow was in view. It wasn't just a piece of a rainbow, but a double rainbow with crystal clear brightly vivid colors. Our neighbor, Nancy was walking outside, telephone in hand. She smiled and dropped the phone to her side. She was calling us to tell about the rainbow. Looking up at the spectacular view, Dan, Nancy, and I stood gazing at the sight.

Nancy commented on the likelihood that we would see something of this magnitude on January 1st, the first new year after Zachary's passing. I knew that I'd not seen anything like this, especially during the winters of Indiana. My mind was frozen but my body stood outside in the unseasonable warmth, gazing at the dynamic sight. Dan, Nancy, and I basked in the glory that shown round about us. The rainbow appeared to arch across our houses. It just had to be a message from Heaven.

Our family had survived Christmas. Zack would always be home for Christmas in my heart and dreams – that I knew. It would take me a few weeks to take down the Christmas tree. I didn't want to touch the ornaments, let alone pack them away.

The new year of 2007 was waiting. Brytni and Jason were newlyweds eager to start their lives together. Joel and Hillary were going to have a baby... Dan and I would be grandparents. There was something exciting to have us look forward to. Together, we moved toward the future.

One for My Baby

Happy New Year, 2007... Reflecting to the beginning of 2006, I reminded myself that just a year before, I had no inkling of what that year was to bring. Never having been one to think "gloom and doom," I found myself in unfamiliar territory. This was my first encounter with thoughts like, "Oh no, what if someone else I love, well...you know" or "Please, Lord, don't let anyone get hurt or sick or....you know." The "you know" was something I couldn't bring myself to think or say for fear that *it* might actually happen again. My safe, predictable old world had been replaced by this new paranoid existence.

Choosing to try to think positively once more, I plunged forward into the uncharted waters of the New Year. After seeing the movie, *Jaws*, when I was a teen, sharks had been something I feared. Now those predators of the deep seemed small next to my future fears. Remembering the frightful music, I thought of how that caused the audience to tremble even though the shark was unseen. I thought of how the music impacted the viewer's emotions. I turned back to Zachary's voice for help. Maybe listening once again to his music would become my comfort for the future. I thought about Zachary's voice and how it had been powerful, even when he was young.

***

Our first house was located on a dead end street. Zachary had a friend named Adam who lived at the end of our road. Zachary was around eleven years old when he came running in the house to ask my permission to go somewhere and sing. Asking him to slow down and explain what was going on, Zack told me that Adam's mom said that Gaither Studio needed another young voice to be in the background of a recording. I called Adam's house to discuss the matter.

His mom, who worked at Gaither's, told me that the studio needed one more voice to complete the recording of the musical titled, "No Phibbin' Mephibosheth, It's Christmas." They would be leaving that evening to go to the studio. She would drive the boys there and back so I needn't worry about transportation. Zack's eyes danced with excitement. Zack had some experience singing at church as well as a couple of weddings. I was aware of Zachary's talent, but more importantly, I knew he loved to sing. Of course he could go with them to the studio.

After Zachary came home, he told me each detail of the evening. Come to find out, the studio had scheduled a special singer to come to sing the lead in the musical, a character named Bo. After the producer heard Zack sing, he called and canceled the other singer. Even though Zack had a cold, his voice had captured enough attention to land the lead.

Zachary talked about the studio all that evening. He spoke of wearing the headsets and getting "cued" when it was his turn. Zachary was thrilled that they paid him to do what he would have done for free.

Zachary said that this part was easy to play because Bo was a crippled boy. "You know, Mom, all I had to do is sing as if I were singing to Amy. I sang the way I think Amy feels sometimes." His cousin, Amy, is Jodi's youngest daughter, who was born with spinal bifida and is confined to a wheelchair. Jodi's three daughters and our three kids grew up together.

Zachary adored Amy and admired her. Amy isn't one to complain about anything. She is someone I think of as being pure of heart.

That night as Dan, Zack, Joel, Brytni, and I gathered to pray as we did each night before bedtime, Zachary thanked God for the chance to sing about helping others. Those nightly prayers, when we asked each child to talk to God about what made today special, remain one of my best memories. Dan and I always told of our special gifts of the day, too. Prayer closed out our day and we learned about some of our children's most intimate thoughts. Sometimes it felt like a window into their hearts. I wondered if God felt that way, too.

When the cassette came out, Gaither's gave a copy to each performer. Of course, I went out and purchased a few to give to family and friends. When I spoke of the recording at school, something interesting happened. My friend and fellow teacher, Marsha, told me that her daughter also recorded with Zachary. Life just seemed like one connection after another.

***

I played the CD Zachary had made for my 50th birthday over and over again. After the accident, the CD was even more important, helping me through the days of emptiness and longing to see Zack. During the holiday months, I'd stopped listening to most music altogether. The music of the holidays echoed memories that had melted me to tears. Maybe I should try to listen once again.

I have to admit that more than occasionally I skipped some of the other song selections to get to my favorites. Zachary's rendition of "One for My Baby" was and remains my preference. I think that it's my choice because Zachary's voice on that song was pure Zack, not *performance* Zack. It's not that I don't like his performance voice because I do, but I enjoy hearing him relaxed; just being himself, as if he were just singing at the piano at home.

***

Prior to making the CD, Zack and I sat in the living room at his old piano bench and talked about what kind of music we liked. Zachary loved classical music, Sondheim, and other Broadway songs. While discussing various types of music, Zachary whipped out a pen and paper and began jotting down the selections I favored and the ones he enjoyed, too. We both agreed that Sinatra's songs were among the great classics of modern time. Several of those songs made that list. At that point, I was sure that the CD was just a pipe dream.

At the birthday party, my dream became reality. As Zachary's CD played, I heard one of my requests, "One for My Baby" … I was thrilled! And it was pure Zack, just as if he were sitting at the piano and singing. I wasn't the only family member to observe the difference in his voice. After a few minutes of listening, Debby and I decided to inquire about the noticeable change.

Zachary told of his struggles to make the song sound as if it were sung in the appropriate venue. He had no difficulties when performing most of the other song selections because they were relatable to his current performance sites, but this song presented him with a slightly frustrating challenge. He had even left the studio to go outside to regroup before attempting to tackle the song again.

Darrell Powell, who owned the studio where Zachary was recording, sensed Zachary's struggle and offered some suggestions. Recommending that they make a few alterations to the studio setting, Darrell advised, "Let's turn off the lights and have you sit on a bar stool. Then just relax and sing." His suggestions worked like a charm. It's odd how changing the setting ever so slightly translated into his making a true vocal connection to the meaning of the song.

One day, after listening to his CD, I called him over the phone to tell him how I thought his interpretation of the song was better than Frank Sinatra's. Being the ever modest Zack, his response was something sarcastic like, "Thanks, *Mom*. That's why Frank's songs were never very successful." Maybe I remain partial because he's my son, but I still believe that Zachary's version is more powerful and moving than ol' blue eyes himself.

***

Over those few months, I found that Dan handled his grief much differently than me. Not that we didn't find ourselves discussing moments of shared thoughts, but not all of our actions were in unison. In fact, some were direct opposites, which is probably why men and women are attracted to each other. Partners aren't always in step.

Even though it was winter, we still tried to walk the neighborhood unless it was icy. Dan shared his thinking about changing jobs. He was the supervisor for the fastest growing area in Indiana and the pressure was becoming unbearable with the long hours and added work load. Our plan for several years had been for me to retire when I turned fifty-five, which was three years from the year 2006. If Dan changed jobs, I wondered if perhaps that wouldn't happen.

The job he was looking at would be a drastic decrease in pay, but much less stress. Money was not as significant as it had been prior to the crash. We'd seen firsthand that money's not important when you are gone from this Earth. If I retired, could we make it on his salary and my pension? Dan assured me that we could still keep the original plan.

If Dan took the new job, it wouldn't begin until March, so we would still have time to talk and pray about this big decision. More life changes…wow, I could hardly stand more adjustments.

Dan and I would go to his sister, Jodi and her husband, Pat's house to escape to water and take a pontoon boat ride. If someone were to ask me to close my eyes and go to my place of peace, I'd tell them water. Whether it would be the ocean or a lake, it doesn't matter. Mountains and water reflect God's way of showing us how little we are in contrast to the world as well as making problems seem small, too. Dan and I had many conversations about wanting to move after leaving their house.

One day after being at Jodi and Pat's, I went into our living room just to look at Zachary's picture and reflect on the past few weeks. After looking around the room, I decided to rearrange the furniture. I thought about what Eric Behrman had told me about not keeping things the same. Perhaps rearranging the furniture in the room with the piano would be a helpful change. Because my sister has such good decorating sense, I called to have her come over to help. We also moved art work around to make the room feel different. After talking things over with Dan, we gave Jason and Brytni our living room furniture and made the room simple, with just two rocking chairs, a couple of book cases, and a few other pieces of antique furniture we'd acquired over the years. We'd move the piano away from its original location as the final touch.

The buffet now held the honored spot where the piano had always been. While dusting the legs of the buffet, I noticed something. From the crouched position, I saw the worn carpet made by Zachary's heel when he played. When the piano was there, the mark went unnoticed, but now the spot was in plain view. I touched that worn place as if it were made of fine silk, shut my eyes, and dissolved into the past. How could I ever have thought to move? This was home. This was where we'd watched the family grow.

As the room began to take its new look, the wall above the piano looked blank. Debby and I decided to take a few of Zachary's things to place into a shadow box. My nephew, David had recommended a designer named Boaz, who had done a remarkable job of framing one of Zack's pictures we'd given him. Our mission was not to turn our home into a shrine, but rather make a shadow box Zachary might have received from Dan and me as a grad school graduation present. I selected the items for the shadow box to take to the framer: a piece of Bach Chorale sheet music with Zack's hand-written notations, a conducting baton, a card telling of the meaning of his name, a black tuxedo bow tie, a pair of Zack's glasses and their black case, and a penny with a music note through the middle.

I was actually excited about how the shadow box would look. After wrapping each item in tissue paper, I'd placed them into a bag. I hadn't cried when I accomplished the task for which I was rather proud of myself. It wasn't until we were discussing with the framer our idea that there was any problem. Removing his glasses from the black leather case brought a shower of emotions.

***

Dan has always had perfect eyesight and I was just slightly nearsighted so I'd thought our children wouldn't need glasses. As it turned out, all three took after their mother in the area concerning vision. Zachary's eyes were the worst of the three. He began wearing glasses when he was in eighth grade. Up until then, he adjusted his eye problem by sitting near the front of the classroom or asking other students for help so any difficulty went undetected. To his credit, I never heard him complain about wearing glasses once he got them. He also took good care of them… except once when he was on vacation with David.

Zack was going to AU at the time. Right after Christmas, Zachary and David made their customary trip to visit my parents at their winter place in Florida. They had decided to go into the ocean for a swim and the water was rough. A huge wave came up from behind and knocked Zachary's glasses off. David and Zack looked all around in the water, but to no avail; after all, it was the ocean.

Hurrying to the shore, Zack phoned me in a panic to help. "Mom, I lost my glasses in the ocean and I can't see!"

I calmly responded, "Why did you wear your glasses into the ocean?"

"Because I wanted to see," Zack replied. I questioned what he wanted me to do about it from so far away and if he'd packed contacts or a backup pair of glasses. Of course, he hadn't, so I phoned our family optometrist to send Zack's prescription to a nearby pharmacy. It all worked out. On a lighter note, Debby and I actually looked for his glasses when we went for our annual Florida visit to my parents in January. Naturally, we didn't find them, but we did find someone else's mangled glasses on the beach which we gave to Zachary as a gag when we returned. He really didn't see the humor in our joke, but we couldn't resist teasing him a little.

Zachary was someone who cared more about seeing than how he appeared. As long as the glasses did their job, he was content. Zachary wore contacts only when necessary or when he was instructed by persons in charge of a performance, although I have to say, he wore them more his last few years of college because some of the female gender told him he looked good without glasses. He must have listened.

***

I had handed those cherished articles to a total stranger in hopes that just a piece of Zack would be captured in art. I explained a little about the dimensions, the items we'd brought, and a little about Zack. I left the double matting up to him except for the colors. Would the framer be able to portray what I'd envisioned? Trust has been a hard thing and something that for me had to be earned. I trusted a stranger which was outside of my comfort zone. I did trust my nephew David so I leaned on that faith in his recommendation.

We picked up the shadow box from the framer a few weeks later. Boaz had added a large letter Z which made the box almost a fourth larger than I'd requested. Despite that, the shadow box was better than I'd pictured in my head. It wasn't at all like a shrine, but truly like a present for Zachary after completing his Master's degree. Debby and I thanked him for his special touch and told him that he, indeed, was talented.

All the way to the van, I expressed my concern about the size of the shadow box. Worry never changes anything. It only gains unwarranted unhappiness. As it turned out, the shadow box looked as if Boaz had seen the room and understood the size needed to complete and complement the accompanying works of art on the wall. The family was amazed by the look of the wall over the piano. The shadow box reflected Zachary's style and taste. To complete the scene, Zachary's photograph in the silver frame (the one that had been on his casket) now rested on his old piano.

While Debby and I were busy rearranging the living room, Dan was working on the downstairs bathroom. He had learned how to lay ceramic tile from Roger, an old high school friend. Dan immersed himself in the remodeling projects. He'd work all day at his regular job and then come home to work on the house, sometimes until midnight.

Dan plumbed the new sink and stool, installed new lighting, plastered and repainted tirelessly. I worried that he worked much too hard and told him so. My concern didn't deter him from his mission. Looking back, I think that Dan took out a lot of his pent up frustration on those tasks.

During February, Valentine's Day seemed to simply come and go. Dan and I may have gone out to dinner or exchanged cards, but actual memories of any events for the occasion failed to make an impression.

Dan's aunt on his dad's side died shortly after the holiday. Going to the funeral in Illinois was hard. Funerals became an obstacle for me; not that I'd ever relished attending a viewing at a funeral parlor prior to Zachary's, but now, they were a real barrier.

One interesting phenomenon occurred outside Aunt Eleanor's funeral. She always loved cardinals and kept her birdfeeder full year round. After the service, the trees seemed to be bursting with those beautiful red birds. I returned to the car before Dan and watched cardinals descend and then rest in those trees. If you couldn't see some of them, you could hear their distinct song. I wondered about the sight and if those birds were a sign. It was amazing!

When we returned home, Dan busily put the final touches on the remodeling of the bathroom. It looked so much larger that we felt that it needed an extra piece of furniture. One Saturday, Debby and I began perusing antique stores for just the right look. We happened to stumble upon an antique music cabinet. It was the exact wood and size needed to complete the look. How odd that it had once been used to store music. Antiques represent old memories… looking around, my eyes landed on a western photo.

***

To celebrate Zachary's high school graduation, our family vacation took a trip out west. Dan and I asked Zack, Joel, and

Brytni what they wanted to do and they responded with a trip in our motor home. Lots of our best times were in that old motor home... hiking, camp fires, games, and making up ghost stories. We made such great family memories on each camping trip.

This outing was the first time we let the kids plan the activities of each day. After all, they were all in high school and had definite ideas of adventures. Zachary, Joel, and Brytni picked up brochures and plotted a wide array of activities from horseback riding to white water rafting while incorporating sightseeing excursions such as Mount Rushmore, Custer State Park, the Bad Lands, and the famous Wall Drug Store. (We were lured there by the signs along the highway until we found the place. We said a prayer at the chapel and sampled our first taste of buffalo meat at their restaurant.) We also scheduled a visit with the Fitts, family friends who lived in Nebraska.

One goal was to just relax and let the road take us away. At one of our stops, Dan took pictures of the kids and me feeding extremely friendly prairie dogs at a prairie dog farm, one of the trip's highlights. Another small side trip took us to an old-time photo shop where we decked ourselves out in western garb. That old-looking portrait remains fixed on our dining room wall.

Joel spent a great deal of time taking snapshots of sunrises and sunsets. Having the photographs developed before we got home helped tremendously. Zack, Joel, Brytni and I worked to compile the memories and photos into a scrapbook while Dan drove home. Because Zachary had the best penmanship, he was unanimously selected (more like drafted) to record the memories. The book was finished before we pulled into the driveway. We'd never done that before but the family didn't want to forget the great family adventure. It was our last family vacation with just the five of us.

***

After those tasks were completed, Dan began another mission. He had uneasiness about the crash site. Would the small cross he'd made when we'd first visited the location of the plane crash be enough of a marker? He wondered how quickly it would deteriorate. Dan planned to construct a large cross out of treated lumber.

As I listened, I thought about Zachary's stone at the cemetery. I remembered my anxiety before the stone was set. Dan and I joined in the need to have the tombstone in place and I remembered how that weighed heavy on both of us. I understood his concern but wasn't sure if I could handle looking at Zachary's name etched permanently anywhere since I still couldn't see it at the cemetery.

At this point in our grief process, Dan and I were just stepping out of each other's way. Whatever each of us needed, we just complied with the other and did it. Dan purchased the necessary materials in order to bring the cross into fruition.

Due to the cold that had set in, Dan couldn't work on the cross in the garage. He brought the cross section of the board inside to the den. I would sit on the couch and attempt to grade papers while Dan took a screwdriver, wood chisel, and hammer to pound in the carving of each victim's name. Sometimes I'd have to stop grading to keep the papers from getting wet from my tears. More often, I simply left the room. My mind questioned Dan's judgment, but he was like a bull charging at the matador who wasn't about to be moved from his target. He was a man on a mission.

After each name was engraved, Dan took Zachary's old wood burning tool from a craft set he'd gotten one Christmas and traced each student's name, with Zachary's name last. How could he write and carve Zack's name when I couldn't bear to look at it? I concluded that men grieve more physically than most women or at least that's how it seemed to me. Dan couldn't protect him any more than I could, but, by golly, he could make sure that Chris, Garth, Georgina, Robert, and Zachary would have a permanent marker at the point where they left this world. We would take and place the cross at the site as soon as the weather permitted.

When the cross was completed, I forced myself to look at it. After all, Dan had spent hours working on it. Looking at those five names, I thought about the other parents once more and about the losses. Four of those young lives had spent a month of the past summer together in Carmel, California. Suddenly, I remembered one funny story Zack had shared with me about that summer.

***

After visiting with Zachary in California the summer of 2005, I listened to him sneeze and blow his nose more than usual. After telling him that there must be something he was allergic to in that house, Zachary decided that he'd sleep on the couch where Chris and Robert were staying. One evening, after one of the concerts, several of the Bach singers came to the home where the boys were staying. Zachary sat down and began playing Sondheim songs at the baby grand piano. The choir members began what, in Zachary's words, was called, "The Sondheim Sing-Along."

Zachary called the night after the sing along to tell me about it. He told of the beautiful blending of their voices and the fun they were having until…the police knocked on the door. Now, I'm not sure, but I think there could have been some alcohol involved, but they were all over twenty-one and not in public. Zachary was shocked by the appearance of the law, to say the least. The officers told them that they were "disturbing the peace" so they needed to "cease and desist."

Zack told me that they should have been charging admission rather than getting threatened with a citation. He stated that that was a memory for the books and then he laughed. His laugh always resulted in me laughing, too. His laughter was contagious.

***

When the weather broke, Dan and I ventured back to the crash site to plant the cross. Debby and Ervin went with us as we trudged across the farmer's field and into the woods. The point of the plane's impact had created a small pond. Dan fastened the cross together with four stainless steel bolts so rust wouldn't be an issue. Debby and I had also selected a natural looking wreath with red berries to surround the date Dan had carved and burned into the cross.

We selected a place on the outskirts of the small body of water where Ervin and Dan dug the hole. They pounded the base of the cross as far into the ground as possible, then secured the foundation with cement. As we stood in the woods, there was an indescribable sense of peace. I'd hoped that the other parents would be glad that the place had been marked. Dan had put so much of himself into the cross.

A few weeks later in March, Dan made the shift to his new job. The work switch would ease Dan's stress and for that I was glad. Besides the salary cut, the job would necessitate several weeks of out-of-state training and offered no vacation time until a year had passed. Selfishly, I was heartbroken. A wave of panic would sweep over me whenever Dan would have to leave for a week-long training session in Oklahoma. Would he make it home safely? I have never enjoyed sleeping alone and now that sleep was hard to come by, those weeks were extremely long. I knew Dan needed to change jobs and I prayed for strength to overcome the anxiety when Dan was away.

Then there was Spring Break... Dan and I had begun taking a trip somewhere warm from the time the kids were in high school. What would happen this year? My parents, who reside in Florida each winter, had called and invited us to come stay with them, but Dan knew that he couldn't go anywhere. He told me to take them up on their offer, suggesting that I take Brytni. Even though she and Jason had only been married a few months, Jason thought that Brytni going with me might help ease her pain as well as mine.

Brytni and I had spent very little time discussing Zachary or the accident. She had not been to the cemetery since the funeral. It was just too hard for his little sis, I think.

On the way to Florida, I found pennies: one in the airport check-in, a couple more going through security, and even another penny when we landed in the Fort Lauderdale terminal. While on the plane, Brytni spotted a Cheerio on the floor of the plane and jokingly proclaimed, "Now that's probably what Zack left for me." We found another penny when walking down the tarmac which I told her must have been for her.

My parents were so happy to see us. Brytni was their only granddaughter so my dad had a tendency to dote on her. We had lots of mother and daughter good times despite the fact that our husbands weren't along. Sometimes, I almost felt guilty if I had fun. I have always loved the beach; the view of the ocean, collecting assorted shells, watching the people, and simply all the sights and sounds. How could I be enjoying myself when Zachary was gone?

On one of those sunny days, Brytni and I decided to take an extended walk on the beach. Brytni hadn't talked much about Zachary. It was good to finally have some alone time with her to listen to her express her feelings and talk about the accident. Up until that time, I hadn't realized how Brytni had felt the need to be so strong for me. She said that immediately after we'd heard the news that I'd literally lost my mind. Brytni told of how worried she was that our family had not only lost Zack but had lost me, too. Up until that beach walk, I hadn't known her true feelings. As we continued our walk, we laughed – and cried – about times we'd shared as a family and how Zachary was the go-to-guy for her and Joel whenever they had a problem.

As our walk drew to a close, my eyes skimmed the crest of the waves as they approached the shore. Catching a glimpse of an object reflecting the sun's rays, I asked Brytni if she saw anything. We both watching in amazement as a penny washed ashore and landed at our feet. Gasping as if I were out of oxygen, I retrieved the penny. Brytni and I looked at each other with shocked faces. Had we just witnessed a penny floating? Could that really happen? Brytni then said, "Oh, I wish Zack had given one to me." Taking two more steps, she found another one at her feet. Had we actually discovered two pennies floating in the ocean, landing on the shoreline at our feet? We both found ourselves asking, "How far away was Zachary? How far *is* heaven?"

Brytni and I shared the story with my parents as well as the rest of our family. We were quite sure that no one really grasped what we'd seen. I wasn't sure that I had comprehended what we had beheld. We didn't share that story with persons outside the family for fear that they would think we were crazy.

Sometimes I am hesitant about discussing such stories as the pennies because people might talk about me or think I'm odd. I then think of Zack. He had chosen to be simply himself regardless of what others thought of him. Zachary was determined to be true to himself even if it caused him to be bullied.

***

Bus rides to elementary school and junior high were often a challenge for Zachary. Joel was into sports and excelled in that area. Zack had athletic ability, but preferred art, writing, and music. I guess that made him the odd man out sometimes.

One day after school, Zachary told of a couple of students who were making his life miserable. These two would torment and taunt him endlessly. Zack related how he hadn't retaliated which made these two bullies all the more angry. He didn't want to ride the bus anymore.

As a mother, I was infuriated at the bullies and wanted to give them a taste of their own medicine… then I remembered what my mom had told me when I was little. "Remember the Golden Rule: Do unto others as you would have them do unto you. Be nice to those who hurt you." Thinking back on when I was little, my mom's advice had worked for me so I'd pass the same advice on to my son. Everyone has been bullied at one time or another in their lives. Bullies have always been around. I'd like to say that the bullying halted, but that wasn't the case. Zack bore the brunt of years of many hateful words over the course of elementary, junior high, and the first few years of high school. I continually encouraged him to be true to himself and his heart.

We talked many times about the bullying issue. I told him that if you remain steadfast in what you know to be right and true, it will all be okay. Telling Zack of how proud I was of him and his talents, we prayed together for God's guidance with these bullies and for their ignorance of their choice of words to others. Words hurt. I drove the kids to school for most of their schooling until they could drive, but, because of my schedule, they had to ride the bus home.

One day, his talent conquered a person's hurtful actions. Zachary raced home after high school proclaiming the good news. One of the longstanding bullies had asked for his help with working on a musical score. This young man also apologized for the countless times he had harassed Zack. "Can you believe it, Mom? He actually *needed* and wanted my help."

I was curious as to whether or not Zack would help the boy who had bullied him. I'm not sure if I would be so accommodating with someone who had been so mean to me. But when I asked him, Zack's response was quick and precise, "Of course I helped him, Mom. If I hadn't, I'd be no better than he had been to me." Sometimes, I felt proud of him in public, but this was a time when I knew I was proud of Zachary in private. Just he and I and our Lord knew Zachary had "turned the other cheek."

***

Brytni and I returned home after Spring Break feeling a new hope inside. We had returned just a day before Easter. Easter had taken on a new meaning for me. It wasn't only about Jesus and His rising from the dead; it had become the holiday that I'd last seen Zachary…his last visit home.

It was almost April 20th, the one year anniversary of the accident. IU had planned a ceremony to commemorate the five musicians. The twentieth of each month weighed heavy in my mind. I found it strange that as that day neared, my heart would race; sleep was even more elusive as I'd assess time by that date. My world revolved around the crash and memories of my first born, Zachary.

Each moment was *one for my baby*. The words to that song marked my path. There was no one in the place but Zachary and me. His life was a brief episode that defined my life which had become…that long, long road.

They Can't Take that Away From Me

The way of Zachary... his bright smile that showed all of his teeth, his contagious laugh, his dry sense of humor and his deliberate stride when he walked into the room, just to name a few things; the thoughts of him can never be taken away from me. Memories... they cling like an indelible embrace. They fasten themselves to your mind and never leave your heart. Memories have helped me through some tough events. No one can take those away from me.

***

The evening of my fiftieth birthday after Zachary had given me the CD, he told how he had prerecorded a lot of the piano parts. When the song, "They Can't Take that Away from Me," began to play, Zachary grabbed me and we began to dance. I am not comfortable dancing with anyone but Dan. Zack laughed and told me to relax and just "follow his lead." I believe he gave up on my clumsy attempt because the dancing stopped and we talked for a while.

"You know how you'd asked me to just play the piano for you," Zack proudly declared, "Well, here it is. I threw in a piano break in this song. What do you think?" Of course, I told him how glad I was that he'd done that. Now I could hear him pound those piano keys anytime and I loved to listen to him play. He'd put a little of himself into each note. I think that some people are just born to play and that was Zack!

***

April was here and I felt like I was drowning. Concerned about the grief tsunamis that had happened over the year, could I withstand the surges of emotions or would those feelings hit me like another giant wall of the water? Sometimes the grief attacks would sweep me away and leave me broken. More often than not, I'd find myself struggling to pull myself together after each wave hit.

Had the accident happened a year ago? Sometimes the days would go by as if they were on a breeze. Other times, it seemed like a single moment would go on without end. The passage of time was an everyday occurrence that I'd found a conundrum. Did others who had suffered loss experience the same time puzzle? I hoped to have the chance to ask the other parents.

IU, in conjunction with First United Methodist Church, had prepared, "A Service of Remembrance for the One Year Anniversary." All the parents and the families of the five students were invited to attend. The invitation was also extended to the school, church, and community. We wanted to talk to the other parents prior to the service. I had corresponded with Laura, Rainelle and Paula. Louise, the pilot's mother, was the only one that I hadn't been able to reach. I wanted to speak with her so badly, to reassure her we understood she and Yatish had suffered as we had, that the crash was a tragic accident. They lost their child, too.

There is a bond forged with others who have suffered the loss of a child and strength can be gleaned from getting together. My emotions were layered with dread of the reminder of the accident and desire to meet the other parents. I found it strange how such contrasting emotions were intertwined.

Driving to Bloomington, my head felt inflated with a year's worth of pain. How could I possibly be able to face the day? My eyes were heavy as sandbags. Tears had become common as breathing and my eyes told of the sorrow. I asked God for strength and endurance for the day that waited for me…for all of us. The memory of the first day we drove to IU slid into my thoughts.

***

Dan and I went with Zachary to scout out the big city of Bloomington. Location and money were deciding factors as to where Zack would live over the next two years. He had told us that he was looking forward to grad school and the chance to live away from Anderson, where he'd grown up.

A fellow church member from St. Ambrose in Anderson was leaving his apartment and Zachary could take over his lease when he left. The building complex had security and was on the bus route so if Zachary opted to avoid parking on campus, alternate transportation was available.

The apartment had two bedrooms with one big enough for that mammoth desk (a prerequisite for any place Zack would live). He could sublet the other bedroom and have the larger bedroom as an office/bedroom. After looking at a few more places, Zack arrived at the conclusion that this complex would work for him.

An elementary school friend, Jonathan, would rent the spare bedroom from Zachary which was great because Dan and I knew his parents, Bill and Diane. They could keep an eye on the boys as well. My philosophy was that you cannot have too many helping hands. Diane and I had several conversations about feeling relieved that we could both look in on Jonathan and Zack. Things fell into place.

Dan, Debby, David, his friend Doug, and I went a few weeks later to help Zachary move out of Anderson for the first time. We made a few trips to a nearby convenience store to pick up some items Debby and I thought were needed. For us, moving into dormitories and apartments had almost become a yearly ritual. We organized the kitchen area from on top of the cabinets to the silverware drawer, making sure that each item had a sanitary spot. When we were finished, the apartment shined and had that fresh, lemony aroma.

Zachary seemed thrilled about really being on his own. I, on the other hand, didn't relish his being two hours from home. Even though he was over twenty-one and would have others checking in on him, I worried that he'd push himself too hard. Zack was bad about taking time to eat or sleep. I made myself a mental note to make contact often to inquire or *nag* Zachary about both, whichever worked. I hugged him but did not cry until we had pulled out of sight.

Later, we discovered the thoughts Zack had written in his journal dated 8/22/04: "My second night in Bloomington... only mild homesickness. Too concerned about entrance exams and possible new job. The living situation is good. Jonathan is very kind. He brought me water while I was studying. Reminds me of Doug."

It broke my heart to think that Zachary had felt any homesickness at all. Why hadn't he told me? But then again, he wouldn't have wanted Dan or me to know something like that.

***

April 20th arrived on a Friday. Dan had arranged to be off that day before he took his new job. I left plans for a substitute. Because Hillary was pregnant, Joel drove her instead of riding with us. Several other family members made the trip, too. Brytni was not yet ready to have much to do with anything about the accident. I understood, but was thankful others made the trip. Once again, we had a small caravan of vehicles going south to IU. It's a scenic drive to Bloomington, with the beautiful rolling hills, but I spent my time mindlessly staring out of the van window and making light conversation.

Gwyn Richards, the Dean of Jacobs School of Music at IU had been in touch with us, as had Mary Beth at FUMC. I wondered about the day and prayed that I'd be able to sit through the services. More than one service had been planned. The first service was to begin at noon at the church with other services proceeding throughout the day.

Prior to entering the church, we waited outside to meet several people, including Chris's parents. Rainelle and I hugged for a long time. We had shared so many conversations over the year that it was almost like touching a piece of what was lost. It was also our first meeting with Chris's dad, Ralph. Even though we'd not talked, you could feel his sweet spirit and his great sense of loss. We found Laura and Bill, Garth's parents, who joined with us in our intense emotional moment as did Paula and Clayton, Robert's parents. Despite our mutual consolation, I still felt razor-sharp pain. I wondered if they could see me bleeding internally.

Among the crowd, I spotted Gwyn and his wife, Barbara. They introduced us to David Jacobs, for whom the Jacobs School of Music at IU is named. He'd flown in from California for the service. How kind of him to do that for these five students. During this past year, I'd seen others extend themselves for us. It gave me faith in people.

Charles Webb began the service with a beautiful organ prelude. I'd learned that Charles had assisted Gwyn the night of the crash. Even though he was no longer responsible to IU as dean, he'd gotten out of his nice warm bed in the middle of the night to be available as needed. And now, here he was once again being generous with his time and talent.

I situated myself on the familiar aisle seat, just in case the need to escape swallowed me up. The cross Zachary had envisioned and sketched on a napkin hung on the wall of the church. It was a reminder of his faith in God. I'd glance at it sporadically to draw strength. As the service began, Jimmy and Mary Beth from FUMC spoke. I could feel their courage intertwined with pain. Again, I remembered how Zachary loved this church… the people made the church. I was so glad they loved him, too.

Students who had known Chris, Garth, Georgina, Robert, and Zachary spoke to the audience in the crowded sanctuary. They spoke from the heart and told tales of humor and regret for what their friends could have been. Each of the stories of these five students carried a familiar theme. All of them had been genuinely kind and compassionate, often extending their time and talents unselfishly to others. I thought to myself that it was no wonder those five were friends.

Much music was involved in the ceremony, representative of the lives lived by the five. An emotionally moving candle lighting piece was included with each person in attendance having the opportunity to light small votive candles in front of each of the students' photos. The church gave each family a large, cream colored candle in a silver holder – ours now rests on Zack's piano by his picture.

As I watched the candles flicker, I thought of Zack's candle at the cemetery by Anderson University. When en route to the cemetery, Dan and I pass his old dorm.

***

Zack seemed to know without a doubt what undergraduate university he wanted to attend. Dan and I wanted him to explore other prospects. He had the grades and high admitting scores, but once he took a look at Anderson University, that was it. Zack said, "Mom, it feels like home."

Being the oldest and our first to leave home, I was relieved that it was AU. I hadn't expected to be so emotional when packing Zack's things for college. He and I stood upstairs in the game room collecting the office items he wanted to take along when Zachary held his large, heavy duty three-hole paper punch. This was not your ordinary paper-hole punch. This sucker could plow through thirty sheets of paper at a time. I borrowed it often from him while putting together booklets for students in my class.

As Zachary lifted the paper-hole punch, I implored him to leave it at home. After all, he was just down the road and he would be leaving it with his "ever-so-responsible mother." I crossed my heart and promised I'd take care of it for him. All of my pleading was to no avail. He smiled at me, wrapped it in newspaper and placed it in the box.

When Dan and I took Zachary to the corner room, top floor of Dunn Hall, I was fighting the urge to cry. Zack was embarking on a new adventure so I put on my happy face. I went on and on about all the excitement facing him. He saw right through me and slipped a note into my hand. "What's this?" I exclaimed, shocked at the interruption of my speech. Zack made me promise not to read it until I got home.

We kissed and hugged goodbye as if we would be miles and miles away. I couldn't believe my first born was going to college. With his note pressed tightly in my hand, I entered the house and read the note: "Go to my closet and look in the bottom drawer of my filing cabinet."

I ran upstairs to the boys' old bedroom, opened his closet door and reached into the bottom drawer of that two-drawer grey metal cabinet. There was a brand new, heavy-duty three-hole paper punch just like his. It had a bright red bow attached with a note that read, "Thanks for always being there for me, Mom. Remember, I'm just down the road. I love you, Zachary." Holding that note and looking up at the empty closet, I cried and cried. Who does that? How blessed I felt to have such a bond with my son. While most of the world would have thought that this was such a bizarre gift, he and I knew it was perfect. Zack listened with his heart, but more importantly, he acted on what he felt.

***

How did we get here? Now Zachary was too far away…outside of the *touch* zone. Were the others feeling the same or was it just in *my* head and heart? The service was beautiful and yet, looking at the crowd, their faces spoke of the related pain.

The church held a lovely luncheon after the service. It was held in the upstairs room where Zachary had helped with so many Sunday morning services. I felt myself looking for him to appear. The people at FUMC and Indiana University could not have extended themselves more for us.

The next part of the scheduled day was a service at the airport. IU had arranged transportation for all of us to go to the crash site. Dean Richards had purchased some flowers for each family to place there – Rainelle had requested Calla Lilies. I told her of Zachary's love for the flower, too. As she handed me one, we spoke of the flower being another similarity between Chris and Zack. They both loved those flowers. Zachary really liked all lilies, but Stargazer and Calla Lilies were his favorites.

***

It was Zachary's Senior Recital at AU. Debby and I were planning a reception to follow. It wasn't going to be elaborate, just cookies, punch and mints. We covered the tables and had a few assorted musical decorations, but the décor lacked that special something that only fresh flowers can give.

Being after five in the evening, the florists were closed, leaving Debby and I to go to the nearest local grocery store. I called Zack to ask him if he had a flower preference. Zachary and I had never really discussed flowers, but he had an eye for detail so I called to get his opinion.

"Oh, I really love the look of Calla Lilies. They just seem to look elegant and not too girlie," Zack responded. "Plus I could possibly use one of them as a prop in a song selection." What were the odds that a grocery store would have Calla Lilies in stock ready for purchase, but they did!

Those distinctive flowers were just the needed piece to complete the tables, while adding a touch of class to the atmosphere. Zachary was thrilled to have the flowers and was so grateful for our efforts. You would have thought we'd special ordered the bouquet. Everything went as planned with the flowers as the icing on the cake. His recital was an enchanted evening culminating his undergrad time at AU.

***

We placed the Calla Lilies at the foot of the cross Dan had made for the students. The pond formed by the plane's impact still had oil floating on the top. Oddly, there were still pieces of the plane scattered in the woods, and some of us numbly walked around gathering those parts. The men cleared away some brush and made sure the cross was secure. The water from the newly formed pond was getting close to its base. Then Paula noticed tadpoles in the water. There would be music in the woods…how ironic and yet, perfectly fitting.

We hugged and cried. Holding hands, we formed a circle and said a prayer for our children, those who had helped us and strength for our families. As we departed the scene, the cardinals and other sounds of nature seemed a little more amplified.

Leaving the crash site, we returned to the Monroe County Airport terminal. Cook Aviation had commissioned a limestone bench to be made in honor and memory of Chris,

Garth, Georgina, Robert, and Zachary. Each name had been etched into the seat of the bench. They had designated a landscaped area close to the entrance of the airport. The extended tribute and support for those five and their families went beyond our belief.

At 4:00 p.m., A Service of Remembrance and Blessing sponsored by IU Episcopal Campus Ministry began outside the airport terminal. The memorial bench was covered by a white linen cloth, reminding me of the pall at the funeral.

When the bench was unveiled, some family members took paper, placed it over their lost one's name, and made a rubbing to replicate the engraving. I could not do this as I was still having trouble looking at Zack's name in stone. In fact, I only touched his name briefly. My sister made a rubbing for me. Snacks were provided by the airport. People could not have been more compassionate.

The day wasn't over. IU and the Jacobs School of Music sponsored a dinner and musical performance. We went back to the hotel to freshen up for the evening events. I was looking forward to meeting some of the people who were to be at the dinner.

Dean Richards had asked if there was anyone in particular that we'd like to see… I wanted to see *anyone* who had connections with Zack. I specifically requested to see Lesli Hansen and Brian Horn. Lesli was the person who had driven the five to the airport. Brian Horn was Zachary's IU voice teacher. Each had written us an extensive letter after the accident. Both had played an important role in Zachary's life over his last years. It was great to trade stories about Zack. The time at the dinner seemed to evaporate.

After dinner, Dan and I met several students who were anxious to see us. My mind spun with emotional overload. I just couldn't digest what I was hearing. Maybe someday I'll meet those students again and be able to grasp their exploits with Zachary. My mind was too full to really hear what they were saying.

Behind a glass case in the hallway of the music building were large black and white posters of Chris, Garth, Georgina, Robert, and Zachary. Each poster had details about the student: degrees, awards, performance venues, and lastly, the birthday. My eyes fixed on Zachary's poster. I found it bizarre that I read each word but when I was finished, couldn't keep hold of anything I'd read.

The IU Jacobs School of Music had arranged a musical community performance of *Fairé: Requiem, op.48*. Rainelle had told me that this requiem was the last song they had heard Chris sing. It was on Palm Sunday just a few weeks before the accident. I didn't know how she and Ralph were going to handle hearing it or singing it.

As we entered the packed auditorium, we were asked if we wanted to sit in our respective vocal parts. They had signs designating seating locations for the parts: soprano, alto, tenor, or bass. Of course sitting in those areas was not required. We could sit anywhere. Not wanting to be separated, Dan and I were ushered to adjacent seats. I needed to hold onto him. The day had been so full of memories.

When the concert began, it was amazing. I felt like I was floating on sound waves. The sound resonated from everywhere: the walls, ceiling and even the floor. Love could actually be felt in the combined voices. When I shut my eyes, I felt Zachary was there with us and his friends in that auditorium. There were even times that I thought I heard his voice. It was a powerfully uplifting, almost incomprehensible and unforgettable experience.

***

Singing had always been a part of Zachary's life. I sang to him from birth; in fact, before he was born. Both Dan's and my parents lived about twenty minutes from our house. I would often sing to Zack and Joel to keep them awake when driving back from a visit, because if the boys dozed off, they'd be rejuvenated when we got home. I did not want to have them think that bedtime was over…not a good idea for a tired working mom.

Zachary was around two years old and Joel was not far behind at one. I usually sang the same songs to keep the boys awake. (Brytni wasn't born yet.) I'd sing, "Jesus Loves Me," "Jesus Loves the Little Children," "Twinkle, Twinkle, Little Star," and a few other familiar melodies.

"Jesus Loves Me" was the song I was singing at the time. All of a sudden from his little car seat directly behind me, came Zack's voice, joining right in with mine. He was on pitch and knew each word! I was amazed and cried the rest of the way home as I listened to the pureness of his tonality. I wasn't even aware that Zack was really listening to me, let alone absorbing the words and the melody. This was the first time his voice moved me to tears but it certainly wasn't the last. His voice was like clear, sparkling glass and felt like pure love. It remained that way throughout his life.

***

A reception followed the concert so that students could meet with the parents of the five friends. Refreshments were once again provided. The IU Jacobs School of Music had set up video equipment to record people who wanted to leave messages about each student. When the video was complete, each of us would receive a copy. IU also gave us a copy of Zachary's poster from the hallway, accompanied by a well-designed black and white poster about the *Fairé: Requiem, op.48* concert. The most fitting touch was the listing of Chris, Garth, Georgina, Robert, and Zachary, inscribed below five white roses. Their lives mirrored that of a flower, gone too soon.

Dan and I said our goodbyes and left for the hotel. We lay in bed and tried to sleep. Blank staring at the ceiling, we spoke about the day. We held each other and prayed. I don't remember sleeping or waking up. The year of being in a trancelike state had passed and I was still numb. Would the next year rekindle any of the old me? I wanted my life back and knew I had to find pieces of it to glue myself back together or I'd go insane. I thought about the little pond formed in the woods… then I remembered water near our home.

***

Our family grew up down the street from an exceptional swimming pool called, The Dolphin Club. I'd been to the club in high school with my friend, Beth. A colleague had told me about The Dolphin Club and had given us a free guest pass to try it out. It was a perfect fit for our growing family with a small wading pool, an intermediate pool and the Olympic size large pool. We took advantage of our close proximity, scraped together a few nickels, and joined.

Zachary enjoyed keeping company with the adults and loved sharing in their conversations. We spent most of their younger years in between the two smaller pools. One day while talking to my friend, Penny, Zachary had entered our conversation and then returned to the pool. She turned to me and said, "I hate that kid."

Of course that comment bristled my feathers and I reacted with something like, "Say, you do know that kid is mine, right?"

Penny answered with something like, "Yes, but I can't understand what he says. He uses too many words I don't understand and he makes me feel so stupid." We both looked at each other and laughed. Some things you never forget.

***

Ralph and Rainelle met us for breakfast the next morning. Have you ever wondered why food follows such events? I believe we're just trying to fill up "the hole."

Chris's roommate, Greg joined us for breakfast, too. Later, he made us CDs of events Zachary had been involved in while at IU and had placed them into a red binder with Zachary's photo on the cover. The depth of Greg's kindness seemed overflowing. We enjoyed his humor and could see why Chris had roomed with him.

Dean Richards also joined us for breakfast. He wanted to make sure that we didn't need anything else. The university had acted over abundantly on our behalf. How could we repay their generosity? His eyes spoke of desire to help. We couldn't believe all they had done to try to help us mend. The dean told us we were not alone in the plight to recover. The university was attempting to heal as well.

Even though healing wasn't something I could see myself accomplishing, I was determined to continue. Zachary would not want me to roll over. He'd expect me to pull myself out of the muck and mire of grief, find life, and move forward.

Material things leave and can be taken from you. Memories are what we leave behind. Zachary had left so many wonderful pieces of himself. Surely he'd find a way to be a part of the future. He was not someone to be forgotten. We have framed pieces of his art work around our home. Looking at those drawings, it's clear that nothing could take him away from me.

***

At an early age, Zack loved to draw. In elementary school, he created a comic strip about a smart-alecky mouse named Figgy. Along the way, Zachary was encouraged to pursue art. I'd once requested Zack to sketch a lighthouse for me while we were driving to Florida. He could draw anything, even when riding in a car!

During his high school days, I received a phone call from Senator David McIntosh's office. His secretary was calling to see how many tickets Zachary's family wanted for the Patriotic Art Exhibit to be held the following week. Confused, I asked the secretary to repeat the question.

Still perplexed, I asked him to explain the situation once more when he responded, "Ma'am, you have no idea what I'm talking about, do you?" I told him that Dan and I really were conscientious parents who took an active role in our children's lives, but we had an extremely modest son who didn't like to brag about his accomplishments – in fact, Zachary explained away most of his accomplishments as, "no big deal." The secretary giggled and went on to tell me that this exhibit *was* a big deal. In fact, if Zachary's picture won, it would hang in the rotunda at the Capitol Building in Washington, D.C. Thanking him for his call, I told the secretary that Zachary's dad and I would be there.

When Zachary arrived home, I asked him about the art exhibit. In his normal calm fashion, Zack relayed the details of his patriotic art as well as stating that he didn't really feel that this was his best work. He had completed it in just a few days and felt that the work lacked the elements needed to win. He hadn't planned to submit it, but his art teacher entered the piece anyway. "Mom, really, it's no big deal."

***

Zachary's modesty was always part of his character. He felt that there was room for improvement in everything he had done whether it was in art, writing, music, or something as simple as organizing a desk drawer. Being a deep seated perfectionist, Zachary was harder on himself than anyone.

He had talent in a variety of areas although Zack wouldn't claim that truth. At one point, Zachary was unsure which avenue to take – artist, writer, or musician. I loved to read his written thoughts. His natural use of our language made the reader easily visualize his meaning.

One of my personal favorites Zachary wrote when he was around thirteen years old. The reason this particular piece remains so special to me is because he described Niagara Falls from a family vacation when Zachary was eight years old. He'd held the moment within for five years before writing it. His short recanting of the memory was entitled, *"Different."*

Night fell. The lights on the falling water kept changing in color, size, shape, and direction, reflecting off the mist made by the plummeting water. People stood from all sides to watch the spectacular show of color and motion. I had waited so long for this moment and now that it had come, I was astonished at what I beheld. The massive gorge cut out by the powerful force of the flowing water was the greatest thing that I had ever seen. It was as if it was supposed to be there.

In minutes, there was a gigantic flow of people standing from all sides to view this amazing waterfall called the Niagara Falls. I honestly can't put into words the way that amazing waterfall affected me, but all the same, here was this spectacular wonder of people from everywhere who came to see and all because it dared to be different.

When my family had planned this vacation we had no idea it was going to turn out the way it did. Even today when I think of the Niagara Falls, I remember how great it was and I hope to go back some day, but what I remember most is what it taught me: The Niagara Falls was so different that it became known worldwide. If everyone in this world was just as different, would that not make this world a better world?

The memory of Zachary daring to be different can't be taken away from me. He followed what he thought was right and abandoned the perception of others. Modesty would not have allowed him to accept how wonderful he really was. Like the Niagara Falls, Zack's life left its own impression on the lives of those who knew him. I'll always, always "keep the mem'ry of" – all the things that made him special. No, no… they can't take that away from me!

See You in a Minute

Young At Heart

After April 21st, 2007, everything was supposed to return to normal, whatever that would be. Dan went to work and I went back to East Side Middle School. Entering the building, I felt out of touch with *myself*. How was I going to teach when I could barely walk? I thought a cup of tea might help so I entered the main foyer leading to the teacher's lounge.

It was a tradition at East Side, if a student was awarded the American Legion Award, their 8x10 photograph would be displayed in the entry hall. Zack had won the distinction. Each day while at East Side, I had passed his photo. Sometimes I could only glance at it due to the heartache. This day, there was more than heartache – there was a penny right under his picture!

***

Zachary, Joel, and Brytni were just a year apart in school. We'd kept involved in their school work and stressed the importance of getting a good education. Being the oldest, Zachary set a stellar example and was a hard act to follow. He won the American Legion Award twice. Each year, Zachary strived for excellence.

In kindergarten, Zachary had a wonderful teacher named Miss Clingenpeel. Zachary loved her so much that when he played teacher at home, he emulated her excellent teaching style to a tee. She knew that Zachary had no difficulties with completing the academic work, but his late birthday made him a little emotionally immature compared to his classmates. We joined in deciding to have him stay one more year in kindergarten at Park Place. This decision resulted in Joel and Brytni waiting a year, too – we didn't want the kids to be in the same grades.

Dan and I have talked often about waiting with Zachary and the difference that "one more year" made for all the kids. It resulted in all positives: better grades, better thinking skills, better athleticism, and the list went ongoing. The choices we make in life reflect in the future.

***

Tea in hand, with that new-found penny in my pocket, I walked back to class. To some degree, I believed that the students saved me. I had to concentrate on helping them so I had to let go of my own pain. I kept thinking about the quote that stated "the best way to stop hurting was to help others." Focusing on something other than yourself is a true blessing in life. Shifting out of the pain gear and into the help lane is not always easy, but always rewarding.

It has been a blessing to keep in touch with my students. I know these students will achieve greatness in their lives. Throughout my teaching, I have known some students would be successful wherever their paths led them. They were smarter than me!

As the school year drew to a close, Dan, my friend and fellow teacher, stopped by my room. With tears in his eyes, he said, "You're going to make it. When this school year began, I have to admit, I had my doubts. God is good, Misty. I see glimpses of the old Misty coming back and that's a good thing."

Thanking him for all he'd done for me, I smiled. It had been a wild year for him, too. Dan had been there when my principal told me the news about the crash. He'd prayed with me and helped me when I had grief attacks. All my fellow teachers and the office staff had given me support when I needed it. East Side had been my cocoon wrapping me in security, love, and genuine kindness. Dan was right. God was good.

The last day of school was June 5th and since Hillary had not gone into labor, her doctor planned to induce. Dan and I were so excited to meet our first grandchild. We knew that they were having a boy. Joel and Hillary had already told us his name would be Camden Zachary. What a tribute to his big brother, Zack. I was sure that if Zachary was here, he would have been so honored by their gesture.

Hillary's family and our family waited for the special moment. We waited – and waited. Hillary and Joel walked the halls and she bounced on a birthing ball. At times, Hillary felt that her labor would begin and then it would just stop.

We waited all day and into night. The furniture and floor of the waiting area of the maternity wing was covered with anticipating family members. The next morning, the doctor came in to tell Hillary and Joel that the baby just wasn't ready and they needed to go home to rest. They were crushed.

On my way back from making a trip out to the parking lot to put away some of the blankets and pillows, I spotted something reflecting the morning sun. It was a trail of pennies! As I bent over to pick them up, I began counting. Thirteen pennies leading the way back into the hospital! Wow, I wondered what this could mean. Dan and Joel were both born on the thirteenth. Did this mean Camden would be born on that date, too?

Seeing Joel and Hillary moving from such excitement to such sadness was difficult, but the discovery of the penny trail seemed like a sign to me. Requesting that Joel hold out his hand, I placed the pennies into his palm. He looked at me emphatically and said, "He better not wait another week. We're ready now." I reached back into his palm and removed one of the pennies and responded, "All I know is that's how many were in the parking lot, but I want one for my angel bank."

Later that same evening, Dan and I took them some Chinese food. Hillary wanted to do anything to move the labor along. They were hoping that Kung Poe might do the trick. Finally on June 12th, the doctor readmitted Hillary. It was their third wedding anniversary, and here they were in the hospital. What an anniversary present if Camden was born on that day!

It didn't work out quite that way – Camden Zachary came into the world at 4 a.m. on the 13th. Some may say that this was a coincidence, but I believe the trail of pennies was Zachary's way of trying to tell us all God was in control.

More and more, pennies became a connection to Zachary and our lives. Dan and I took a trip to Hawaii to celebrate our thirtieth wedding anniversary. We found some form of money each day of our two week stay. Some of the most amazing were: two pennies that seemed to be waiting for us when we hiked to the top of Diamond Head and the pile of change while waiting in line to see the USS Arizona at Pearl Harbor. There was this pile of change sitting on the curb in front of us. Tapping the person on the shoulder in front of us, I asked if the money belonged to them. They didn't answer right away. I think they were contemplating keeping it, but their response was that it wasn't theirs. It only stood to reason that there would have been lots of angels at Pearl Harbor. The pile totaled eighty cents.

The last penny found while on our Hawaiian trip was among the most meaningful for me. We were about to leave the island of Maui without a penny discovery. Just when I was about to board a small tram, I spotted a bright shiny new penny right at my feet. I had looked everywhere and then it seemed to appear out of nowhere. Dan knew it, too. We had been blessed with *258 angels* during that excursion.

A few days after Camden Zachary was born, Dan's brother Bob called him to say that our sister-in-law LeDonna was in the hospital and it didn't look good. We threw a few things into a suitcase and left.

Bob greeted us with sad eyes and told us that she was already brain dead. I'd not witnessed anyone die and LeDonna was the first. She was a remarkable mother to Jessica, Heather, and Alexis, and a wonderful example of strength and courage. Recalling our last conversation, I prayed that her girls would know and remember their mother's love, her laugh and desire to live.

My dad's brother, Dick, passed that same week. LeDonna's and my uncle's funerals were on the same day. Dan and I had to split up to attend both ceremonies. So many times, I had to ask myself, "What are the odds?" Throughout the days of our family's enduring loss, I felt and experienced the power of prayer, the warmth of friendship, and longed for some other connections to Zachary.

During the fall of 2007, I began to feel a deep need to meet Georgina's parents. Dan and I had met the parents of the boys who had been on the plane, but not the girl... not the pilot. I'd been forwarded an e-mail announcing a dedication concert for two baby grand pianos in Georgina's name. Telling Dan about the news, I expressed my desire to meet the Joshi's. They had lost their child, too.

I called Gwyn Richards – he was anxious to arrange a meeting between the two families. The concert was to be on Wednesday evening, October 10th at Auer Hall in IU Jacobs

School of Music. Dean Richards contacted the Joshi's, and found they wanted to meet with us as well.

It was a good meeting! While we hugged, the feeling of loss the Joshi's had endured was transferred back and forth to Dan and me. As we shared the meal, we spoke of how we'd felt so empty and alone. We also had many similarities including having two boys and one girl. Louise and I spoke of how girls call home often and share details of their day. The sorrow of loss during that talk was clear.

The most unusual moment occurred when I asked about where Georgina fell in the birth order of their children. Louise responded that she was their first child. I told them that Zachary was our eldest, too... in fact, Garth and Chris were also eldest children. Robert was an only child, so we had all lost our first-born child in the accident. The moment was a shocking revelation to all four of us. We sat silently at the table not moving. The thought had rendered us speechless.

Dan, Yatish, Louise, and I attended the concert together with several IU staff. Dan and I were also honored to meet Tenzing and Avatar, their two boys. This was to be the first and last time I saw Louise. She died December 27, 2007. Dan and I were so blessed to have had the opportunity to have met such a fine lady.

The next few months came and went. Holidays, I thought, were supposed to be easier after the first year and yet the second celebration of each event was more difficult. The hardest holiday, Christmas, seemed even emptier without Zachary. How could this be when our family was growing? Even in my sadness, I found eagerness in celebrating Christmas for the first time with our first grandchild, Camden Zachary, and now, to add to the excitement, Brytni was expecting in March. There were so many firsts for me and our family; yet, my heart still ached for my first born. The festivities were filled with joy. It was paradoxical that I could feel happiness and sorrow mixed together. There were days that I felt lost in Christmases and holidays past as winter melted into spring.

On March 25, 2008, *my* baby girl Brytni gave birth to our first granddaughter, Lily Ann. Brytni and Jason named their first born, Lily, after Zachary's favorite flower. Zack had sung a solo from Secret Garden called "Lily's Eyes." Brytni loved Zachary's rendition of that song. Both of Zachary's siblings named their oldest child in his honor. What a testimony to their love for their brother!

Since that time, Dan and I have been blessed with two more amazing grandchildren: another granddaughter, Kendall Jo, and another grandson, Connor Laird. Both families have a boy and a girl. Over the course of the past four years, our grandchildren were born about nine months apart. Each family appeared to be taking turns having babies. Babysitting has become the joy of my days! Children keep you young at heart. You can see things in a new perspective through their eyes.

***

When Camden was around two and a half, he came to our house for the evening. The two of us were downstairs playing when I decided to get some of the old toys stored in the attic. Brytni's old room has an easy attic access so I took Camden and went upstairs. Camden was a good listener. Instructing him to sit at the doorway, I entered the attic and came out with an old Fisher Price School House. "Ta-da! Look what Meme has found for you, Camden," I exclaimed. "You sit right there while I clean it up for you to play with."

Camden looked at me and said, "That was Zachary's."

I was dumbfounded. I asked him, "What did you say?"

"That's Zachary's" was once again his answer.

I hadn't thought about which of the kids had received the house, but now that he mentioned it, that was true! "Yes, but your daddy and Aunt Brytti played with it, too."

"But it was Zachary's," Camden nodding his head, answered once more.

I didn't know what to say next. It had been Zachary's, but how would Camden have known that, especially since I barely remembered that fact?

When Dan got home, I had Camden tell Dan whose school house that was and he told him, too. Once again, I thought about what I'd heard about small children and pets being able to see and hear what adults cannot. I longed for that insight.

***

April 20th, 2011, Dan, the Carducci's and I were standing with Dean Richards by the bench at IU. Two students came by to leave flowers at the foot of each tree. We stopped them to ask about their recollections.

Their most remarkable memory was about the Saturday after the crash. The event was in the Music Art Center during the performance of *Beethoven's Ninth*. The MAC has numerous chandeliers hanging over the first few rows of the auditorium. Zachary and Georgina were to have participated in the concert. Once the music started, something odd happened. First, one of the light fixtures began to swing; then a second, then a third, and finally a fourth and fifth chandelier joined the others. None of the other light fixtures were swinging; just the first five. It was so noticeable that it was reported in the newspaper.

Dean Richards was at the performance and said that he had witnessed the swaying light fixtures. He also said that was the only time to his knowledge that the phenomenon had happened in the history of the auditorium. After that, the dean took us to the auditorium to see those chandeliers. The laws of human nature tell you to reason something like that away, but I choose to believe that those five students wanted everyone to know that they were just fine: more than fine.

Big family events continued to go on as they should. The fact is that time waits for no one. Each day brings a new adventure.

There is a book that I used to read and sing to my kindergarten students called, *Down by the Bay* by Raffi. It's a book that I now read to (and sing along with) my grandchildren, and the ending seems to parallel my life. It ends with, "Did you ever have a time when you couldn't make a rhyme? Down by the bay." That line struck me the morning before my daughter's 28th birthday at 3:36 am... is that my life now? I simply have lots of times when life just doesn't make sense. That's because I am not in charge of my life. I have to learn to let go and know that God sees the big picture and it's not always going to rhyme.

I was in panic mode when I realized that I was having my daughter's birthday party at our home and had for some unknown reason forgot to purchase her a birthday card. Now that is a rarity for me because if I see a card in the store that relates to anyone, I buy it. How I could have not purchased one for Brytni was beyond me, but since Zack had been gone, my memory's not what it once was. After cleaning the house, setting the table (which I had done the night before with my sister so as to make sure that it had that "autumn touch of class"), I hurried off to a local Christian book store which was only about five minutes from our home. After selecting two cards (because of course I couldn't make up my mind), I found myself at the store's checkout.

I preface the next *wave* by stating that although I totally and profoundly love having my other two children, their wonderful spouses, and my magnificent, smart, joyful grandbabies together, I also can't help feel an earthquake-of-a-gap when

Zachary is not present. I was trying hard to omit this from my brain because I didn't want to be sad. After all, we were having a celebration at our home in less than an hour. At the checkout, the clerk showed me the five dollar bonus items available to club members. I, of course, am a member and always looked for bargains. Up until this point, I really felt that I was in control of my emotions. "I got this," I said to myself, "No problem."

The clerk revealed the bargain Veggie Tales DVD. In my mind, the plan of action was set: I'd get two Veggie Tales Videos as Halloween treats for the grandkids (one for each of the families) and Brytni's two birthday cards, and be on my way.

The clerk also pulled out a video about a Christmas homecoming with Neil Patrick Harris on the cover. My pulse began to quicken. My brain said, "Don't think!" (You see, Neil Patrick Harris looks very much like Zachary. I find myself sometimes just watching shows that Neil is in just so I can *kind of* see Zack. I know that Neil is not Zack at all, but I still want to see him (Zack)… so I watch.) I realize that all of that sounds strange; nevertheless, I bought the video.

On my way out of the store, purchases in tow, the tidal waves of grief hit. It swept over me and I found myself engulfed and going down fast. I could scarcely breathe for a few minutes (seemed like forever). I made every effort to hurry to the truck before breaking down in the parking lot.

"Hold it together," I said to myself. "You're almost there."

My eyes, thick with tears, blocked my view. I needed desperately to catch my breath… then came the good part. Yes, I said, "Good part." There, in front of me, just a few inches in front of my feet, shining so bright that it couldn't be overlooked, was a nickel. I stopped, drew in a breath and smiled.

"There you are," I found myself saying out loud. I picked up the nickel, unlocked the door to the truck, and sat down. I truly thought about the distance between us…that Zack wasn't that far away. At that moment, nickel clutched tightly in my hand, I thanked God for small miracles that helped me keep swimming to the surface and through the wave. No sinking time. I had a party to throw.

Sitting in my truck, I felt my panicked breathing begin to slow, wiped my eyes, and called my friend, Beth. I left her a message that simply said to keep me in her thoughts today. Joel and Brytni and their families were coming over. I knew that she'd understand when she heard the message.

The party went off without a hitch. My husband, Dan, was so wonderful to help in all the preparations as well as the clean up. I was learning to survive.

Autumn turned to winter, and with the change of season came different memories, with varying emotions. I thought about snowball fights, snowmen, sledding, catching snowflakes with our tongues, waiting and watching for Santa, the list went on and on… and of course, memories of past Decembers with Zack.

***

One cold, winter evening in December, Zachary decided to come home for a visit accompanied by three of his college friends: Doug, Leah, and Lee. It was a school night for me and Dan had to go to work the next day, too. I was less than thrilled to have the late night company even though his friends were always fun.

Parading through the family room and into the exercise room, he asked if he and his friends could use the hot tub. I expressed my concern for the lateness of the evening and told him that we were getting ready for bed, but reluctantly relented.

Without hesitation, Zachary flung open the French doors and took off the cover to the hot tub. He and his friends took turns changing in the downstairs bathroom. Next Zachary rushed upstairs with me to gather up some beach towels.

After they were in, Zack shut the doors and put on some music. He also asked if we could fix them something to eat and drink. Dan and I looked at each other and shrugged our shoulders. Brytni was home from Purdue and had been working as a waitress so he recruited her as well. All of this was out of context for Zack, so I was in unfamiliar territory. In another way, I was sort of relieved that he was doing something out of the ordinary and taking time for fun.

Dan and I told them to clean up and lock the doors before leaving. To their credit, they left the room as they found it. I'm not sure what time they left but their laughter filtered up to our bedroom that night. It sounded like good friends telling stories and enjoying the evening away from school. At the time, I was less than thrilled, but looking back, it was a blessing to catch a glimpse into his college days.

***

And then there are other holidays... Christmas still seems to me to be the hardest. I think that our daughter, Brytni, said it best. She stopped by to have a cup of coffee on the way to finish her shopping for the holiday and could tell that the morning had been a little rough for me.

Brytni said, "Christmas always is the holiday that I think about Zack the most. I think that it's because he loved the season so much and that he did it the right way. He worshiped his way through it." I could see Dan wiping his eyes in the background.

We all knew that this was true. Zachary immersed himself into finding just the right music to express the birth of our

Lord. The celebration of birth! He wanted the choir at whatever church he was directing to experience the holiday of Christmas in a deeper, more profound way than the surface commercial atmosphere that surrounds all of us. Looking back on each of our choir practices, I recall the way he shut his eyes and felt the words and music flow. He would tell us to read the words. Listen to the meaning behind the music. Sing with passion!

Each holiday and at least once a week we go to the cemetery. Visits there are so surreal. We live so close that we pass by often. Some days, the scene has been set for others who are going to walk into this nightmare. The blue canopy over the open grave can be seen from the road. The chairs set close to the opening... so close you can see the depth of the grave. The vault that the casket will be placed inside, then sealed by the groundskeeper. Whenever I drive by and see these sights, I am transported back in time to that spring day when I was that person at the cemetery. Unbearable grief is all I can feel. I feel myself trying to pull away from those memories. The pain of it all is a vast abyss into which I can feel myself falling. But I don't – I gather hope and remember the good things in life.

Unfortunately, dealing with death is part of life. July 4, 2011 was spent in the hospital waiting for what the family knew was going to happen. Dan's dad died in the early morning hours of my 56th birthday. He was just about a month shy of being 82 years old. Dan's dad, Raymond Novak, Sr. had a heart attack when Dan was 17, suffered his first stroke when he was only 58, and his second stroke two years later. The last three years of Ray's life were spent in a nursing home due to his rapidly decreasing health.

It was Ray's last two weeks that left its deepest mark on my life. He was hospitalized for the second time in less than a month with pneumonia. One of the very compassionate nurses from the nursing home had told Dan that it would probably be pneumonia that would take Ray. His body had become so weak that it just couldn't fend off the reoccurring disease.

During the course of the long, long two weeks, Dan was determined to be at his father's side. His brothers, Ray-Ray (Raymond, Jr.), Mike, and sister, Jodi took different shifts at the hospital. Even though she didn't feel that good herself, Dan's mom, Rory managed to be at her husband's side each day. Somehow God gave Dan the strength to be at his bedside most of those two weeks. Often times, I felt unsure of my place throughout the ordeal. Sitting with the family, cooking or picking up food, transporting Dan's mom, Rory back and forth to the hospital – all of that just seemed like busy work. It was the nightly prayers that felt right.

I'd not seen someone die slowly. In reality, Ray had been dying for the past three years. He called out, "Help me! Help me! I don't want to die!" numerous times during those last days. It was tortuous to watch…you felt so helpless. Dan and his brother Ray were there for their father's last breath. Dan told of praying and holding his dad as he peacefully slipped away.

Having experienced having someone we loved die so differently, Dan and I spoke later about the painful process of each one. Zachary's death was shocking and over in an instant while his dad's was slow and lingering. Dan said that even though it was tough to watch his dad suffer, he felt that slow death offered some rewards. Dan had the chance to hold his dad, to care for him, and to tell him everything he wanted to say. Slow death affords you the time to prepare yourself for the loss and gather acceptance of the reality of death and life. With rapid, shocking death, the person you love is ripped away from you… here one minute, gone the next.

Personally, I don't believe that I would have been able to see Zack suffer like Dan's dad. Zack and I were blessed with a great relationship. I feel that I told Zack everything I wanted to say. My last words to him were, "I love you and I miss you. Be careful and call when you get there." I had given him a hug and a kiss. What else could be said? Yes, he was here one day and gone the next...and yet, to have seen him struggle for his last breath...I believe that fate is what it is.

Ralph, Rainelle, Dan and I continue to make April 20th a date to gather and reflect on our children. Rainelle and I have so much in common. One of our deepest shared feelings is to be where our boys were last. Even though it's hard, we feel a need to be at the crash site. Not everyone feels the same way – there isn't a right or wrong, but rather the acceptance to do whatever it takes to deal with loss. Rainelle and I take Calla Lilies and listen for the sounds of nature. For us, it has now become a place of peace.

Dean Richards, his wife Barb, Charles Webb, Jennifer Naab and other staff personnel at IU Jacobs School of Music continue to be as gracious as that first day. The bench with the students' names inscribed on the top has been moved to the grounds outside of the music building. Five Redbud trees have been planted with plaques commemorating each of those five talented people, forming an arc around the bench.

Events and honors continue to come Zachary's way. In September 2010, the week of Zachary's birthday, AU held a special performance by five cellists. One of those five was Hannu Kiiski, a Professor of Cello at the Sibelius Academy, one of the largest conservatories in Europe and one of the most prestigious in the world. Zachary had been a guest in his home in Finland while on tour with the Anderson University Chorale. Professor Kiiski dedicated a piece to Zachary and to Garth. He spoke of Zachary's talent and his kind personality while staying in his home. It was such an honor for Dan and me to meet Hannu and his wife after the performance.

Two songs have been composed in his honor. Doug Beam, Zachary's roommate for three years while at AU, wrote the song titled, *Spirits*. Doug wrote the music and additional text. Most of the text was by a fellow called William Shakespeare. Doug dedicated the song to Zack and Garth. The other song, "A Clear Midnight," was composed by John Harbison and dedicated to Georgina, Chris, Garth, Robert, and Zachary. Louise and Yatish Joshi had commissioned the piece for all five of the students. Both pieces continue to be performed in a variety of venues. We all received autographed copies of the piece from the composer.

Dan and I also received a letter accompanied by a CD from a faculty member of IU's Jacobs School of Music named Edwin Penhorwood. In his letter, he told of being commissioned by Southern Mississippi University in April of 2010. His composition, *An American Requiem*, was created to reflect the devastation of Hurricane Katrina, but Mr. Penhorwood also included a Movement 11, Elegy, in memory of those five departed students. His letter was sent along with his love, prayers, and good wishes. We hope to meet Edwin Penhorwood one day to personally thank him.

Zachary's accolades continued. The William L. Clements Library at the University of Michigan contains original resources for the study of American history and culture. Zachary's friend and mentor, Duane Diedrich has a collection of historical items housed in the library in impressive leather bound book-like boxes. Duane created a new box honoring Zack, including one of Zachary's musical compositions, arrangements, recordings, pictures and articles about him. Broadening its appeal, the box also included other historically significant items such as one of Karen and Richard Carpenter's autographed scores along with a recording contract, a note written by famed Irish poet and songwriter Thomas Moore to artist G.S. Newton, an archive of letters written by classical conductor Leopold Stokowski to American composer and conductor Phillip Lambro, and several items from American conductor Erich Leinsdorff. These significant documents were included to entice interested parties to view pieces of Zachary's life included inside that book-like box. Dan and I remain indebted to Duane Diedrich for his genuine friendship and generosity.

***

Christmas Eve of 2005, Zachary had left a voice mail for Duane to wish him a Merry Christmas. After Zachary passed, Duane had been so kind as to have made copies of that message. I am reluctant to delete voice messages now. The message may be the last time to hear someone's voice again.

During one visit in our home, Dan, Duane, and I were discussing Zachary's artistic ability. We have framed artwork throughout the house. Duane and Zack had talked about many things, but Zack had not shared his ability to draw. As Duane and I were perusing through several of Zack's early pieces, we came across a picture with words written in smoke: *Old soldiers never die; they just fade away.* Duane loved the picture and the saying because he was quite familiar with Douglas MacArthur. Duane and MacArthur had been friends.

We insisted that Duane keep the picture. It felt like that art work was predestined for Duane. That piece of artwork is slated to be hung in the MacArthur museum in Norfolk, Virginia. Duane's friendship and thoughtfulness continues to amaze us. He's a font of knowledge and has a dry sense of humor making it easy to see why Zachary and Duane had been friends despite the difference in ages.

Neither age nor appearance were determining factors for friendship to Zachary. It was astonishing the variety of persons Zachary called friend. He had the ability to make everyone feel important and valuable. Zack looked beyond outward appearances and into the heart. What a trait to possess!

Over the years, we have continued to look for hope and pray that God will grant us the courage to move forward and aid others as much as we have been lent that formidable helping hand. Night panic attacks, night sweats, flashbacks, and that *hole* are still part of my life after more than five years. I find myself questioning whether or not some of these things simply come with age or are these things part of the aftershock, so to speak. I guess I'm just not sure.

There is a lot of truth to being young at heart. When I was a little girl, I loved fairy tales. Rodgers and Hammerstein's *Cinderella*, was one of my favorites (and now a favorite of my granddaughter Lily, who often breaks into the song, "Ten Minutes Ago.") The underlying theme that good prevails still holds true in my heart. No matter how long my life will be, I hope that I try to find the best in everything and everyone. My life still contains more good than bad. Losing a child…nothing I think could be worse. The tragedy of the loss has taught me many things; some of them I already knew, but since the accident, I've come to a deeper grasp of their meaning.

Epilogue:

You Raised Me Up ~ Danny Boy

Parents are held accountable for raising children, but in a lot of ways, children raise the parents, too. Children don't come with a maintenance guide or an owner's manual. We sought help from grandparents and great-grandparents, colleagues, and friends. Advice compiled from all angles was incorporated; yet, looking back, most of time, our family learned *together* and grew with each of life's milestones and challenges. Dan and I learned as much or more from Zachary, Joel, and Brytni than they did from us. With God's help, we raised each other up.

As the years tumble by, I know that I'll always miss Zack's physical presence. I'd be lying if I said that I don't still look for him in a crowd or expect that he might be coming through the front door. I think that I'll always be waiting for him to appear.

I'd like to say that the second year after Zachary passed was easier, but it wasn't… in fact, it was harder. Maybe the reason it was more difficult was because I was no longer numb and the reality of his passing was staring me in the face. I'm not sure. The years that have followed the second seem to have softer edges that have been dulled by time.

There isn't a minute that passes that I don't call to mind some old memory of him or our family times together. God gave me the honor of being Zachary's mom for 25 years. I know that on the morning after the accident, that chill I'd felt was Zachary. I believe that he came to me and tried to let me know that he was all right. His hugs transcend time… sometimes I can still feel him.

No longer is death something I fear or dread. Some people have asked me, "How can you go on without Zachary?" I wasn't given the choice to be buried with him although I have to confess that I wanted to go with him for a while. No, fate is out of my hands, but death has given me a wake-up call about life.

This journey since the plane went down on April 20th, 2006 has taught me some clear lessons:

- Grief can swallow you up if you let it. Will there ever not be a time when tidal waves of emotion sweep over me and I can't catch my breath? After years of being swallowed up in the quicksand, sometimes *I think I can…* is the only thought that registers in my head and heart. I try not get sucked under by the pain. Hold on to faith and hope, ask for God's help to move, and escape its clutches.

- Prayer is essential for each day and throughout the day. God remains with me even though I had times when I was totally confused with the hand life had dealt me. Believing in God gave me the strength to move each day.

- Material things aren't important. Things fade and it is true that you can't take them with you. Remember to soak in the moments and memories. They are the *things* that matter most.

- Think before speaking. This is the hardest action for me because so much of what I say is out of habit. Try not to ask, "How are you doing?" My answer to that question for two years was, "I'm doing." That was all I could do… just try to exist. Also, no one has experienced the same kind of loss, so avoid comments like, "I know just how you feel." Even though the five parents lost our children on the same day, our time spent with our children was not exactly the same. Our loss happened simultaneously, but our experiences weren't identical.

• <u>Be a good listener</u>. If you are a true friend, you will <u>listen</u> when a grieving person needs to talk. Just listening is a gift. Throughout these days, weeks, and years, I learned about *true* friends and the meaning of the word, friend. Friends stand by you even when you look like hell and act like a zombie. Friends hold you up when you are falling down. They remember meaningful dates and particular things that have been painful and won't change the subject when you want to talk about the person who died. Friends listen and pray for you and with you. I have been blessed with some great friends.

• <u>Live in the moment</u>. We are not guaranteed tomorrow. Life doesn't permit us to determine our destiny. If I had been given a choice, I wouldn't have walked this path.

• <u>Believe in miracles</u>. I know that miracles come to pass and have in our lives. Pennies, rainbows, cardinals, and other miracles are everywhere, if we choose to see them. I take comfort in knowing signs are all around.

• <u>Greet each day as a gift and each person as a blessing</u>. Zack always greeted us with a warm smile and genuine hug. Try to follow his lead.

• <u>Talk less with words and more with actions</u>. This may sound very cliché: Treat people the way you hope you would be treated. When I was a little girl, my mom taught me the Golden Rule: *Do unto others as you would have them do unto you.* If we could always practice that, the world would be in good shape, right? If *I* could always practice that, I'd be in better shape!

• <u>Be remembered for your smile, not your frown</u>. I have had to learn to wear different faces. You can't always go around feeling and looking sad, although it is a struggle figuring out how to be happy again. Happy is the best face.

• <u>Watch more sunrises and sunsets</u>. Try to take in the beauty of nature whether it be watching the birds or viewing the change of seasons. Dan continues to take lots of pictures trying to capture the wonders of God's world. He took a picture of the sunrise on the birthday of each of our grandchildren. Finding the beauty in the things surrounding us is a natural mood booster.

• <u>Be thankful and cherish each moment</u> …especially times with friends and family. Try to take a mental picture for your memory bank.

• <u>Death of a loved one is never easy, whether it's fast or slow</u>. Perhaps the lesson that I learned is that no matter what happens, *be kind when you leave someone*. It may be the last time you see them. Have no regrets.

• <u>FAITH, HOPE, AND LOVE ARE EVERYTHING</u>! Faith in God, hope that I'll see Zachary again one day, and love for my family and friends has helped me live each day.

I can only hope that my life will have made a fraction of the impact that Zachary has made and continues to make in the lives of others. Was Zachary right with our Maker? I do feel that Zachary lived his life praising God and using his God given talents for the Lord. I continue to take comfort in knowing that fact. I, too, continue to praise the Lord for the abundant blessings in my life.

The last few lines of the poem found among his possessions have become my life's code:

On the day of my death,
What I am will be mine forever!
The purpose of my life is not just to be happy,
It must be useful, honorable, compassionate;
It must have made a difference
That I have lived!

Together, we raised each other up… a little closer to Heaven… a glimpse of eternity.

Acknowledgments

Thank you:

Most Gracious and Loving, God, my Savior, Jesus Christ and the Blessed Holy Spirit, for unfailing love and peace in the midst of life's storms. Thank you for your gift of eternal life. Without You, I am truly nothing.

Dan, my wonderful husband, without your love, strength and support I'm unsure if I would be standing today. You truly ARE my better half.

Joel, Hillary, Brytni, and Jason, my children and in-laws who continue to amaze me each and every day. All of you kept me forging ahead, praying for me with your loving spirits. I'm so proud to be your mom and mother-in-law.

My sister, Debby, who has been with me since birth and continues to be the person I turn to daily. You continue to walk this journey with me, experiencing each step. Thank you for your love, courage and unending strength. Thank you for being more than my big sister. Thank you for being my friend!

My Parents, Robert and Ellen, to whom I will always be grateful for introducing me to Jesus and for living your faith. Your recitation and singing of scripture continue to inspire me.

Elmore Hammes, my friend and editor, whom God sent with listening ears and an open heart. Without our *weekly* work sessions at Panera Bread, this book would not have been completed. Thank you for your tireless support, endless patience and professional assurance which helped me record the nightmare of my life. You gave me the hope that this book may provide help to others.

Sandi Patty, my friend who graciously wrote the foreword to this book. Thank you for being an anchor for my family and me in the best of times and in the depths of despair. Our families continue to intertwine as we move along life's path. There was a special bond from the moment we met. You and your entire family emit love. Thank you for sharing that marvelous voice with the world as God shines through you.

Jon McLaughlin, watching you mature and grow as an artist from a young age to now, I feel blessed. Thank you for making your music such a powerful catalyst, expressing what mere words can't describe. May you continue to inspire others with your many talents.

Abby Beard, the little girl next door who grew into such a talented graphic designer. Thank you for using your skill to design the images for this book.

Beth Smiley and Gloria Scharnowske, my two friends who listened to my painful journey without passing judgment. I thank God for connecting our paths at Madison Heights Junior High and keeping us linked together throughout our adult years. Thank you sharing the laughter and the tears.

Alberta Pettigrew, my friend who ran to my rescue and continues to be a support in my life. Our families have shared many adventures from house boating trips, Beach Boys concerts, Chicago excursions, and much more. Thanks for sharing and caring.

Terri Ginder, my friend who continues to bring love and laughter into my life. You brighten each day with your genuine heart and precious spirit. Thank you for always understanding and being my buddy.

My family and friends too numerous to mention, for your prayers, profound encouragement, love and support. God has surrounded me with a cushion of love which you are all a part. Thank you for giving my life softer edges.

15799551R00155

Made in the USA
Charleston, SC
21 November 2012